The Shaman's Secret

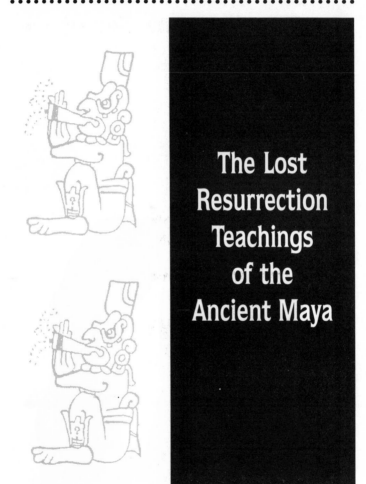

The Lost Resurrection Teachings of the Ancient Maya

Bantam Books   New York Toronto London Sydney Auckland

THE
SHAMAN'S
SECRET

Douglas
Gillette,
M.A., M.Div.

This edition contains the complete text
of the original hardcover edition.
NOT ONE WORD HAS BEEN OMITTED.

THE SHAMAN'S SECRET
A Bantam Book

PUBLISHING HISTORY
Bantam hardcover edition published June 1997
Bantam trade paperback edition / November 1998

The author is grateful for permission to use the extensive quotations that appear on the following pages:

Pages ix, 144, 146, 147, 160, 161, 162, 163, 179, 190, 196, 197, 200, 208, 209, and 210.
Reprinted by permission of Simon & Schuster from *Popol Vuh: The Definitive Edition of the Mayan Book of the Dawn of Life
and the Glories of Gods and Kings,* translated by Dennis Tedlock. Copyright © 1985 by Dennis Tedlock.

Pages xv, xvi. Reprinted by permission of Simon & Schuster from *The Fever Coast Log* by Gordon Chaplin. Copyright © 1992
by Gordon Chaplin.

Pages 3, 4. From *The Mysterious Maya* by the National Geographic Society. Copyright © 1977 by the National Geographic
Society. Reprinted by permission of the National Geographic Society.

Page 18. From *Man and His Symbols* by Carl G. Jung. Copyright © 1978. Reprinted courtesy of
Ferguson Publishing Company, Chicago.

Page 46. From *The Tao of Physics* by Fritjof Capra. Copyright © 1975, 1983, 1991. Reprinted by arrangement
with Shambhala Publications, Inc., 300 Massachusetts Avenue, Boston, MA 02115.

Page 83. From *Bhagavad-Gita As It Is,* abridged edition, with translations and elaborate purports by His Divine Grace A. C.
Bhaktivedanta Swami Prabhupada. Copyright © 1968, 1972 by the Bhaktivedanta Book Trust, International Society
for Krishna Consciousness. All rights reserved.

Page 84. From *The Idea of the Holy* by Rudolph Otto. Copyright © 1982 by Rudolph Otto. Used by permission
of Oxford University Press, Inc.

Page 99. "The Surangama Sutra," from *A Buddhist Bible* by Dwight Goddard, editor. Copyright 1938, renewed © 1966 by
E. P. Dutton. Used by permission of Dutton Signet, a division of Penguin Books USA, Inc.

Pages 124, 125, 211. From *Systematic Theology,* volume III, by Paul Tillich. Copyright © 1963 by The University of Chicago.
All rights reserved. Reprinted by permission of The University of Chicago Press.

Pages 201, 202. Reprinted by permission of Warner Books, Inc., New York, New York, U.S.A., from *Bless Me Ultima*
by Rudolfo Anaya. Copyright © 1972 by Rudolfo Anaya. All rights reserved.

Pages 245, 246. From *Cortes: The Great Adventurer and the Fate of Aztec Mexico* by Richard Lee Marks. Copyright © 1993
by Richard Lee Marks. Reprinted by permission of Alfred A. Knopf, Inc.

ISBN 0-553-37779-5

Published simultaneously in the United States and Canada

Bantam Books are published by Bantam Books, a division of Bantam
Doubleday Dell Publishing Group, Inc. Its trademark, consisting of the words
"Bantam Books" and the portrayal of a rooster, is Registered in U.S. Patent
and Trademark Office and in other countries. Marca Registrada. Bantam
Books, 1540 Broadway, New York, New York 10036.

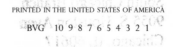

For Olga Valero—
my wife,
my inspiration,
my passionate Huasteca

ACKNOWLEDGMENTS

I wish to gratefully acknowledge the people who have supported me the most in writing this book: my enthusiastic, attentive, and excellent editor, Brian Tart; Ryan Stellabotte, his skilled and solicitous assistant editor; Leslie Meredith, my acquiring editor; the art and production departments at Bantam; my agent, Candice Fuhrman; Jared Kieling, with whom I consulted on the proposal; the many scholars, artists, and institutions who have granted me permission to use their original materials; Joy Parker, for her wonderful and insightful endorsement; my wife, Olga Valero, and my mother, Marie, for their emotional support; my friends, Don Jones and Mark Proesel, for their careful reading of the manuscript and for their many helpful, even inspirational comments. Don especially brought much wisdom and theological insight to the writing; my superb photographer, Rudy Vetter; my skilled and conscientious computer typist, Lorie Julian; and, finally, the Mexican people—among the warmest and most spiritually gifted people I've known.

CONTENTS

Make my guilt vanish,
Heart of Sky, Heart of Earth;
do me a favor,
give me strength, give me courage
in my heart, in my head,
since you are my mountain and my plain;
may there be no falsehood and no stain,
and may this reading . . .
come out clear as dawn,
and may the sifting of ancient times
be complete in my heart, in my head;
and make my guilt vanish . . .
and however many souls of the dead there may be,
you who speak with the Heart of Sky and Earth,
may all of you together give strength
to the reading I have undertaken.

(Contemporary prayer of
the Quiche Maya shamans)

Prologue

From my childhood something about ancient Mexico and Central America—something both bright and dark, the substance of dreams and nightmares—had stirred my imagination. I began at an early age to read everything I could about these Native American civilizations that had flourished in the deserts and jungles of a continent undreamed of, and untouched by, the rest of the world until Christopher Columbus literally ran into it by sheer accident. The ancient Maya especially held a powerful fascination for me, and as the years passed my energies focused more and more on these most mysterious of ancient peoples and on the secret wisdom of their lost spirituality. Even before I left on my first expedition to Mexico—the first of many to that spirit-haunted land—I knew something I was going to discover there would change my life.

I clambered over pyramids in the dense jungles, oppressed by almost unbearable heat and humidity and swarms of stinging flies and mosquitoes, descended into stifling tombs to speak with the dead, caressed the ancient stones with reverent fingers, pored over reproductions of ancient manuscripts, and reflected on moonlit Caribbean shores. The ancient wisdom teachings of the vanished Maya began to speak to me. They spoke through the painstaking work of the anthropologists, symbol-system and language experts, and the "dirt" archaeologists who, like me, had been drawn to a mysterious *something* about the Maya that seemed to seep from the stones and rise as a supernatural presence from the magical hieroglyphs.

These hidden teachings of the long-dead shamans also spoke to me through the encoded symbolism in the carvings and sacred architecture of the ruined cities, and through my background in the fields of comparative religion and mythology and depth psychology. These disciplines handed me powerful tools for "decoding" the carvings and temples, the statues and paintings, and the mysterious death-resurrection poems left by those who believed they would live again. While sitting on the dusty limestone steps of vine-shrouded pyramids, a mournful yet tranquil presence would often fall gently around me, and I would listen for the sound of distant flutes, of rattles now turned to dust, and the clacking of human thighbones from terrifying and wonderful rituals long past.

The understanding that gradually dawned on me, the puzzle that was filling in and taking shape before my eyes, was that the Maya shamans had encoded in their art and writings a system for transforming the human soul into a durable being capable of defeating death and embracing immortality—a kind of "resurrection technology." This technology included sacred objects, ritual practices, and achieving altered states of consciousness in which oneness with the Divine Being was possible. I also realized that the very act of my seeking to recover and reconstruct this lost technology was changing *me*. I was discovering something within myself—an iridescent core—and a more vivid, passionate, and courageous way of living. I found myself being drawn downwards into a macabre realm of shadows and, at the same time, released into a dimension of astounding peace and light. I was entering the frightening and miraculous world of the ancient Maya and beginning to see and hear at least a part of what they saw and heard in their ecstatic communions with their frightening and soothing gods.

My journey is far from complete. But it has already yielded treasures of the spirit far more powerful and important even than ancient artifacts. It has given me a new way to live my life *here,* a vision of what may lie on the other side of the darkness that will inevitably overtake me, and—just perhaps—a method for making the fearful crossing from the life I know to the one I hope for.

I have written this book to share with others what I have discovered, and to impart more of that lost world's magic than has been accessible up to this point. This book has four major purposes. The first is to make the reader more familiar with the ancient Maya resurrection teachings that we have been able to reconstruct from the art and writings of the shamans—their myths and images, their core beliefs, and their instructions for living, dying, and being reborn. The second—really an aspect of the first—is to try to help the reader imaginatively *enter* the Maya universe and experience that universe as the Maya themselves did. The third is to suggest ways that we might apply their powerful insights and soul-transforming wisdom to our own spiritual lives. It is my hope that, in the process, this book will challenge its readers, and disturb and move them.

As strange as it may sound, the fourth—and most important—purpose of this book is to help readers find new ways to destroy death and live forever. This book takes the Maya at their word and affirms the truth in *some* form of their method for achieving immortality. In various ways throughout the book I invite the reader to ask the question: What if the Maya knew something about the nature of God, about the purpose of human life, and about life after death and how to achieve it that we, as a civilization and a people, have forgotten? And what if that something really is, as the Maya believed it was, indispensable to our ultimate well-being?

INTRODUCTION

November 17, 1839, marks the birth of American archaeology. It was on that date that the American adventurer John Lloyd Stephens and the British artist Frederick Catherwood, having hacked their way through nearly impenetrable jungles, narrowly escaped death at the hands of murderous bandits, and racked with fever, began clearing the mysterious site of the ancient Maya city of Copan, deep in the mountains of western Honduras. Shrouded in thick vines and underbrush and infested with disease-carrying insects, the ruins presented the greatest challenge the two explorers had yet faced. The work was slow, the discovery of new buildings and monuments aided only by the occasional clang of their machete blades against previously hidden stones.

Stephens and Catherwood paused often to wonder at the unearthly beauty their hard work was gradually uncovering. In a now famous passage from his book about his rediscovery of Maya civilization, Stephens described how he was overwhelmed by the palpable feeling of mystery and the melancholy spirit of Copan:

> It lay before us like a shattered bark in the midst of the ocean, her masts gone, her name effaced, her crew perished, and none to

tell whence she came, to whom she belonged, how long on her voyage, or what had caused her destruction; her lost people to be traced only by some fancied resemblance in the construction of the vessel, and, perhaps, never to be known at all. The place where we sat, was it a citadel from which an unknown people had sounded the trumpet of war? or a temple for the God of peace? or did the inhabitants worship the idols made with their own hands, and offer sacrifices on the stones before them? All was mystery, dark, impenetrable mystery. . . .

This same sense of mystery still haunts the forested paths, the moss-covered stones, and the tumbled monuments of Copan and other ancient Maya cities. While Stephens's "lost people" had left behind an incredible wealth of art objects, sacred scriptures carved in stone, vibrant murals, painted ceramics, stelae, statues, and an awe-inspiring architecture, for the most part, they had remained mute for the hundred years and more since Stephens's discovery of them. What these ancient people thought, what they believed about their gods, what they felt about their lives continued as a "dark, impenetrable mystery." After a century of research, scholars had deciphered only a few hieroglyphs, mostly dates and calendar signs, and just scratched the surface of the symbolic meanings of some of the carved and painted images.

But suddenly in the 1970s the painstaking work of decades reached a dramatic breakthrough. In a series of meetings in and near the ruins of Palenque, called the Mesa Redonda conferences, Maya scholars from various disciplines, including archaeology, linguistics, art history, and epigraphy, came together to make a coordinated assault on the unyielding script of the ancient Maya. Building on the work of previous scholars, Linda Schele, Gillett Griffin, Floyd Lounsbury, Peter Mathews, David Joralman, and others finally cracked the hieroglyphic code. Suddenly the complicated iconography started to make sense. Images could now be connected to other images and vast patterns began to emerge. The hieroglyphic inscriptions began to speak, and dynastic family trees, terrifying rituals, and metaphysical poems began to materialize before the wondering eyes of anthropologists and language experts. Revelation followed revelation, and a universe of secret wisdom, an untapped spiritual resource of tremendous power and terrible beauty, opened onto unsuspected depths.

We now know that the overarching reality for the Maya—the

thing that colored every aspect of their lives, defined their goals, and determined the final destiny of their souls—was this sense of terrible beauty—a kind of beauty that, through a combination of savagery and splendor, evokes feelings of awe, "holy dread," and of supernatural wonder. For the ancient Maya, the universe and life itself were an awesome art form imagined into being by an ecstatically visioning God. When, in imitation of this divine creative ecstasy, the Maya shamans produced their own works of art, they believed they were participating in the ongoing creation of the cosmos, "giving birth" to God, and guaranteeing their own eternal lives.

The Maya believed that the Divine Being was the very soul of all things—animate and inanimate—and that the world was the materialization of Its exuberant drive to express Itself in a kaleidoscopic multiplicity of forms and entities, including the gods and demons.

The most important gods—those who were central to the great life, death, and resurrection drama of the cosmos—were the beings the Maya called First Father, First Mother, and their three sons—First Lord, First Jaguar, and K'awil. First Father, First Lord, and First Jaguar had made a series of descents into the Underworld to sacrifice themselves to the Lords of Death, and then rose into the Overworld in glorious resurrections that had carried the whole created cosmos with them. First Mother presided over the final apotheosis of dead souls who, like the "Lords of Life," had defeated the forces of darkness and won their own ascents into the realm of light.

The third son of the Creator Couple, K'awil, was the god of ecstatic consciousness, spiritual transformation, cosmic energy exchange, and materialization or manifestation. It was through K'awil that revelation happened, and it was through his Lightning-Serpent strikes that human souls were transformed into true shamans, what the Maya called "authentic human beings."

The gods had a dark, diabolical side that the Maya knew as the "Lords of Xibalba," or the Lords of Death. As the shadow side of the Divine Being, the demons expressed the "wrath" and the "beautiful terror" of God—a terror the shamans believed was a part of His/Her/Its core essence.

The underlying force that energized both the gods and the created world the Maya called ch'ulel, or "life force," "life-essence." Both the gods and the created world depended on a constant circulation of this supernatural force. Blood—called itz—was the primary carrier of ch'ulel.

The most effective way the Maya believed they could keep the divine life force circulating, and thereby keep the world not only alive but in a continuing process of resurrection, was human sacrifice—especially the decapitation sacrifice. The prelude to this awesome core of Maya spirituality was the sacred ballgame. Played by opposing teams who assumed the identities of the gods and demons in sunken I-shaped courts designed to replicate the Abyss of the Underworld, this fearful "passion play" reenacted the cosmic life-and-death struggle between the Lords of Life and the Lords of Death. The final "play" of this dark ritual was the decapitation sacrifice of the losing players, who in their deaths merged with First Father and his sons to proclaim the final mystery—that only through sacrificial death can new life be born. The blood of the sacrificial victims poured into the Otherworld where its *ch'ulel* fed the gods and demons.

As revolting as human sacrifice certainly is for modern people, it was the central—and culminating—religious act for the ancient Maya. Much as we might want to avoid facing it, an honest—and even beneficial—entry into the spiritual world of the Maya requires that we find a way to see it through their eyes and experience it as they experienced it. The brutality of human sacrifice must not keep the spiritual treasures of the ancient Maya from us, any more than the horrors of the Christian Crusades, Inquisition, and witch burnings should blind us to the beauty and wisdom of this religious tradition. But more than that, human sacrifice is the final key that unlocks the very essence of the ancient Maya spiritual vision.

For the Maya, sacrificial rituals were the climactic steps in a carefully crafted resurrection technology they believed would ensure the immortality of the soul. Life could only be victorious if it engaged death fully and embraced the darkness of the Divine Being as well as Its light. Then the miracle of rebirth would manifest from the hidden depths of the *ch'ulel*-charged energy fields from which the gods themselves had arisen. Life would soar upward from the abyss of death into the light-filled Overworld, and resurrection would be the final destiny of the human soul.

Maya salvation was not cheap; nor was it democratic. Not every soul made it to eternal life on the other side of death's portal. While First Father, First Lord, and First Jaguar had begun the resurrection, manifested the model of rebirth, and created a source of cosmic life force for human souls to draw upon, each soul bore its own personal responsibility for grasping the eternal destiny the gods offered it.

·   ·   ·

The principles of myth-and-symbol interpretation created by the fields of comparative religion and mythology and Jungian—or depth—psychology allow us to see hidden patterns in the ancient myths and discover their potential meanings for our own lives. Using these ways of interpreting ancient images and symbols allows us to see deeper than the anthropological findings alone can see, while at the same time respecting what the myths may have meant to their original creators.

The founder of depth psychology, Carl Jung, believed that ancient myths have the same basic psychological meanings for all people in all times and places, regardless of their particular cultural backgrounds. Like the scholars of comparative religion, he believed that we can discover universal patterns in the world's myths, whether those myths come from ancient Greece and Rome, India, Africa, or the Americas. He called these universal patterns "archetypes." According to Jung, these archetypes are the living ingredients of every human soul. In the end, they are the organic building blocks of what Jung called the "Self"—the mysterious, never fully knowable divine center of the soul where God and human beings are one.

When we use this Jungian tool of interpretation to understand the Maya myths, we can see that the Maya gods and demons, whatever else they may be, are depictions of the structures of our own souls, and the stories of their relationships with each other are expressions of the interactions between the psychological and spiritual forces within us. This powerful modern insight directly parallels what the Maya shamans themselves believed: that the gods, goddesses, and demons—and the universe itself—dwell within the soul just below the threshold of normal awareness.

Amazingly, these powerful teachings of the ancient Maya have been almost completely overlooked by those seeking ways to use the wisdom of exotic religions to enrich their own spiritual lives. With all the attention paid in the last fifty years to the spiritualities of the Far East and even to those of the Native Americans, no one has thought to look south of the border. This strange omission is partly due to the fact that Maya spirituality is only now emerging into the full light of day. But there may be another reason the spiritual gifts of the ancient Maya have been passed over: What we *have* known for a hundred years now about their myths and symbols has perhaps been too disturbing, too frightening, and too directly challenging of our self-images, of our domesticated and perhaps sugarcoated views of ourselves, the universe, and God. But after more than half a century of psychologies that have encouraged large numbers of people to face their dark subconscious secrets and integrate their shadows, we may be ready at last to receive the disquieting gifts the Maya have to give and embody them in our own spiritual lives.

The greatest spiritual strengths of the Maya—their facing of the harsh realities of suffering and cruelty, their conviction that creation and destruction, good and evil, and life and death are inseparable and ultimately interchangeable, their belief that we can find the light only by embracing the darkness fully, their anything but "cheap" salvation, and their aesthetic experience of life—*could* complement and fill out our own spiritual traditions in a powerful way. The Maya experience of living in a sacred cosmos infused at every turn by an unseen spiritual dimension of unutterable force and beauty could help modern people reenchant the world and their own lives. The Maya resurrection teachings could satisfy the hunger for meaning and vividness so many of us feel, unnaturally marooned as our culture has taught us to be in a sterile universe devoid of divinity.

In addition, as more and more people shake off the spell of an exaggerated materialism and turn their thoughts to the possibility that there really may be life after death, and if there is, that they had better begin preparing for it, they may find the Maya resurrection teachings speaking to them with a profound, and perhaps startling, relevance.

Pronunciation Guide to Maya Words

Maya vowels are pronounced like the vowels in Spanish, as follows:

a is like the *a* in "father"
e is like the *e* in "heh!"
i is like the double *ee* in "tree"
o is like the *o* in "hello"
u is like the double *oo* in "zoo"
u also functions as the English *w* when it appears at the beginning or end of a word. For example, *U*axactun is pronounced *W*axactun, and aha*u* is pronounced aha*w*.

Each vowel is a separate syllable.

Maya consonants are a little different from English consonants, as well as from some Spanish consonants.

x is pronounced *sh*. For example, I*x*-Chel is pronounced I*sh*-Chel, Chac-*X*ib-Chac is pronounced Chac-*Sh*ib-Chac.

The letter *c* is always pronounced like the English *k*. For example,

> *c*auac is pronounced *k*auak,
> *C*oba is pronounced *K*oba, and
> *c*izin is pronounced *k*izin.

The consonant *tz* or *dz* is somewhat difficult for both English and Spanish speakers, but is pronounced as it looks.
j is always pronounced as a hard *h*. For example,

> *J*aina is *H*aina.

The accent in Maya words almost always falls on the last syllable. For example,

> Pacál
> Uaxactún
> baktún
> huipíl
> itz'át
> sak-nik-nál

The adjective *Mayan* refers exclusively to the various languages of the Maya peoples. Otherwise, the people, their cultures, civilizations, and literary and artistic products are referred to as *Maya*.

TIME LINE FOR THE MAYA AREA

DATES	PERIODS	EVENTS
1530	Spanish Colonial Period	The writing of the *Popol Vuh*. Spanish Conquest.
925	Post-Classic Period	The hegemony of Chichen Itza and the florescence of Uxmal and Dzibilchaltun.
	Classic Period	Gradual collapse of the Classic Period cities. Altar L at Copan.
800		Bonampak murals. Six-Sky-Smoke at Tonina.
		Reign of Bird-Jaguar at Yaxchilan.
700		Reign of Eighteen-Rabbit at Copan.
600		Reign of Pacal at Palenque.
250 A.D.		Teotihuacan influence, especially at Tikal.
B.C.	Pre-Classic Period	Izapa on the Pacific Coast.
1000		Olmec influence on the budding Maya civilization.
1800		The emergence of village life.
3000	Archaic Period	Hunting, fishing, and gathering.

CHAPTER 1

Rediscovering a
Lost World

Working at the ancient site of Palenque deep in the tropical rain forest of southeastern Mexico in the spring of 1949, the Mexican archaeologist Alberto Ruz Lhuillier made a discovery that would revolutionize our understanding of the nature of the Maya pyramids. But far more important to those seeking spiritual truth, Ruz's discovery led to the recovery of a central part of the ancient Maya instructions for preserving the essence of the human spirit after death and then resurrecting it into eternal life. These instructions had been hidden for a thousand years by the vine-choked forest and by our own ignorance of the mysterious hieroglyphs and the meaning of the religious symbolism of this vanished civilization. Along with the ancient Egyptians and modern-day Tibetans, the Maya carefully encoded the instructions for gaining eternal life into their architecture, their paintings, their hieroglyphic inscriptions, and their tombs. Ruz's discovery was far more than a triumph of archaeology. It was the beginning of the recovery of the Maya secret knowledge about how the soul can face the ultimate terror, dance on the brink of death, negotiate its way through the trials that await it in the suffocating blackness of the grave, beguile those forces and beings who wish it dead—finally and forever—and rise again in a paradise beyond its wildest dreams.

As it turns out, this knowledge about how to overcome our physical deaths also included instructions for how to live fulfilled lives here, how to experience our own resurrections while we still move within the terrible and wondrous sensuality of the things of this world. As all authentic spiritual traditions have seen, life's victory over death is something we must achieve *here* or we will not have it "over there," and the soul's triumph in the "eternal now" of the Otherworld that stands behind, beneath, and above every moment of our lives reshapes us in our earthly forms into beings capable of grasping an eternal destiny.

Ruz stood on the top platform of the Temple of the Inscriptions and gazed out across the green sea of trees that stretched as far as the eye could see from the shelf beneath the mountains on which the ancient city of Palenque had been built, a gigantic generator of spiritual force in the heart of the jungle. Then he turned away from the blue sky and the green forest and made his way into the Vision Chamber of the great pyramid. In the humid darkness of this "holy-of-holies" the deified kings of the city, in ecstatic trance, had communed with their ancestors and with the gods and demons of the Otherworld.

Ruz saw that the floor of the Vision Chamber, unlike those of most Maya buildings, was not finished with stucco. Instead, it was made of flagstones. And he noticed that one of these flooring slabs at the rear of the chamber had strange holes bored into it. He correctly guessed that these holes were handgrips and that the stone had been made to be removed. He realized with a start that something lay beneath the floor.

When he lifted the slab Ruz found what appeared to be a rubble-filled pit. But as he and his workers began breaking up the hard-packed fill and removing it inch by inch, they uncovered a step—then another, and yet another. Excitedly, but with painstaking professionalism, Ruz and his team began the laborious task of clearing what began to seem like an endless stairway that descended precipitously into the bowels of the pyramid. For three archaeological seasons they worked, finally realizing that this mysterious stairway would take them all the way down to the very heart of the temple, and, according to Maya belief, into the depths of Xibalba—"the Place of Fright."

The rubble fill was packed so tightly and Ruz worked so carefully that he was able to clear only eight steps a month. But at last, in late May of 1952, the workmen hit a wall of stones with an offering cache of painted plates, jade beads, and a pearl. We now know this cache was left by the ancient shaman-priests to formally mark the entrance to the dreaded Underworld, and that the wall and the almost desperately

A view of the Group of the Cross from the Temple of the Foliated Cross at Palenque.

packed rubble of the stairway were meant to seal the dark Lords of Death below to try to keep them from erupting through the core of the pyramid and unleashing their fury on this world. The portal the shamans had opened behind the wall—and for whatever reason—had had to be closed.

Beyond the first wall lay another, and beyond it a level corridor. The workers labored feverishly to clear this hallway. Then they stumbled upon a horrifying sight—the bones of five individuals who had been sacrificed and left in the eternal darkness as offerings and guardians. But offerings to whom and guardians of what?

Beyond this site of human misery was yet another wall. Working to clear this further barrier to the powers of the Underworld, one of the workmen's crowbars suddenly struck empty space. Ruz stepped forward, widened the hole the workman had made, and saw a huge triangular stone, eight feet high and five feet wide. Ruz pressed his face against one edge of the stone and shoved a light through the opening. His heart stopped.

The dazed archaeologist later wrote of this most breathtaking moment of his life:

> . . . out of the shadow arose a vision from a fairy tale. . . .
> First I saw an enormous empty room that appeared to be
> graven in ice, a kind of grotto whose walls and roof seemed to
> have been planned in perfect surfaces, or an abandoned chapel

whose cupola was draped with curtains of stalactites, and from whose floor arose thick stalagmites like the drippings of a candle. The walls glistened like snow crystals and on them marched relief figures of great size. Almost the whole room was filled with the great slab top of an altar, on the side of which hieroglyphs painted red might be distinguished, while on the upper surface only the fact that it was entirely carved could be made out.

At first Ruz believed he had discovered an underground chapel, perhaps a "dreaming place" as the Maya called such hidden sanctuaries. The dreaming places were secret rooms where kings and priests believed they transformed into their *uayob*, or animal spirits. In the case of the divine kings, these *uayob* were usually jaguars, the earthly incarnations of the Otherworld Sun, the Lord of darkness and human sacrifice.

Three days later, on Sunday, June 15, 1952, Ruz and his workmen pushed the triangular stone aside and descended into the fairy-tale room. Ruz wrote:

> I entered the mysterious chamber with the strange sensation natural for the first one to tread the entrance steps in a thousand years. I tried to see it all with the same vision that the Palenque priests had when they left the crypt; I wanted to efface the centuries and hear the vibrations of the last human voices beneath these massive vaults. . . . Across the impenetrable veil of time I sought the impossible bond between their lives and ours.

As Ruz and his colleagues moved into the room and gazed at the huge carved slab, twelve by seven feet, they could make out something of the hallucinogenic tangle of images cut into the yellowish-white limestone, a type of stone the ancient Maya believed to be charged with divine power. They could see the figure of a man apparently falling down the length of a giant tree—what we now know was the Maya World Tree—into the skeletal jaws of an Underworld monster, the White-Bone Snake. A magical bird sat perched atop the tree, and the whole image was surrounded by sky symbols.

This massive slab lay on top of another even larger stone that was supported above the chamber floor by four sculpted pedestals. Ruz drilled a small hole through the massive stone and discovered that it was hollow. Archaeologists, engineers, and workmen alike looked at each other in wonder. It began to dawn on the awestruck men jammed into this dank underground chamber that they had something other than an altar on their hands.

Toiling day and night below the crushing psychological weight of the artificial mountain above their heads, and already deep within the Maya Underworld, they gradually pried up the carved slab and slid it to one side. And there, in the fish-shaped hollow carved into the bottom stone and painted bloodred were the jade-bedecked bones of a man, a giant for his day, a man who could only have been a king, and a great one. Ruz had won the prize of all archaeological prizes—an intact royal burial! After years of controversy about the identity of this king, most experts now believe he was Pacal, the greatest of all Palenque's rulers.

At the time of Ruz's astounding discovery scholars believed the Maya pyramids were only temples, and that, unlike their Egyptian counterparts, they were not built to be the tombs of god-men. But since the opening of Pacal's tomb archaeologists have discovered many more royal burials at the hearts of Maya pyramids. Far from being memorials to in-

Pacal's burial chamber beneath the Temple of the Inscriptions at Palenque.

dividual egos, we now know that for the Maya the pyramids were generators of tremendous spiritual force, that they were portals to the Otherworld made even more potent by the presence within them of deified ancestral kings. The Maya believed that the divine kings were the sources of abundance for their cities and that they could manipulate the forces of life and death to secure the fecundity of nature, commerce, and crops—especially maize. What these men were in life they were even more so in death, assuming that they won resurrection in the Otherworld. From their hard-won divine apotheoses beyond the grave, the ancestral dead heard the prayers of their descendants, advised and counseled them, and interceded for them with the gods. Pacal's pyramid was even fitted with a "spirit tube" that ran from his burial vault up to the Vision Chamber at the top of the temple so that the king's soul could ascend from the Underworld when called by the ecstatic visioning of his descendants.

Maya funerary art was never just art in the sense of decoration or even in the sense of pious memorial. Instead, it was intended to remind the dead soul of its potential immortality and to provide it with instructions for how to achieve resurrection. The carvings on Pacal's sarcophagus lid and on the walls of his burial chamber, even the fish-shaped cavity of his casket, were intended to guide his spiritual essence in its contests with the Lords of the Underworld. By reading the images and their accompanying hieroglyphs Pacal could remember his own individual identity and achievements and actualize his personal triumph over death in that dreaded land of utter darkness and final annihilation under the surface of the earth.

Along with recently deciphered funerary ceramics and resurrection texts from stelae, temples, and pyramids, and the decoding of Pacal's sarcophagus lid, we are now able to understand the broad outlines and even many of the details of the Maya secret knowledge for achieving eternal life. It's clear now that the discovery of the Maya treasures is much more than literal archaeology. Instead, it is about the archaeology of the soul, the unearthing of the great truths about life that we somehow already know, but that we've buried or forgotten in more superficial concerns.

Our rapidly advancing understanding of the Maya hieroglyphs is allowing us to see the Maya as they actually were. Far from being the peaceful, dreamy priests and stargazers of popular fantasy, they can now be restored to their proper place among all the other great peoples of ancient Mexico and Central America—what anthropologists call "Mesoamerica"—as the merchants, politicians, warriors, and the bloody practitioners of that most dreaded and horrific but central part of ancient Mesoamerican spirituality—human sacrifice. Even more cruel in some respects than the infamous Aztecs, the Maya often tortured their victims for days, weeks, even months before finally forcing them to play rigged ballgames that reenacted the creator gods' final triumphs over the Lords of Death. Then, as the Maya put it, they "harvested" the heads of their victims. As strange as it may seem, it was in part this darker side of their spirituality that enabled them, through a combination of careful observation and educated reflection, and wild, ecstatic vision rites, to develop the technology for helping the soul survive after death.

The much later Aztecs of central Mexico knew the mythic realm of the Maya as "the land of the red and black inks," or the land of the books of hidden wisdom. The Yucatan itself was known as "the red land," the place of rebirth across the eastern sea. Indeed, the Maya area to this day is a magically beautiful land where miracles seem probable. It still shimmers with the illusive presence of the Otherworld. It is a landscape that still seems charged with *ch'ulel* and *itz*. It is a countryside haunted by the ruins of past supernatural glory when the great temples, plazas, and ballcourts opened life-giving and death-dealing portals to the Otherworld and filled the charged atmosphere with the vibrations of spiritual dimensions above and below the earth plane. Even today the ghostly roof combs of ancient temples loom above the treetops, startling and shaking all who encounter them.

In prehistoric times the Maya learned to cultivate beans, squash, peppers, chocolate, tobacco, and—above all—maize. They also harvested the wild sources of hallucinogenic drugs that aided them in their Otherworldly vision journeys. They created a system of raised-field agriculture in which they dug intricate networks of canals and heaped up the rich organic mud between the canals to form wonderfully fertile fields. The languid, organically rich waters of the canals were an all-pervasive entrance to the Underworld for the Maya, and from their raised-field agriculture they learned that the realm of death and decay beneath their feet, and oozing up between their toes as they toiled in the canals, gave birth to abundant life here in the daylight world of sun-baked earth and soaring green corn plants.

The history of the Maya is shrouded in the mists of antiquity. But we are learning more and more about it all the time, thanks to the now rapid deciphering of their hieroglyphic writing as well as significant advances in "dirt" archaeology. We know that they were the inheritors of the spiritual traditions of the first Asiatic hunters who crossed the ancient

The major Maya sites.

land bridge from Asia into Alaska and then made their way through this uninhabited hemisphere to the tip of South America. The possibility of sea crossings from Asia becomes more and more likely too as archaeologists and anthropologists gain new respect for the seafaring capacities of ancient peoples.

We don't know when these people first set foot in what was then a truly new world for human beings, but there are sites in South America that could date back over fifty thousand years. We do know that the first Indians brought with them from their Asian homeland important aspects of their spiritualities: shamanism; ancestor worship; a belief in the quadrated nature of the universe with a vertical fifth dimension at its center; the idea that various levels of spiritual reality exist above and below the earth; the conviction that jade, flint, and pyrite crystals could be used to communicate with the spirits; the tradition of ecstatic trancing to open the Otherworld and release its deadly and life-bearing energies; the practice of human sacrifice; and an unshakable belief in the survival of the soul after death.

The first civilization to arise in the Americas was that of the Olmecs who lived along the Gulf Coast of Mexico in what are now Veracruz and Tabasco states. The Maya inherited much of the spirituality of these more ancient people. The Olmecs developed a cult of the divine jaguar (later, one of the Maya Twin Gods, First Jaguar) that missionaries and traders carried with them as far south as Peru. We don't know much about the details of this cult because we are not yet able to read the Olmec hieroglyphs. But from hundreds of figurines, the imagery of Olmec altars and thrones, and paintings found in caves throughout Mesoamerica we've been able to grasp at least the outlines of a frightening faith.

A being of mystery and terror, the jaguar was almost certainly the Olmecs' primary deity. He appears to have been for them what he was for the later Maya, a vision from the demon-haunted regions beneath the earth where life and death and light and darkness gave rise to each other like the black and gold markings on the jaguar's pelt. The Jaguar-god lived in caves, especially those with pitch-black pools of water in their lower reaches. These pools of water in the deep interior of caves were entrances to the realm of death and spiritual transformation.

When the Underworld slid up above the earth at night to become the star-studded sky, the patterns of the constellations were thought to be the Jaguar-god's hide, now seen in all its diabolic immensity. But the Jaguar-god also bore in his terrible darkness the promise of resurrection and rebirth for the living and the dead, for he was also the Underworld Sun—more golden in the Underworld than black, and destined to rise at dawn as the Lord of Life.

The Olmecs may have believed, as the Maya did, that by identifying with both the darkness and the light of the Jaguar-god, and becoming one with it, the human soul could achieve eternal life. Many Olmec figurines and sculptures have been found that appear to depict were-jaguars—human beings caught by the sculptor in the act of transforming themselves into the awesome Lord of Death and Life through rites whose gruesome nature we can guess from later Maya practices.

Along with the Jaguar-god, the Olmecs passed on to the Maya other aspects of their religion as well. One of these was the terrifying ballgame, a drama of real death and hoped-for resurrection. Another was a belief in the stupendous creative power of the cosmic World Tree, the vast central pillar that the Creator-god—called First Father by the Maya—in orgasmic ecstasy, had thrust upward at the beginning of time to lift the sky off the earth and begin a new world. This is the same tree that appears a thousand years later on Pacal's sarcophagus lid.

The Cosmic Monster in whom the Maya also came to believe, and the Feathered Serpent who gradually evolved into the mighty Quetzal-coatl of the Aztecs and who still inspires the art and imagination of modern Mexicans, were gods who first achieved concrete expression among the Olmecs. It's certain that these and other aspects of Olmec religion, now forever buried in the mud and swamps of Gulf Coast Mexico, continued to flourish through the dark flowering of other Mesoamerican spiritualities, among them those of the Zapotecs, the Teotihuacanos, the Aztecs—and the Maya.

As the Olmec civilization gradually faded back into the swamps from which it had first emerged, these other peoples began to take the stage of history and develop civilizations of their own. And in the vast lands to the west, south, and east of the Olmec center a new god arose. In its generic form scholars call this god the Principal Bird Deity. The Maya later called it Itzam-Yeh—"the Bringer of Magic." This god was a cosmic monster-bird with bright, tropical plumage, a spirit-mirror on his forehead, razor-sharp talons, and wings that ended in the heads of sacrificial victims. For his worshipers he symbolized the wild, untamed powers of nature—all those forces that make life so dangerous and uncertain for human beings. Like the Jaguar-god, the Principal Bird Deity was the source of both life and death, creation and destruction. And, as with the Jaguar-god, he was a divine being with whom the shaman-kings sought ecstatic union through visions and trances. Many of these non-Olmec kings, including those of the early Maya, wore his mask; and the first Maya royal headdresses with their magnificent flowing feathers were meant to depict the monarch's mystical oneness with the god.

It is this monster-bird that appears perched atop the World Tree on Pacal's sarcophagus lid and who is depicted in the much later Maya

An Olmec shaman riding his jaguar spirit familiar into a trance state.

book the *Popol Vuh* as the supreme enemy of the gods of resurrection and the new creation. It's certain that as the Maya cities sprang up there was an early form of religious warfare between the followers of First Jaguar and those of Itzam-Yeh. The *Popol Vuh,* a product of the winning side, shows the Jaguar-god, now the Hero Twin Xbalanque, along with his double, or brother, Hun Ahau, defeating the monstrous Bird-god as they prepare to bring the new world to birth and aid in the creation of human life. Maya sculptures from the Classic Period depict losing ballplayers who are about to be decapitated as the cosmic bird, while the victors are represented as incarnations of the Twin Gods.

By the second century B.C. many of the Maya cities had already emerged from the forests and jungles of the Peten region of the Yucatan peninsula. First among them was the gigantic city of Tikal, whose Maya name was Yax Balam—"First Jaguar." Mighty Tikal/Yax Balam was dedicated to the Jaguar Twin.

About this same time in central Mexico Teotihuacan, the first truly metropolitan city in the Americas, came into being. Today the vast expanse of its ruins and the enormous size of its pyramids still astound visitors. The sacred kings of this, the sixth largest city in the world at the time, assembled huge armies and established an empire that reached as far south and east as Tikal. Wherever they went, the Teotihuacanos took their god of war, Tlaloc/Venus. Under the influence of Teotihuacan, Tikal began a kind of warfare known as Tlaloc/Venus warfare. In Tlaloc/Venus warfare raids and military campaigns were timed to synchronize with the yearly cycles of the planet Venus (the baleful star of death and human sacrifice), which for many Mesoamerican peoples had close ties with Tlaloc, the god of rain. Tikal and other Maya cities had long identified Venus with the Twin God known as First Lord (Hun Ahau)/Chac-Xib-Chac, foremost of the Maya rain and fertility gods— and also the god of human sacrifice. Through their unearthly powers and their combination of the forces of death and life, Yax Balam and Hun Ahau led first Tikal and then other cities to victory on the battlefield. Victory on the battlefield meant an abundance of sacrificial victims; and an abundance of sacrificial victims meant prosperity for the worshipers of the Twin Gods.

By the late eighth century A.D., however, the great Classic Period cities began to falter, and by the early ninth century they had one by one ceased to be generators of spiritual power, and winked out of existence. We don't know why this happened, though several factors may have contributed to this sudden, mysterious collapse of a great civilization. Inten-

The roof comb of Temple IV at Tikal, rising above the jungle treetops.

sifying warfare, overuse of natural resources, drought, and malnutrition may have finally eroded the Maya's confidence in their shaman-kings. There is evidence for popular uprisings, and it's easy to imagine massacres of the nobles who had been the rulers, priests, and artists—unfortunately, those very people who had known the formula for resurrection. We know that non-Maya or "Mexicanized" Maya people from Tabasco and central Mexico invaded, and that these new peoples flourished for a while in great urban centers like Chichen Itza. But by the time the Spanish conquered most of the Maya lands in the 1540s hardly a trace of the once-great civilization with its profound and ancient spirituality was left.

What the Maya themselves had not destroyed of their own occult wisdom the Spanish finished off. Diego de Landa, the first bishop of Yucatan, collected the remaining Maya books and burned them in a huge public bonfire. He also enforced Church laws so severely that he was recalled to Spain in 1568 by the Inquisition for his harsh treatment of his Maya charges. The Spanish conquistadors rounded up the Maya from the lowland cities and drove them on forced marches into the mountains to the south. Those who remained became the slaves of the conquerors. With the burning of the books and the destruction of the last Maya cities, what was left of the Maya secret wisdom was lost.

Almost. Over the centuries that followed four books, or codices, that had survived the ravages of Bishop Landa and the Maya peasants came to light, along with Landa's attempts to translate some of the hieroglyphs and to record the life and rituals of the very civilization he had destroyed. A fifth, Post-Classic Period codex that had been translated into Spanish during the Colonial Period also made its appearance. This was the now-famous *Popol Vuh,* or "Book of Counsel." This translated codex reflects the beliefs of the Mexicanized Quiche Maya and represents a tiny fraction of a once-vast world of myth and resurrection teachings that made up Classic Period Maya spirituality. With all its limitations the *Popol Vuh* still gives us some important insights into that lost world and helps us to interpret the religious imagery of the ancient tombs and temples, funerary ceramics, and hieroglyphic texts. The other major surviving source for our knowledge of ancient Maya spirituality is the heavily Christianized collection of prophecies known as the *Chilam Balam.*

Even though a rich universe of mythology and occult wisdom is gone forever, the efforts of archaeologists, anthropologists, language experts, comparative religion specialists, and depth psychologists are enabling us to put many of the pieces of the ancient Maya resurrection technology back together. What has emerged is a picture of the human soul that is dazzling in its beauty, awesome in its scope, and both profoundly disturbing and powerfully inspiring in its implications for our own lives—both here and beyond the grave.

CHAPTER 2

A Terrible Beauty

At first the visitor to Chichen Itza sees only rock glaring in the noonday sun. The rock is elaborately carved, so much so that it is hard at first to make out individual images. The hordes of tourists and local vendors hawking their blankets, statuettes, and trinkets cover the ruins at this hour, and make taking a closer look even harder. But then it's lunchtime back in the air-conditioned hotels. The crowd thins, the sun begins its long afternoon descent, and hidden Chichen begins to emerge. Something seems to seep out of the stones and rise from the dusty earth. As the carnival atmosphere of the tourists and vendors melts away, it is replaced by the real spirit of this ruined city—what can be described as a kind of beautiful terror. Chichen Itza is an eerie, majestic, and deeply disturbing place. And it is full of snakes.

They are everywhere, serpents of stone that have slithered into this world from the nightmares and visions of the ancient shamans and artists. Some of these monstrous serpents raise their rattled tails to support temple roofs. Others slide up balustrades or lie draped in petrified waves along the tops of walls, sleeping, as if satisfied with the gore of the human sacrifices they have consumed. Still others gag up the heads of shamanic oracles—long-dead ancestors who returned to warn and counsel the living. The ancestors rise from the black gullet of

Two serpent columns from the Temple of the Warriors at Chichen Itza.

the serpent of all serpents, the White-Bone Snake—the Serpent of Death—whose gaping jaws draw all living things down into the snaky Underworld.

The Post-Classic Itza Maya who built this city in the tenth century and ruled a Maya empire from it were obsessed with snake energy. They saw death in the snake's belly, but they also saw new life in the serpent's ability to grow out of its smaller self, shed its skin, and take on a larger life. They saw feminine energy in its seductive curves and liquid movements, and male power in its phalluslike shape and its angry thrusting. And when the snake-demons spewed up the wisdom-bearing heads of deified ancestors, for the Itza it was like the ejection of semen that brings new life.

But there was something more to the Itza's obsession with snakes than this. A trip to the great ballcourt—the largest ever built—makes it clear what this something else was. As soon as the visitor steps onto the vast playing field where, personified by the ballplayers, life and death struggled, death won, and then was suddenly and miraculously overcome by life, he or she feels the powerful presence of danger and the possibility of the impossible. The most terrifying and wonderful of Chichen Itza's snakes are carved here in the side walls of the ballcourt on friezes that depict the death and resurrection game and its frightening end.

In the center of the action in these sculptures is the answer to the serpent-energy obsession of Chichen Itza. Here we see a kneeling ballplayer dressed in the costume of a monster fish—the same Otherworld fish in whose form Pacal had been buried centuries before. This fish monster was the first manifestation of the Twin Gods when they were resurrected from the dead in Xibalba. The kneeling ballplayer's fists are clenched—and for good reason. He has just been decapitated.

His killer stands nearby facing the headless trunk, clutching the sacrificial knife in one hand and the severed head of the "terminated one," as the Maya called their sacrificial victims, in the other. The terminated one's head is sprouting quetzal feathers, while the Underworld itself is erupting from his severed neck. Through the hallucinating eyes of the Maya believers, his spurting blood, coursing in jets and torrents, has transformed into snakes that strike the air and test the atmosphere of this world with their forked tongues. And from the center of the neck wound the great stalk and arching tendrils of a huge water-lily (or calabash) plant—the awe-inspiring sacred plant of the Underworld—soar into the sunlight and explode into blossoms.

For the Maya of Chichen Itza, the "terminated one's" sacrifice unleashed the terrible beauty that dwelled at the core of a Mystery before which all created things reeled in wonder and terror. The Underworld with all its horror and its promise of new life lay just beneath the surface of this world. It was always pressing upward, searching for a portal, a way up onto the earth plane where it could work its dark and exuberant magic. Hacking off the terminated one's head opened just such a portal, and through it, the Lords of the Underworld poured their dangerous soul-stuff—their *ch'ulel*. Using the victim's own blood, they fertilized the dusty earth with their *itz*—the sticky, slippery substance that carried their divine energies throughout the universe.

For the Maya every human being was a tiny model of the im-

The decapitation scene from the great ballcourt at Chichen Itza.

mense cosmos. The gods and demons lived in the mysterious hidden realm beneath the surface of the skin just as they lived beneath the surface of the earth. The Underworld with its darkly fascinating beauty and its death-and-life-bearing monsters rose from the depths of every human soul.

Many otherwise normal people have had frightening experiences of the surface of reality suddenly falling out from under them, revealing a mysterious inner essence. In these experiences a tree no longer looks like a prop for a well-kept yard. Instead, it unexpectedly reveals itself as a living presence. For no apparent reason a familiar street takes on an alien look, displaying a strange intensity of color and form. A person we thought we knew backwards and forwards reveals a depth of feeling that shocks us into realizing his or her true "otherness." And the nightly dreams and nightmares everyone has are intimate messengers from a haunting inner world that is both us and *not* us.

While many people are afraid to talk about their experiences of extraordinary reality, many others—among them modern abstract painters—have written movingly about the Otherworld within. Giorgio de Chirico wrote:

> . . . every object has two aspects: the common aspect, which is the one we generally see and which is seen by everyone, and the ghostly and metaphysical aspect, which only rare individuals see at moments of clairvoyance and metaphysical mediation. A work of art must relate something that does not appear in its visible form.

Franz Marc wrote that the goal of art is "to reveal unearthly life dwelling behind everything, to break the mirror of life so that we may look being in the face."

Mystics and theologians of all religions have described similar intuitions about a divine reality—both terrible and wonderful—that exists beneath the surface of official religious teachings. The Protestant theologian Paul Tillich said that events and places can suddenly become "transparent," as he put it, to the "God beyond God" who lives behind them.

What these artists and mystics have described is a way of experiencing beauty that is much more than "stopping to smell the roses." This beauty is far more than sweet. Instead, it is ferocious, wild, and wonderful in the same way that our most powerful dreams are. It is the terrible beauty of black holes swallowing galaxies, of forest fires burning out of control, of ice-locked continents, of childbirth. In its most basic form, this ferocious beauty that presses up from our own mysterious depths draws us to movies that depict stalking, torture, and murder; glues us to our TVs when stories of cruelty and violence appear; and urges us to pause when we pass an accident scene.

The ancient Maya lived within such a vision of terrible beauty every moment of their lives. It was a way of seeing as the gods saw that allowed them to peel back the layers of reality until the Otherworld core that also bore the possibility of resurrection emerged through the portal they had opened.

The *Popol Vuh* tells the story of the four creations of the world and human beings. Each creation was an improvement on the one before, as the creator gods, meeting in council, struggled to re-create themselves in human form. By the dawn of the present age, which began on August 13, 3114 B.C., according to Classic Period Maya texts, the gods finally succeeded—but too well. They created human beings that knew as much as they did, and as the *Popol Vuh* says, "then they saw everything under the sky perfectly. . . . They understood everything perfectly . . . and this didn't sound good to the Builder and Sculptor [the creator gods]. . . ."

Like the biblical god of the Old Testament the divine creators were alarmed by their success. So they attacked the first man and damaged his "sight" so that he could no longer have godlike knowledge. The Maya believed that written language, books, and learning on the one hand, and ecstatic spiritual experience on the other, were the two complementary ways that human beings had painstakingly developed to reclaim their original divine sight. The Garden of Eden story in the Bible makes it clear what the Hebrew God was really afraid of—that human beings would

Stela 11 from Yaxchilan, showing King Bird-Jaguar wearing a Chac-Xib-Chac mask. The artist has shown the mask in an X-ray or cutaway view.

gain the secret knowledge of eternal life. The *Popol Vuh* implies that this same divine fear was the real motivation for the gods' attack on their own creations. But through their two-pronged resurrection technology—developed through human cleverness and wisdom—the Maya found the way to restore their *in*-sight into the true nature of things.

The Maya preoccupation with restoring godlike vision and, through it, reclaiming the hidden beauty of their divine soul-essence, expresses itself in many ways. One is their creation of elaborate masks and costumes, which they believed were aids to supernatural empowerment. We ourselves get a hint of the eerie, supernatural effect masks can create at Halloween. But the impact the ancient Maya masks made must have been of a much greater magnitude.

With the exception of a few jade mosaic pieces, no ancient Maya masks have survived the ravages of time; but we know from their depictions in stone that they were elaborate surrealistic masterpieces of unearthly beauty made of brightly colored feathers and wicker frames with painted modeling over them. The ancient artists painted complex symbolic patterns in orange, green, yellow, red, black, white, and blue—the color of the watery Underworld—on their fantastic creations. Usually,

Lintel 26 from Yaxchilan,
showing one of Shield-Jaguar's
wives dressing him for battle.

the masks were attached to headdresses that made their symbolism even
more complex and added to their supernatural power.

One of the most dramatic and moving scenes that illustrate a
shaman-king's masking comes from the ruined jungle city of Yaxchilan.
On one badly damaged panel from the side of a temple, we see King
Shield-Jaguar and one of his wives facing each other, saying good-bye.
Her ornate shawl has slipped off her shoulder. He's already dressed in his
padded cotton armor, ready for battle. She's handing him a magical jaguar
mask—the emblem of his namesake and *uay*. The jaguar's muzzle is crin-
kled in a snarl, baring its teeth. A startling aspect of this depiction of
Shield-Jaguar's masking by his elegant young wife is that her cheeks are
stained by streams of blood. She, too, is wearing a kind of mask—one
made of her own sacred *itz*. She's just finished the bloodletting ritual in
which she has pierced her tongue with a stingray spine and drawn a rope
with thorns attached through the hole. By her bloodletting sacrifice she
has done what she could to ensure her husband's victory.

Often the Maya sculptors depicted these portable generators of divine power in cutaway and X-ray views to show that the mask's wearer
kept his personal identity even as he was transforming into a previously
hidden Otherworld being through the power of the disguise. Gods, too,
sometimes appeared wearing one another as a mask. From the depths of
the masks the eyes and mouths of men or gods showed through, provid-
ing fleeting glimpses of a humanlike intelligence underneath all the layers of phantasmagoria, and indicating that the real identity of these
combination beings was the underlying one. Or was it? The masks and
headdresses were also certainly designed to show the inner Otherworld
outside—externalized—and overwhelming the human one.

Fantastic costumes usually accompanied the masks and head-dresses. An important part of many of these costumes was wicker-frame backracks, often decorated with high, sweeping arches of quetzal feathers to identify the wearer as the Principal Bird Deity. Sometimes these backracks represented wondrous mythological events. Archaeologists have recovered several paintings and sculptures of kings in the costume of First Father—the dying-resurrecting Maize-god and the embodiment of the ultimate Mystery—wearing a "creation backrack." This kind of backrack shows the universe as it was at the moment of creation and includes images of the so-called Jaguar-, Reptile-, and Monkey-god thrones.

Examples of costumes that depict the gods, the monsters of the Underworld, and *uayob* abound on painted funerary ceramics and in carved stone monuments. Some of the most haunting are the stelae of King Eighteen-Rabbit, the greatest king of Copan. Eighteen-Rabbit had more need than most of the Maya shaman-kings to affirm his resurrection identity with First Father and the other Lords of Life because not long after he finished his death-and-resurrection portrait gallery—his "stations of the cross"—he was captured in battle by his archenemy, the king of the nearby city of Quirigua, tortured, and sacrificed.

Pacal is shown on his sarcophagus lid wearing the net kilt of First Father that he appeared in when he was reborn at the dawn of the new universe. The meaning of this coded image was that at the very moment of death the resurrection process can begin. This sculpture was for the eyes of Pacal's soul so that it could remember that resurrection is hidden in death, that death wears the costume of life, and that he—Pacal—could live again.

The Maya shaman-kings, priests, warriors, and others also wore body paint. The color schemes of the paint carried symbolic meanings. The shamans often painted their faces with the features of gods or demons, and marked their arms and legs with "mirror/brightness," "blood," and *ak'bal*—or "darkness"—signs. Those marked with *ak'bal* signs were often doomed to die sacrificial deaths.

The masks, costumes, and body paint of the Maya were all designed to bring the invisible power of the gods into this world through the person wearing the magical symbols. They conveyed spiritual power by being the externalized images of the terrible beauty within the human soul and beneath the surface of the earth. They were ways of playing with the layers of reality so that the dark-bright essence of things could be seen and faced. As such, they were all parts of the secret resurrection technology.

The Maya's fascination with the hidden beauty below the surface of the world appears in the construction of their pyramids as well. Digging into the depths of Classic and Post-Classic Period temples, archaeologists have found even more ancient structures entombed beneath the more recent facades. These more ancient pyramids are often covered by gigantic god-masks, molded out of plaster and painted bloodred. Now we know that the Maya did not destroy their earlier pyramids. Instead, they built succeeding generations of temples on top of existing ones. In this way they concentrated and amplified the divine energy that thrust up through the pyramids' core from the Underworld, increasingly thinned the membrane between this world and the Otherworld, and made opening the portal at the temple's heart progressively easier.

The Maya preoccupation with the awesome soul-essence at the center of all things also appears in their near-identification of the Underworld with the Otherworld. Scholars used to believe that these were two different "locations." Now we know that while the Otherworld signified the invisible divine realm in general, and the Underworld an especially terrible aspect of it, the Maya used the two ideas almost interchangeably. For them, "spiritual" and "divine" usually meant "under," "below," "dark," "mysterious."

Their quest for insight also led the Maya to search for the secret connections between things. They believed that all things were interrelated and ultimately joined into one stupendous whole. One of the most dramatic instances of this way of experiencing the world is the relationship the Maya believed existed between human beings and maize (corn). The fact that 80 percent of the Maya diet was maize was not lost on the ancient shamans. They created the myth that the gods had made human beings from white and yellow maize and their own sacrificial blood. The mythmakers saw a striking parallel between the human head and the ear of corn. For this reason noble Maya families elongated the heads of their babies by binding them between carved pieces of wood, and arranged their hair to resemble corn tassels. The Maya saw a connection between harvesting maize and "harvesting" heads, which is the reason they usually preferred the decapitation form of human sacrifice.

The shaman-priests taught a method of disciplined observation and reflection to kings and nobles, artists and writers, to enable them to see the secrets the gods had tried to conceal from human beings when they had damaged the sight of the first man. This recovery of the lost ability to "understand everything perfectly" led to a kaleidoscopic experience of the world in which all things, no matter how chaotic they appeared, still formed discernible patterns.

This recovery of the divine vision was an essential part of the resurrection technology. For by seeing as the gods saw and experiencing all the dimensions of reality as they did, the human soul was taking the first step toward attaining the gods' consciousness and becoming one with them. The Christian theologian Saint Paul thought this oneness with the Divine was an essential part of rising again with Christ, and he often claimed that he had "the mind of Christ." Buddhists today seek salvation by developing "Buddha Consciousness."

Along with seeing the hidden connections between things, gaining divine sight allowed the Maya to discern truth from falsehood, and appearance from reality. This applied to all the usual categories of human interactions, but it extended to a deeper "existential" reality as well.

According to the ancient Maya, things are never what they seem. Or rather, they are always *more* than they seem. At the core of the Maya's instructions for resurrecting the soul was their belief that even life and death are not what they appear to be. The one changes into the other in a hallucinogenic, dreamlike way. Good is exposed as possessing the germ of evil within it, and evil is seen to miraculously give birth to good. All creations, including human creations—societies, institutions, and relationships—carry the seeds of their own destruction; and out of destruction and loss new life emerges. As was true for the gods in their myths, the Maya believed that sacrificial death of the most gruesome kind was the necessary prelude to rebirth, and the tortured sacrificial victims, in the twinkling of an eye, became gods on the other side of death's dreaded portal. Profound paradox was built into this way of deep seeing, a paradox that dramatically expressed the core Maya concept of cosmic duality.

In this vision of terrible beauty, creation and destruction, life and death, and what human beings call good and evil are locked in mortal combat, and the triumph of goodness, creation, and life seems far from certain. At the same time, these deadly contestants are ultimately two sides of the same mysterious, underlying reality.

The ancient Maya believed that, probe as deep as we will, peel back the layers of the world as far as we can, we will still confront the undeniable fact that everything is shot through with this chilling paradox. When in our own deaths we come face-to-face with the demons of the

Underworld, we will discover that they are the very gods of our most fervent hopes. The diabolic Lords of Xibalba are also the Lords of Life.

The religion of the ancient Maya was dramatically different from most of the world's other religions, at least on the superficial level of their official dogmas. Most of these faiths subscribe to one form or another of dualism, as opposed to the duality of the Maya. In the dogma of dualism the forces of creation and life are believed to be the irreconcilable enemies of the forces of destruction and death. The Western Christ-Satan myth is the most well-known example of this belief. But dualism appears in Judaism, Islam, Hinduism, and Buddhism as well. For those of us raised in the Judeo-Christian and Moslem traditions the roots of dualism go far back into the ancient past of our civilizations. They have their origin in Greek thought and, even earlier, in ancient Persian spirituality.

But the first Asiatic hunters who peopled the Americas came to the New World long before the rise of the religions of dualism in their Old World homelands, and their Maya descendants were believers in the more ancient faith of duality. Native Americans refined this more ancient faith over a period of thousands of years in total isolation from the rest of humankind, untouched by the new religions of the Near East, India, China, and Europe. As a result, ancient Maya spirituality, and the resurrection teachings that developed from it, find their closest parallels in the predualism religions of ancient Egypt and Tibet.

Religious beliefs are never just intellectual ideas. They always have powerful emotional impacts on our lives, whether we are aware of them or not. They shape our daily behavior and often determine how we think about ourselves and the significance of our lives—or the lack of it. It matters what beliefs about ourselves, the universe, and God we have inwardly accepted. Interestingly, our real beliefs may not be the same as those we *say* we hold.

The consequences for the way we live here on earth—with ourselves, one another, and God—and for our fates after death that these two different spiritual systems—dualism and duality—bring with them are serious. If we believe in dualism, we will probably spend much of our earthly lives trying to deny the dark side of things in general, and of ourselves in particular. But if modern psychologists are right, this denial of our shadow sides—usually our aggressive, angry, even cruel desires—leads to a split in our souls, a split that produces most of our modern neuroses. Dualism also promotes a spirituality of sweetness that rings hollow, a vision of beauty that is shallow, and an ideal of perfection that forces us to be constantly at war with ourselves.

The ancient Maya wisdom of duality could lead us to feel more totally alive, to a more intense and fuller expression of all of our emotions, and to a deeper satisfaction with our lives. The spirituality of duality nurtures a sense of our "groundedness," of feeling solid and real. As psychologists have said, just because we try to cut ourselves off from feelings we have been taught are dangerous, those feelings don't go away. Instead, they rebel and cause us to suffer from feeling unreal and false. They also leave us torn by inner conflicts that we all too often take out on others.

Embracing duality in our spiritual and emotional lives does not mean acting on every bloodthirsty whim. It means engaging ourselves, others, and the Divine with energy and vitality. It meant to the Maya, and it could mean for us, seeing deeply and honestly with passionate hearts and thereby reclaiming our ecstatic Godlike essences. The Maya believed that the real death was the death of the soul, of the wonderful human capacities to feel and to think, and through intensity of feeling and clarity of thought to become real as the gods are real.

For the ancient Maya, the aesthetic ideal of terrible beauty rather than moralistic perfection was the highest value and the purest and most powerful expression of God in human life. This Maya way of experiencing God stands in stark contrast to the religions of dualism that emphasize morality as the highest value and the most important quality of the Divine Being. The kinds of morality put forward by these religions vary, from strict laws that are intended to enforce conformity to group beliefs and practices to lofty ideals like Christian love and Buddhist compassion. But unless love and compassion are understood deeply, and unless they follow rather than come before the painful and joyful work of the soul— work that ultimately demands for its completion embracing the awesome mystery of God—they end up rupturing the soul. According to the Maya, to the extent that human beings can embrace the fullness of an integrated vision of spiritual Reality they can achieve an unsurpassable richness of spiritual experience and depth of soulful passion.

This climactic ideal of the beautiful rather than the good was not an amoral acceptance of evil in the human soul and in human actions. The aesthetic ideal expressed a deep morality of its own that put it on the side of the victorious God of Life, while at the same time engaging his dark, death-dealing aspect with complete realism. This aesthetic morality affirmed that all human beings are the artists of their own lives and that all those seeking eternal life need—here and now—to become educated, courageous, and passionate cocreators with the Divine Being.

Often Western civilization's utilitarianism and moralism struggle

The so-called judgment mural from Bonampak, showing tortured captives being prepared for sacrifice.

with each other for cultural dominance; but separately or together they both deny the sacred origins of beauty. Our culture's hostility toward the spiritual value of beauty has led many people to conclude that beautiful things are alluring but suspect, that meaningless work is somehow morally superior to self-satisfying creativity, that vocational fulfillment is beside the point—the point is money—and that sensual and sexual joy— the most immediate products of the aesthetic ideal—are less than fully human. The Maya believed they were more than human.

The ancient shamans and artists led the way on the road to immortality, and it was their insights and ecstatic visions that shaped Maya art and spirituality. Shamans were known as "*itzers*"—those who could bring forth the divine substance and direct it to create abundance and life. Painting, sculpting, writing, and mask-making were all forms of "*itz*ing." And they were all designed to teach those who had eyes to see the secret instructions for surviving death and achieving resurrection.

The artist's paint was a form of *itz,* and his painting a kind of "anointing," a direct parallel to the shaman-king's anointing of the temple-pyramids with the blood of sacrificial victims. Both painting and sacrifice brought forth new life. In the Maya imagination the creator gods themselves, who had begun the present cosmic era by painting three hearthstones on the center of the sky with paint made from their own blood, were divine artists, and the world was the aesthetic manifestation of their ecstatic vision.

Even when it depicts terrifying beings and events or ecstatic rituals and altered states of consciousness, Maya art is regal, graceful, and dignified. The paintings on funerary ceramics show tortured captives dancing with boa constrictors and cutting off their own heads. But the artists' form and line—like the Maya ideal of the soul itself—shows a kind of vibrant calmness, and an awake and energized tranquillity.

The famous murals of Bonampak, deep in the jungles of the Usumacinta River basin, are the best preserved of all Maya wall paintings. When they were first discovered in 1946 they were completely encased in obscuring sheets of calcite from centuries of rainwater leaking into the chambers in which the paintings had been done and dissolving the limestone of the ceiling and walls. Visitors to the painted rooms used to throw kerosene on the walls to make the calcite temporarily transparent.

Using this method for photographing and studying the murals, archaeologists missed a lot of detail. They believed that the scene with the blue-green background and rows of serene nobles and naked petitioners was a depiction of a trial of some kind. Recently the Mexican government has cleaned off the calcite, and a team of art historians, with the help of computer-enhancement techniques, has created full-color images of the paintings as they originally looked. What has emerged is startling. Instead of a pleasant background, perhaps intended to convey an atmosphere of spaciousness, anthropologists now realize that the blue was meant to portray the waters of Xibalba and to show that the scene takes place in the Underworld. Instead of supplicants' hands lifted up to plead for justice from impartial judges, we now see tortured captives whose fingertips are dripping blood from having had their nails pulled out. The "judges," we now know, are Maya lords who are about to send the captives to their sacrificial deaths. We can now see that the captives are lifting their hands not so much to plead for mercy as to look with horror at their mangled fingers.

In ancient Maya belief, we are all called upon by the gods to become one with them and live forever. In the simplest and the most dramatic happenings of our lives the Lords of the Otherworld are giving us opportunities to create resurrection events for ourselves. But, according to the ancient Maya, we must engage our own hidden depths in order to succeed. Those hidden depths embrace a universe filled with terrible beauty and divine power, and one that is vitally, miraculously, and ecstatically alive.

CHAPTER 3

A Living Cosmos

Most human beings have had experiences in which they've looked up at the night sky and felt the sense of a mysterious presence in the black vastness above. Or they've stood on a high hill and gazed in wonder at the shimmering landscape beneath their feet, a landscape that seemed somehow alive in its very essence. Or they've been caught in a violent storm and felt their mortality in the face of seemingly malevolent powers far greater than their own fragile lives.

These kinds of experiences communicate to us something of what the ancient Maya felt about the world in which they lived. For the Maya the sky, the sea, rivers and streams, the earth with its towering mountains, its fertile valleys, its frightening caves, weather patterns, even the stones themselves were alive and pulsed with *ch'ulel*. Everything throbbed with the wild, undomesticated presence of creator gods. The whole dizzying pageant of nature—animate and inanimate—was the ongoing manifestation of these beings—themselves merely aspects of a Divine Being who, through Its eternal rapture, imparted ecstatic aliveness to the world. The creator gods, in turn, were made up of humanlike and animal-like characteristics and also of a mysterious additional quality, a quality of unearthly otherness that could be experienced directly only through the mystery of sacrifice, in the fearsome bright gushing of human blood. A cosmic drama of life and death was taking place within the Divine Being and unfolding with urgency and passion in every aspect of the natural world and of human life.

The most dramatic and sweeping depiction of this living cosmos that we have is a painting on a Classic Period offering plate that originally may have been used for the owner's bloodletting ceremonies and was later buried with him as a kind of "Book of the Dead" that would guide him when he confronted the Lords of the Underworld. The painting on this now famous tripod plate shows the structure of the Maya cosmos as it was shaped in every aspect of its being by the great life-and-death struggle between the gods and demons. It even provides a kind of blueprint of the human soul and the unfolding of its potential immortality. In fact, the Maya believed that offering plates were one of the physical manifestations of the soul. The scenes they painted inside the plates were understood to happen within the soul, which itself was a microcosm of the universe.

Meant for the eyes of the dead man who commissioned it, the tripod plate provided a set of images with which he could identify himself and his own life's journey. By identifying himself and the events of his life with the cosmic drama and its triumph of the Lords of Life, he could win his personal resurrection.

The outside of the plate is decorated with water signs, lily pads, and shells, and is painted to represent the awesome waters of the Underworld-Otherworld. The placement of the Underworld-Otherworld around the entire outside surface of the plate depicts the Maya belief that this dual spiritual dimension completely surrounds and enfolds this world

The outer rim of the tripod plate, with waterband, water lily, and shell symbols depicting the surface of the Otherworldly ocean.

The interior of the
tripod plate.

of normal space and time. The Underworld-Otherworld, much like the well-known Australian aborigine "Dream Time," existed in an alien form of time and space that modern theologians have called the "eternal now"—a time-space forever repeating its sacred patterns without beginning and without end.

The physical inspiration for the profound insight that the Underworld-Otherworld enfolds the earth dimension was the Yucatan peninsula itself. The peninsula-dwelling Maya saw the surrounding sea as the timeless realm of the gods and the earth as a gigantic turtle (or crocodile) afloat on its infinite surface. For the Maya, the Underworld-Otherworld was the mysterious dimension from which all things on earth arise. The rim of the tripod plate is painted red to show the *itz* nature of this supernatural water that encircles our daily lives.

Inside the plate we see the three-layered structure of the universe as it has emerged from the Elsewhere and Elsewhen of the Otherworld. Here we see that the Otherworld has divided into a more or less distinct Underworld, the earth plane, and an Overworld. The unearthly happenings of the Underworld and Overworld have flowed down into the bottom of the plate, where they engulf the earth dimension.

On the upper inside wall of the plate—in the Overworld—the artist has pictured the Cosmic Monster—the huge two-headed snake-crocodile whose rear head is the sun and whose front head is the planet

Venus. This Overworld monster's clawed legs thrash the sky as it surges around and around the plate-universe on its eternal journey.

Along the lower inside wall of the plate gape the jaws of the White-Bone Snake—that same beast into whose gullet Pacal is falling on his sarcophagus lid. Stuck in the throat of this, the greatest portal to the Underworld-Otherworld, which the Maya also called the "Black Transformer" or the "Black Dreaming Place," is the head of a humanlike god. The head is spurting water lilies and blood, symbols of the life-death at the core of the universe. This disembodied head is the final goal of all shamanic journeys through the Black Transformer. The very heart of the Maya cosmos, it is envisioning and manifesting the entire scene painted on the inside of the plate, with all its rich mythological images. The cosmic drama rushes upward from this Underworld head to soar into the highest Overworld heaven.

As the symbols and the nearby hieroglyphs indicate, the bottom third of the scene is the Underworld proper. It is filled with bloody water, on top of which floats a layer of what the Maya called "black water"—the underground water of the earth plane that seeps up into it from its Underworld source in the form of cave pools, muddy canals, and jungle-shaded streams. This bloody black water fills the mouth of the Black Transformer Serpent. It is clogged with what the hieroglyphs call "black water lilies," decaying plants whose decomposing remains create abundant life in this world. Something mysterious is taking place in these putrid but fertile waters of the Black Transformer portal: Death is transforming into life.

Rising from the bloody head at the center of the Underworld is the figure of a man with a head shaped like an ear of corn. This strange, unearthly figure is almost certainly the Maya Creator-god, First Father. We know from other evidence that First Father originally had the form of a tapir or peccary, but that after he was sacrificed by the Lords of Death in the Underworld and resurrected by his sons, the Twin Gods, he became the soul of the sacred maize plant and took on the appearance of a handsome young man with an elongated head. In this scene, we can see that First Father with his ear-of-corn head is in the process of resurrecting because he is wearing a belt with three stars on it. These stars may be the three stars of the constellation Orion's belt. If so, for the Maya, they marked the split in the so-called Cosmic Turtle Shell from which First Father was reborn in the myth of creation.

According to the myths, after the Xibalbans had sacrificed First Father, they hung his head in a calabash tree where it miraculously came to life and caused the tree to bear fruit. The myths go on to say that one day, a daughter of one of the Underworld demons—"Blood Woman," the moon aspect of First Mother—came to see the miracle of the living skull and the fruiting tree. The head of First Father seduced her and then impregnated her by spitting into her hand. From this "immaculate conception" First Lord and First Jaguar were born.

The artist of the offering plate painted two Underworld demons upside down, hanging from the underside of the watery surface of Xibalba. These terrible beings seem to be gazing in wonder and fear at First Father as he emerges from the cracked Turtle Shell, victorious over death. The ancient Maya belief that the Underworld was a mirror reflection of this world was probably inspired by gazing into pools of standing water. Even today, the visitor to the ruined city of Dzibilchaltun, peering down into the dark waters of its sacred cenote, or well, can see the upside-down images of its pyramids lurking between the lily pads that cover its surface. Farther down in the dark water, he or she can see the entrance to Xibalba itself, the black mouth of the vast underground cave system that underlies much of the northern Yucatan.

Lunging upward from the black waters of the earth plane is the firstborn son of First Father, First Lord, in his aspect as Chac-Xib-Chac, god of sacrifice, rain, blood, fertility, and the planet Venus. He, like his father below in the Underworld and like his brother above on the earth plane, is ascending from the dimension of death. All three figures appear from the waist up, their lower bodies still submerged in the Underworld-Otherworld realm from which they are rising. First Father, resurrecting from his own cracked Cosmic Turtle Shell head, is the primal, timeless model of life's triumph over death.

The Christian writers of the New Testament, who through their scriptures created their own kind of "Book of the Dead," depicted their dying-resurrecting god in the same way, saying of him that he was "the firstborn of many brothers" whose resurrection had been "predestined" through God's "foreknowledge" "before the foundation of the world."

Rising from the imagination of First Father, First Lord/Chac-Xib-Chac breaks the surface of the earthly waters and carries the resurrection into this world. Chac-Xib-Chac rears above the earth plane, a gigantic apparition whose bug eyes are still staring into the Otherworld reality from which he has come. He grips a sacrificial ax in his right hand. But his left hand is missing and his wrist is gushing torrents of blood that flood the earth.

First Lord/Chac-Xib-Chac has just won resurrection for his father and has put the Lords of Death under his power. He has limited their ability to cause suffering and destruction in the world he is about to help create. He is continuing the resurrection on the earth plane by the ecstatic vision *he* is having in the center of the plate, brought on by the blood sacrifice of his left hand. If the account in the later *Popol Vuh* is an accurate guide to this Classic Period scene, First Lord has been forced into this bloodletting ritual by his archenemy on the earth plane, Itzam-Yeh—the *uay* of Itzam-na, the cosmic shaman and the ruler of the Underworld. In the *Popol Vuh,* Itzam-Yeh, as Seven Macaw, tore off First Lord's arm and put it in his cooking pot. In this Classic Period scene Itzam-Yeh may have snapped off First Lord's hand with his fearsome beak and eaten it.

First Lord/Chac-Xib-Chac's massive loss of blood has put him in an altered state of consciousness that the artist has shown as a combination Vision Serpent and World Tree that rises up from the top of the god's head. This terrible Serpent-Tree divides into two blood-spurting branches. The left branch lashes out as an undulating snake body and head with gaping mouth. The right branch thrusts upward, and from an eruption of blood bursting through the serpent's skin, the third resurrection figure emerges, First Jaguar, the brother and *uay* of First Lord/Chac-Xib-Chac.

For the Maya, the Serpent-Tree that rises from First Lord's ecstatic visioning was a rich symbol for the *ch'ulel*-charged center of the universe and of every human soul, that which gave both of them life and the potential for rebirth. Since First Lord is actually a product of First Father's imagination, it is really First Father who is raising the World Tree through his son. This wondrous Tree had its roots in the Underworld. On the earth plane it shaped all time and space. Its topmost branches spread into the Overworld where they organized the space-time of the heavens and set the star fields in motion. In the Maya imagination this miraculous Tree manifested on earth as the giant ceiba. In the Underworld it appeared as the calabash—or cacao—tree, which, in the Blood Woman story, had been brought to life by First Father's vision-making head. The World Tree manifested in the night sky as the Milky Way in various forms, including the Crocodile Tree and the Canoe of Life and Death. It was the joyful expression of First Father's phallic energy, and its sap was his life-bearing semen. It was the pathway by which shamans, shaman-kings, and the dead could travel between the Underworld, the earth plane, and the Overworld, and it was the Xibal Be—the "Road of Awe"—along which Pacal is falling into the Underworld in his sarcophagus portrait. The World Tree was

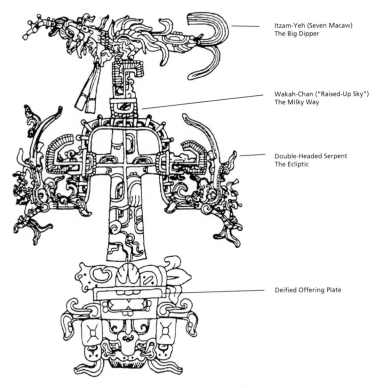

Itzam-Yeh (Seven Macaw)
The Big Dipper

Wakah-Chan ("Raised-Up Sky")
The Milky Way

Double-Headed Serpent
The Ecliptic

Deified Offering Plate

The World Tree as depicted on Pacal's sarcophagus lid.

also First Father's body—the Cosmic Corn Plant, which the Maya
called "First-Tree-Precious."

As the scene on the tripod plate shows, the Vision Serpent manifested the snake form of this fabulous phallic Tree. While vision serpents
came in many different forms, they all expressed various specialized aspects of this one great Tree-Snake.

First Jaguar rises from the right branch of the Serpent-Tree from
a leaf-shaped eruption of *itz*. He throws his head back, roaring and flailing at Itzam-Yeh with outstretched claws. The monster-bird flutters just
above the top of the Tree. First Jaguar has chased Itzam-Yeh from his
perch in the Tree's branches. The Principal Bird Deity has a look of panic
on his face, and is bleeding from a terrible chest wound, no doubt inflicted by First Jaguar. The Bird-god is almost certainly dying.

In the *Popol Vuh* Itzam-Yeh is pictured as the "false sun" of a savage,
out-of-control nature ruled by the Lords of Xibalba. First Jaguar appears
as the "true sun" who, along with First Lord, defeats the Bird-god aspect

of these destructive and deadly forces. By defeating the Lords of the Underworld both in Xibalba and on the earth plane, the Twin Gods made the universe as safe as it could be for the new creation to begin and human life to emerge.

First Lord, like his father—and *as* his brother—has won the world's resurrection by *imagining* it. He has achieved his victory on the earth plane by envisioning First Jaguar's destruction of Itzam-Yeh.

The man who commissioned this amazing plate was educated. He was trained in the Maya way of deep seeing. In the tomb, his soul would have gazed into the plate, scanned the symbols, and acted with cleverness and courage to outwit the Lords of Death, just as the Twin Gods had done. Through his training in seeing the hidden patterns in the universe, and through his ecstatic oneness with the triumphant gods of life, the dead man could have gained his individual resurrection.

Of course it is impossible to enter fully the mind of a long-dead person from an alien civilization. But we can try to know some of what he knew and see some of what he saw in this offering plate as the eyes of his soul peered into its mysteries.

We can be sure that this long-vanished Maya noble saw in the plate the unfolding of the great drama that shaped and fueled the universe. He would have immediately recognized that resurrection comes only through suffering and sacrifice. Salvation, the dead soul would have recalled, is not cheap. It is paid for by the shedding of one's own blood—literally and figuratively.

He would have seen depicted in his offering plate the aliveness of the universe—the mysterious Underworld-Otherworld, the soaring Overworld, and the rancid and fertile earth. He would have recalled that the earth's turtle shell often burst open to allow the forces of life to erupt from the fertilizing Underworld. He would have remembered that the earthly form the forces of life and creation take is the Vision Serpent/World Tree/Cosmic Maize Plant. He would have known that this shimmering, energy-charged Serpent-Tree, called into being by bloodletting rituals, was as central to the life of his own soul as it was to that of the cosmos.

From these and other insights the dead man would have recalled on a deeper level that the cosmic drama depicted on his offering plate was really the story of his own soul's journey, and that First Father/First Lord/First Jaguar's victory in the Otherworld was the gods' act of grace by which his own resurrection had been made possible. He would have gathered courage to face the Lords of the Underworld from his realization that his own rebirth would come from the very wellsprings of death, as had First Father's, as did the corn plant's.

When First Father raised the World Tree he "entered" and became the Tree. His act of entering, or perching, in the Tree's topmost branches as the new Principal Bird Deity magically organized all space and time and sent ripples of *ch'ulel* radiating out in every direction.

The three levels of the universe—Underworld, earth plane, and Overworld—like a fertilized egg dividing, immediately formed themselves into first four, then eight vertical partitions, so that the cosmos took on the appearance of a segmented sphere. The four quadrants, each divided in half, became magnets that attracted specific kinds of spiritual energy to them. These energies then portrayed themselves as colors. The later Maya believed in nine levels of heaven and nine levels of hell. But in the Classic Period these were originally the eight segments of the cosmic sphere plus the vertical World Tree/Vision Serpent center.

The gods and other divine entities, like the World Tree itself, divided into four so that from that moment on each would have five aspects, colors, and faces. In this way, the life-giving center could be present everywhere.

As the universe came alive, its three levels and nine segments were flooded with divine blood. Vast, unseen umbilical cord serpents began carrying *itz* to all the segments and dimensions of the new world. An awesome process of snake-energy exchange and transformation among the three levels of reality was set in motion. If the Maya shamans could manage the spiritual machinery of this supernatural irrigation system well, voluptuous and dangerous rivers of *itz* could now flow from the Otherworld onto the earth plane and erupt at various "power points," or portals.

For the Maya, the Universe was an exuberant celebration of fractals. Everything repeated itself in an endless variety of forms and sizes, and all things were mirror-image transformations of the same underlying life force. The giant turtle that was the earth was also the "First True Mountain" of creation from which maize had burst forth. This Turtle/Mountain was also the temple-pyramid (the "living mountain," as the Maya called it), which, in turn, was the Cosmic Turtle Shell of the Underworld-Overworld from which First Father had emerged at his resurrection. The watery cleft in the Cosmic Turtle Shell from which he arose was also the clefts in earthly mountains, water-filled caves and cenotes, the cleft of the sacred ballcourt, and the hole in the earth in which farmers planted their maize kernels and from which the corn sprang. The maize kernels themselves were known as "little skulls"—fractal incarnations of First Father's life-bearing severed head, cleft to release an upwelling of life force. All clefts, canals, rivers, streams, and female sexual organs were fractals of First Mother's vagina *and* the crack in First Father's head. Likewise, the Vision Serpent/World Tree/Cosmic Maize Plant, all earthly trees, corn and other crops, snakes, and the penises of men and animals were images of the Milky Way phallus of First Father.

All of these things were fractals of the renewing, re-creating, life-bearing center. This center did not have a single location. Like the mystics' definition of God—"God is a circle whose center is everywhere and whose circumference is nowhere"—the Maya center was anywhere a human being could enter the altered emotional state of blood-ecstasy. Then the seemingly solid universe would suddenly reveal its true dreamlike nature, and a portal would open to the *really* Real.

The Maya used many objects and places as tools to help them open their portals to divine reality. They used natural features such as caves and cenotes, hills and mountains—anywhere they could find patterns that reminded them of the divine center. They also created their own man-made fractals. Among these were the temple-pyramids. These were often built over caves with standing water. Where caves were not present, they built their pyramids over underground "dreaming places" and the burial vaults of ancestral shaman-kings, like Pacal. Often the Maya architects and artists created whole ranges of living mountains complete with their own plateaus and cleft valleys. All Maya pyramids were equipped with artificial cave mouths in the temples at their tops. Ballcourts with slanting walls and center markers, designed to offer glimpses of the mythic events occurring in the Underworld below, also created cleft portals. Sunken plazas with ceremonial stairs down which sacrificed victims were thrown to the demons of Xibalba activated the same death-resurrection technology. All of these architectural wonders were meant to amplify the powers of the natural power points in surrounding mountains and valleys in order to guarantee the ongoing flow of *ch'ulel* and keep the resurrection of the world going.

Along with this permanent portal machinery the Maya also used portable transporters, especially mirrors and offering plates. Inherited from their distant shamanic past in Asia, mirrors made of polished pyrite crystals helped the shamans see more deeply. After taking trance-

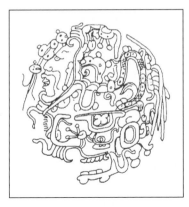

An offering plate as a portal to the Otherworld,
showing a vision serpent rising from its center.

inducing drugs, they gazed into their mirrors and saw the deeper layers
of reality hidden within their own souls and behind the illusory surface of
the created world. Perhaps like the Christian Saint Paul, they longed for
the time when, instead of "seeing in a mirror darkly," they could turn
around and see the Divine Being "face-to-face."

Offering plates worked in a similar way by giving the dimension-
traveler a road map to Otherworldly destinations. Often these plates depicted specific places in the Otherworld that the shaman wanted to reach.
Sometimes, as in the case of the tripod plate, the paintings on these
portable transporters showed the hoped-for Vision Serpent rising from
the target portal. Occasionally the portal appeared in the bottom of the
plate head-on, opening to swallow the shaman into its fearful depths.

Another way the Maya opened the portals to the Otherworld was
by sounding conch-shell trumpets. These trumpets, cast up by the Otherworld ocean and fashioned into portal-opening instruments by the
shaman-artists, were often elegant works of art. When the shamans blew
the sacred conch-shell trumpet in bloodletting ceremonies and funerary
rites, and as their armies went into battle, the unearthly sound an-
nounced the arrival of the death state, enlightenment, and the approach
of the Underworld. The eerie notes tore the fabric of normal space and
time and heralded the eruption of the Divine Life onto the earth plane.

Although anthropologists and language experts are still trying to
understand the ancient Maya portal system, it seems likely that all the
portals depicted in Maya art and architecture were really different manifestations of the two primary portals. These great "stargates" lay at either
end of the World Tree/Vision Serpent—one at its foot in the southern
sky and the other in its branches in the far north. The southern portal was
the White-Bone Snake/Black Transformer/Black Dreaming Place, the

entrance to the Underworld. The northern portal the Maya called the 01 Portal. This was the portal through which the souls of newborn babies entered the earth plane from the Otherworld. The 01 Portal opened near the place in the sky where First Father eternally burst forth from the Cosmic Turtle Shell.

Transformation of the soul took place in the Underworld, on the other side of the Black Dreaming Place. Resurrection happened through the 01 Portal. This harrowing, life-and-death pilgrimage of the soul took place through the terror of being swallowed by the White-Bone Snake, digested in its poisonous innards, and then vomited up—a new being. Snake-energy either killed the soul or made it a god—more whole, more real, and more alive than before its encounter with death.

Stars have always fascinated human beings. Our species has always turned its eyes to the heavens, scanning its awesome depths for the miraculous. The night sky and whatever inhabitants it may harbor other than ourselves draw us up in wonder and dread.

The Maya shamans saw in the mysterious, liquid movements of the constellations and the Milky Way, especially on certain momentous nights, the annual unfolding of the terrifying and wondrous struggle between the gods of life and the demons of death. The shaman-kings dedicated their ballcourts in the dead of night on these sacred dates, as the stars wheeled into position in silent splendor. From the inscriptions on his stelae, we know that Eighteen-Rabbit of Copan timed the erection of his huge stone portraits to correspond with the stars' cyclical reenactment of the primal drama.

Everywhere the Maya looked they saw traces of the great story. In the hushed beauty of the night sky, they could watch in awe as the story unfolded in all its terrifying magnificence. To look up into that awesome void was also to stare down into the Underworld-Otherworld and back in time to the moment of creation.

The Maya shamans saw in the ecliptic—the invisible path of the sun, moon, and planets—the wondrous and menacing body of the Twin Gods in their Cosmic Monster form. The shaman-kings held a double-headed serpent bar clasped to their chests in ecstatic trance to show that they were masters of the ecliptic serpent's power. The astronomers saw in the Big Dipper the story of Itzam-Yeh's arrogance and tragic end; in Gemini, First Father and First Mother's lovemaking, long before the birth of human passion; in Orion, the three hearthstones the gods had painted to begin the new creation and the crack in the Cosmic Turtle Shell First Father had stepped through as the original Lord of Life.

As the Milky Way slowly turned in the sky, and rose and set, they saw their universe come into being. On certain fateful nights they saw how, from a position low on the southern horizon, the Milky Way formed a lighted arch above a black pocket in the sky and became the jaws of the White-Bone Snake. They saw the black pocket as the Black Transformer itself, usually invisible to human eyes, but on these special nights dreadfully apparent. Later, on these same nights, as the Milky Way reared in the sky like a gigantic serpent about to strike, they watched the miracle of the raising of the Vision Serpent/World Tree and the paving of the glittering Xibal Be, the highway that led to the realm of death.

On other nights, the shamans could see the Milky Way becoming the mythic Canoe of Life that carried the spirit of First Father to the place of creation and resurrection. At 12:30 A.M. they could watch the celestial Canoe unload its precious cargo at the Cosmic Turtle Shell. Then, by 2:30, when the Milky Way began its plunge below the horizon, they gazed in horror as the Canoe of Life became the Canoe of Death.

Time for the Maya, like space, was mysteriously alive, and like space with its fractal power points and portals, it was uneven. It gathered itself into awesome moments, days, years, and vast cycles in which the hidden events taking place in the Otherworld made themselves immediately felt in human lives.

We, too, sometimes feel the strange, living quality of time, especially at important turning points in our lives, like birthdays, New Year's celebrations, marriages, divorces, and deaths. At these and other times we gaze back with longing and nostalgia, remembering what has already happened to us and wondering what is in store for us in our uncertain futures.

But it isn't just the *events* of time—past and future—that may move us in such moments of higher awareness. It is time itself, which, when we allow ourselves to really enter it, may feel like a living thing, far more ancient and enduring than we are. In moments like these time seems to have a will and direction of its own.

For the Maya, time was the chronological enactment of the great story of death and rebirth, which in the eternal now of the Otherworld took place "above" time. The hours, days, months, years, decades, and the larger cycles of time the Maya could discern were the endlessly repeating patterns of the rhythmic comings and goings of divine beings. As the sun, the moon, the planets, constellations, and the Milky Way moved, the shamans could see time unfolding itself in the sky. And as the rainy and dry seasons swirled around each other and grappled for power, time forced all things on earth to play a part in the cosmic drama.

Time, like space, was quadrated, and the shape of the universe was as much the shape of time as it was of physical structures. By quadrating, time animated every part of the cosmos. Like space, time expressed itself in fractals. The hours of the night were the nine refractions of the Lord of Death. Months of twenty days each, called *uinalob*—"human beings"—were the gigantic replicas of human fingers and toes. The twenty-day months were fractals of four hundred-year periods, called *baktunob*.

For the Maya every day was the awesome manifestation of the Cosmic Monster's journey from east to west across the arch of heaven. As it dragged its bloated crocodile-snake body across the sky, it created the hours of the day and the movements of the sun, moon, and planets. Its front head—the planet Venus—had an elephantlike snout, a scrawny, dangling beard, terrifying rows of teeth, and hooded eyes that were closed as if savoring the bloody sacrifice it was consuming. It had deer ears and hooves. The rear head of the Monster—the sun—was shown upside down, as if in painful resignation to its role as the sacrificial victim of the crocodile-deer. This sun head had a blunt nose, puffy eyes, and a skeletal jaw—signs of the torture it was enduring in the belly of the crocodile. Its forehead was an offering plate—a symbol of the sacrificed soul. Between the "death star" and the tortured sun the planets clogged the Cosmic Monster's intestines.

The Maya shamans created two different calendars that, as they interacted with each other, revealed the hidden connections among all earthly and Otherworldly events. One calendar was especially sacred. It directly expressed the divine drama, which measured itself out in the form of ever-recurring cycles of 260 days, divided into thirteen months. The other calendar, like our own modern calendar, was made up of 365 days. This calendar was called *tun*—"stone"—because at its completion the Maya raised stelae in its honor. It was divided into eighteen months.

As the days of the two calendars engaged each other like the gears of a vast machine, they produced a holy fifty-two-year cycle, which for the Maya was filled with dread. The shamans believed that the end of each of these sacred cycles threatened the destruction of civilized life, and every Maya city took precautions to avoid this catastrophe.

According to the shamans, human events were best timed to resonate with the subtle vibrations as well as the great upsurges of divine power, as the gods created, destroyed, and re-created the patterns of time. The Maya seers recommended the most *ch'ulel*-charged dates for specific human actions like planting and harvesting, marrying, naming children, dedicating ballcourts, ritually activating and deactivating the living mountain-pyramids, erecting stone monuments, and going to war.

At the same time, they saw that *human* actions affected the Otherworld and reshaped the very fabric of time and space. The building of temple-pyramids, plazas, and ballcourts changed the divine power grid in nature, and important human happenings caused shifts in the flow of time.

The ruins of Copan are haunted by a sense of time—and its catastrophic end. On the top of a mound at the northern end of the ancient ballcourt entrance to the Underworld is a mysterious monument archaeologists call Altar L. Altar L is an eerie witness to the unknown disaster that overtook the city. On the south side, facing the ballcourt, the carving is complete. We can see a depiction of U-Cit Tok (the last king) and Yax Pac (his great ancestor) seated across from each other involved in some kind of ritual. But on the north side, the artist began to work, sketched the figures in, and then, practically in midstroke, dropped his

Altar L from Copan.

tools and left the site—forever. The date of Altar L—the last recorded date at Copan—is February 10, 822 A.D.

We ourselves live at the close of an age, a moment in history in which romantic hopes and powerful fears rise to a climax as one millennium gives way to another. The disasterizers among us envision a universal catastrophe that will end human life as we know it. The optimists expect a new golden age in which our societies will be transformed into utopias.

Some of the Maya priests appear to have predicted the end of the present creation for December 23, 2012. Others calculated the end for either October 15 or 23 of the year 4772. And yet those with perhaps greater powers to fathom the "not as yet" foresaw that this, the age of true human beings, would last at least 142 nonillion years.

But are predictions of the end of the world genuine prophecies or are they something else? There is certainly a deep emotional and spiritual wisdom about the belief that the world ends every now and then. Such a belief grips the human soul at its very core and engages it with a vital, living universe. It can cause us to experience space and time as a living thing that moves and changes like a great serpent periodically shedding its skin in cosmic cataclysms, and then making everything new.

Still, the feelings of terror and hope so many people have felt throughout history about the end of the world, instead of being history, may really be outward projections of our own personal deaths and anxiously awaited rebirths. Perhaps the end the Maya predicted is really a cataclysm within the soul as the dark portal of its annihilation looms before it and it both dreads and yearns for its "moment of truth." It could be that our hopes and fears about the end of the world are coded messages from our souls warning us through their own form of hieroglyphics—images and symbols cast up in dreams and moments of deep reverie—that we need to get on with our own personal resurrections. Maya wisdom, deeper than priestly speculations about the end of history, says exactly that. And the ancient resurrection teachings make a further point: If we do not get about the business of being reborn now while we have the chance, when we die we will be truly dead—and not for a while, but forever.

When first exposed to the beliefs of ancient spiritualities about the nature of the universe, many modern people may react with feelings of ridicule and disgust. But we may need to take another look. For example, the three-layered structure of the Maya universe with its seemingly childlike picture of an upside-down Underworld may seem unscientific and naive until we realize that mythological descriptions of things are always projections onto the world of our own psychological structures and makeup. Jungian psychologists might see in the upside-down Underworld a representation of Jung's idea of the shadow, the reverse, or mirror image, of our conscious attitudes and our supposedly good qualities. Like the ancient Maya, Jung believed we must defeat our personal demons and the demons that afflict our whole species. But we must do it in a way that allows us to embody some of their fierce qualities in our own lives.

From this perspective, the inverted Underworld appears as the shadow side of both our personal unconscious and the "collective unconscious," that universal aspect of ourselves that dwells below the surface of our personal unconscious. There, hidden in the dark waters of the Black Transformer, lurk our demons. We fear these complexes and archetypes for good reason. They usually try to kill our joys, our hopes, our plans, our loves and relationships. Unfortunately, most of us do not have the resurrection technology to turn their attacks into life-bearing victories for ourselves. Jung might also have seen in the Maya Otherworld that mysterious and haunting presence at the core of each human being that he called the Self, the image of God within.

The Maya belief, shared by all ancient spiritualities, that human beings are microcosms of the universe, and that all things mirror each other and are interconnected, finds confirmation in modern psychology, philosophy, and science. Jung translated the ancient saying "as above, so below" into the psychological truth "as within, so without." Careful reflection will reveal to most of us that our outer worlds *do* tend to mirror what is going on inside of us. The philosopher Alfred North Whitehead claimed he had proved mathematically the interconnectedness of all things. He called this theory "causation at a distance." He said that events in distant galaxies had a cause-effect relationship with events in our daily lives because everything in the universe is tied to everything else. The new field of fractals as well as modern cosmology say the same thing. Both claim that in the primal fireball from which the cosmos exploded in the big bang all the patterns and forces we see today were present. Both have demonstrated the fact that though the universe is much larger now, it has kept its ancient unity.

The Maya belief that time and space are a single time-space and that time has a "shape" is echoed in Einstein's thought. The hallucinogenic, ecstatically alive quality of the world the Maya experienced is confirmed by modern subatomic physics. When subatomic physicists look closely at the particles that make up atoms, they observe startling and mysterious things. They see that a single subatomic particle can appear at one and the same time in two different places—without ever having divided. A solid particle is also a wave of energy. These tiny waves or particles emerge out of a matterless dimension, form as congealed bits of pure energy, and then disappear, sometimes in millionths of a second. Using Hindu imagery, the physicist Fritjof Capra comes closest to the Maya vision of a living cosmos made up of shifting forms of energy when he writes:

> The Dance of Shiva . . . symbolizes . . . the cosmic cycles of creation and destruction. . . . Shiva reminds us that the manifold forms in the world are . . . not fundamental, but illusory— like the subatomic particles of which our universe is made—and ever-changing—as he keeps creating and dissolving them in the ceaseless flow of his dance. The Dance of Shiva is the dancing universe; the ceaseless flow of energy going through an infinite variety of patterns that melt into one another.

Some people may object that the Maya were claiming that the cosmos is *literally* alive, while Capra and other physicists are using images of the universe's aliveness as metaphors. But even if this is true, questions about the origins and ultimate nature of energy itself remain. What, as the German philosophers wondered, is "the thing itself"? Science alone cannot answer this question. Only theology—and mythology—can.

The belief that the material world is surrounded by a mysterious Otherworld finds confirmation in modern cosmology, which has shown the mathematical probability that other space-time worlds exist, and that before the big bang—in a dimension known as the "Planck Era"—all things dwelled in a spaceless/timeless Elsewhere and Elsewhen.

The ancient Maya belief that there are portals between dimensions of reality finds scientific support in the theory of wormholes. These mathematical constructs are tunnels that carry enormously powerful cascades of light and energy between black holes—which suck everything around them into their bottomless depths—and white holes—from which this superenergized material explodes. As far-fetched as such an idea may sound, we need to remember that before the existence of black holes was proven, they too appeared only as mathematical formulas.

The apparently naive belief of the Maya shamans that by looking up into the night sky they were actually looking back at the events of creation has been validated by modern astronomers. We now know that the farther out we reach with our telescopes the farther back in time we are seeing. We have now "time-traveled" to the birth of the first galaxies nearly fourteen billion years ago. Finally, the Maya conviction that our world is engaged in a process of mutual enrichment and unfolding with the Otherworld that results in a kind of evolution through various cosmic eras by repeated patterns of birth, destruction, and rebirth is confirmed by modern cosmology, evolutionary theories, and by Whitehead's process philosophy.

If we scratch the surface of our high school science and the short-hand explanations by which most of us live our daily lives, we will find a world very different from the one we've been led to believe in. We may even feel a little betrayed that we have been duped into believing in a domesticated, explainable universe, safe from the inherently unknowable and irreducibly mysterious, safe from the darkness, and safe from blood. But, whether we like it or not, the universe of our most advanced sciences is disturbingly similar to the cosmos the ancient Maya imagined. And if the Maya saw so deeply into the true nature of the universe, perhaps their intuitions about the fate of the soul after death were equally accurate.

CHAPTER 4

Blood and Ecstasy

Six naked gods crouch together over bowls piled high with strips of paper in the timeless Void of the Otherworld. Beneath their feet words are gathering out of the ether to create an undulating floor of hieroglyphs—the mysterious, concretized language of an Abyss beyond the reach of all finite minds. Deeper than these, monstrous apparitions of supernatural splendor vibrate like nuclear reactor cores, radiant symbols for Otherworldly places that exist only in the imagination of the unnameable Something or Someone that gives them a borrowed reality.

Looks of wonder and horror steal across the faces of the gathered divinities. Suddenly, the feathers on their plumed headdresses shudder as they snap their heads back in preparation for the fearful moment. Their mouths drop open as they raise the terrible instruments of self-sacrifice high above their heads. Then, together, they plunge the elaborately carved, razor-sharp spikes through their penises. Their blood splashes into the Void. Lightning cracks, and the total blackness of the boundless Otherworld ocean flashes an electric red. The gods leap into the light from the neon background. The creation of the world has begun!

This is the scene on a now-famous Classic Period vase from Hue-

The Huehuetenango vase depicting the creator gods, including the Twin Gods, drawing blood from their penises in order to resurrect the universe.

huetenango, Guatemala. It depicts one of several versions of the first moments of Creation as the Maya saw it. In this, the primary portrayal, the universe burst into being from the *ch'ulel*-charged imaginations of the creator gods in the midst of the visions they had induced through the terrible rite of bloodletting. For the Maya, one way or another, the universe—and human life—were the products of the fierce love of a Divine Being whose blood-rapture had hallucinated the creator gods themselves into existence. This fierce love was so powerful it had turned nothing into something, and through self-inflicted suffering had kick-started the resurrection of life from the abyss of eternal death.

According to the Maya, this fearful self-sacrifice of the Divine Being had provided the life force that created, sustained, and forever re-created the universe and human beings. For their part, human beings were obligated to participate in this original divine sacrifice by repeating it in their own self-sacrificial rituals, thereby keeping the creative energy of the Divine Being circulating throughout all the levels of reality. In the process, the soul was empowered to engage in sacred acts of cocreation, to "give birth" to the gods on the earth plane, and to achieve a oneness with the Divine Being that would guarantee its survival after death.

We know what came before and after the scene on the Huehuetenango vase from the many depictions of bloodletting rituals the Maya painted on their ceramics and carved on their temple walls, as well as from eyewitness accounts by the Spanish conquerors. These bloodletting ceremonies took different forms and had various purposes. But they were all excruciatingly painful, and designed to create a state of shock that would induce hallucinatory visions of power and beauty.

The Maya let their blood on many minor occasions—the birth of a child, the dedication of a new house, the first planting of the season.

Lintel 17 from Yaxchilan, showing King Bird-Jaguar and one of his wives, Lady Balam-Ix, engaged in a bloodletting ceremony. Bird-Jaguar is drawing blood from his penis, Lady Balam-Ix from her tongue.

But they saved the most awesome forms of bloodletting for state events, high religious festivals, and the creation of works of art. They prepared themselves for achieving the altered states of consciousness that were central to these rituals by secluding themselves, fasting, abstaining from sexual contact, and taking hallucinogenic drugs such as balche, peyote, toxic mushrooms, and morning-glory seeds. They pierced themselves with richly ornamented obsidian or flint spikes or stingray spines that were crowned with shimmering mini-quetzal-feather headdresses. These "bloodletters," as anthropologists call them, were divine beings with personalities and wills of their own. They were all manifestations of the original supernatural bloodletters that had materialized in the gods' hands from the energy fields of the Otherworld moments before the terrible ritual of creation.

After they had opened a wound with the bloodletter, the Maya drew heavy hemp ropes, often with thorns woven into them, through their bleeding members. They leaned over offering plates filled with strips of paper. When the paper was saturated with *itz* it was set on fire. The sacred smoke that billowed up from these offering plates formed clouds of materialized *ch'ulel* in imitation of the rain-bearing storm clouds of the Overworld. Sometimes the smoke became the bloody placentas through which the gods could be born into this world. Usually, the rising column stretched itself into the rearing Vision Serpent through whose open jaws a divine Reality emerged to speak words of wisdom, empower with its supernatural energy, and inspire with rapturous images of truth and beauty—images of life, of creation, and of Being. These vision serpents were the vehicles of transformation and the "machinery" that allowed the shamans, gods, and deified ancestors to move in and out of the various dimensions of sacred Reality.

Blood could be drawn from several areas of the body, including the arms, thighs, and hands. When it was drawn from the hands in what researchers call "scattering rites," it was sprinkled into offering plates that symbolized the earth, in imitation of the planting of maize kernels. Scattering rites were acts of sympathetic magic designed to stimulate the corn to yield a bountiful harvest.

The most sacred sources of human *itz* were the ears, the tongue, and the penis. The Maya shaman-kings, scribes, artists, and others opened their ears in order to hear the gods' oracles and revelations. They opened their tongues to be able to speak what they had heard. And they opened their penises in order to participate in the divine pro-creation of the cosmos—to re-create their own lives and the lives of their kingdoms and people.

The images of the original divine bloodletting on the Huehuete-

Lintel 2 from La Pasadita, showing Bird-Jaguar and a village chief performing the scattering rite.

nango vase are profoundly sexual. For the Maya, the offering plates of blood sacrifice were miniature versions of the universe, symbols of the "blue-green plate, the blue-green bowl," as the *Popol Vuh* calls the earth and sky. By ejaculating their bloody semen into the potential world the creators are impregnating it with the divine "soul-stuff" that will quicken it to life. By burning their *itz* the gods will transform their *ch'ulel* into the world-making Vision Serpent.

Modern people brought up in the Judeo-Christian tradition may be sickened by the central importance the Maya attached to blood rituals, but as scholars of religion like Mircea Eliade and Joseph Campbell have pointed out, a primeval sacrifice dwells at the core of all spiritual traditions. Christianity is awash in the "blood of the Lamb" that, according to the theologians, has re-created the world. And all the more ancient religions that Christianity is based upon portray blood sacrifice as the foundation for the creation of the cosmos. In ancient Mesopotamian and Canaanite religion, the creator gods killed and dismembered the original goddess and made the earth and sky from her body. Her blood became the rivers and streams. In the ancient Persian religion, Mithraism, the god Mithra sacrificed a cosmic bull to make the world, and in the Dionysian mysteries the worshipers of the god tore apart a living goat and drank its blood in order to renew their souls. The wine of Dionysus, like that of the Christian Eucharist, was really divine blood. Even the Jewish tradition, which has staunchly opposed blood sacrifice ever since the destruction of the Temple of Jerusalem in 70 A.D., has as its foundation myth the near human sacrifice of Isaac by his father, Abraham. Some scholars believe that the original version of this story carried the sacrifice through to its bitter end.

Another Classic Period Maya vase shows the newborn universe unfolding from the vision that followed the Divine Being's bloodletting ritual. Found at Acasaguastlan in Guatemala, this magnificent ceramic depicts the ecstasy of the Sun God (an aspect of the Twin Gods) as he sits in the Otherworld, legs crossed and hands folded on his chest in the rapt pose of Maya shamans in bloodletting trance. He clutches two feathered Vision Serpents that snake through his arms and rear up on either side. These serpents symbolize light and darkness, life and death, the Overworld and the Underworld, and depict the duality at the core of Maya spiritual experience. The serpent on the Sun God's right glitters with mirror signs and blood-symbols for supernatural brightness. Strangely, mysteriously, the Sun God himself emerges from its mouth. The serpent on the left wears signs for darkness and the waters of the Underworld.

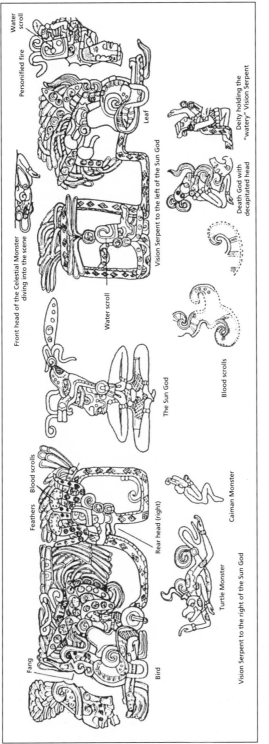

A schematic drawing of the Acasaguastlan vase, showing the world coming into being from the ecstatic vision of the Sun God.

The vision this serpent manifests is a leaf and a human being. Entwined in the coils of these two world-making snakes are animals, humans, the Cosmic Monster, and a death god holding a severed head.

The Underworld serpent shows that plant life and human beings spring from the dark, watery regions below the earth plane. The bright serpent shows God imagining Himself into being in the Overworld. The image of human sacrifice proclaims the resurrection technology by which a shaman could enter the Underworld-Otherworld and rise again into eternal life.

The creation spirituality depicted on the Acasaguastlan vase is amazingly similar to Hindu beliefs. In Hinduism the created universe is the vision of Brahma, who, as he sleeps in the timelessness of the "unmanifest" world, breathes his dream into concrete, physical form. He even imagines himself into his dream—as all the things he is creating, but especially as human beings. As he first emerges into this visionary world he appears as a figure with three faces. The face on the left is his destructive and deathly aspect, the one on the right his creative and life-bearing side. The face in the middle is himself in the grip of his vision.

Taoism also provides a remarkable parallel to the Maya creation depicted on the Acasaguastlan vase. Corresponding to the two vision serpents of light and darkness, Taoism's first act of creation is the manifestation of all the pairs of opposites—ultimately the opposing forces of creation and destruction, life and death.

It is easy to see the Asiatic origins of Maya spirituality in these and other parallels from the religions of India, China, and Japan. The Jewish, Christian, and Moslem religions, perhaps less honest about the inherent duality of the Divine Being's creative rapture, still assume that behind the sacred Word by which God manifests the world is his imagination. The world as it is is ultimately the expression of his exuberance and passion.

The Maya believed that it fell to the shamans, in creative partnership with the Divine, to concentrate and channel the *ch'ulel*/blood-energy of the Otherworld. In a sense, the shamans were like modern engineers. But instead of nuclear power plants and electrical grids they used pyramids and Vision Serpent portals. Instead of electron flows they used *itz*. The spilling of blood, like the throwing of a giant breaker switch, brought life-giving energy pouring into the universe from the underlying force fields of the Otherworld.

In part, this bloodletting was a process of simple engineering. But it was also the expression of an emotional contract. Since the gods had shown their love for their creatures with such overwhelming intensity by the ferocity of their original, and ongoing, self-sacrifice, human beings had to pay them back in kind. In addition to this payback scheme, the Maya also let their blood to petition the gods and deified ancestors for help and advice, to conjure the energies they needed for their world-making tasks, and to achieve their ultimate creative goal—ecstatic oneness with the great Mystery.

Probably the most common motivations for bloodletting took the form of acts of piety and prayers of petition. These are still the most common motives for approaching the Divine today. Acts of piety—words of gratitude, confessions of sins, and so on—assume that a vast gulf exists between human beings and the Divine. God is infinite; we are finite. God is perfect; we are sinful. God is self-sufficient; we are dependent. All religions teach that the awareness of human creaturehood is a vital aspect of our relationship with the Divine Being, and that if our pious impulses are genuine, they can bring a sense of relief and reconciliation to the soul. The problem is that for many people these feelings are often superficial. Too often we either mumble our prayers with little awareness or feeling, or we display them to others to gain status and power. The great spiritual teachers have always warned against this kind of insincerity. Jesus frequently called the pious of his day a "brood of vipers" and he advised his followers to:

> Beware of practicing your piety before men in order to be seen
> by them; for then you will have no reward from your Father who
> is in heaven.

Bloodletting as practiced by the ancient Maya made genuine piety more likely. Self-inflicted physical pain, and the altered states of consciousness that came with it, made expressions of thanksgiving, confession, and repentance much more than lip service. Real pain must have transformed even self-aggrandizement into something more than mere theatrics.

Likewise, when the ancient Maya asked the Divine Being for help, what they had to go through to get it made their petitions far more than the neurotic bargains so many modern people try to make with a god they often don't really believe in and with whom they almost never bother to consult—until disaster strikes.

When the Maya let their blood to ask for help, they were seeking a concrete vision and an overpowering emotional experience of the Divine Being. On a carved lintel from Yaxchilan a queen, Lady Xoc, still holding the bloodletting instruments she has just finished using, gazes up at the ancestral warrior she has conjured from the fanged mouth of a terrifying Vision Serpent. The warrior emerges fully armed, brandishing a shield made from a flayed human face and the spear of Tlaloc/Venus warfare. Lady Xoc has sought—and received—the fearful energy of a threatening warrior-god.

This lintel from Yaxchilan, and others like it, point beyond acts of petition to bloodletting as a method for conjuring supernatural forces. Although petitioning and conjuring are closely related, conjuring requires more active involvement on the part of the petitioner. It demands that the vision seeker use his or her imagination to reach deep inside the soul and focus on the vision or energy he/she is trying to actualize. This involvement with the inner world was certainly the central dynamic in bloodletting rituals whenever the shaman-kings constellated—or brought forth—the World Tree. It was also essential to the mysterious rites that gave birth to the gods on the earth plane.

An eerie phrase often appears with these carved or painted scenes in which the gods are shown materializing in clouds lined with drops of blood. These placentalike clouds hover above the heads and shoulders of the shaman-kings who have called them forth. The phrase calls these conjurers the "mothers" of the gods and says that through their bloodletting they have actually given birth to the divine beings. If the interpretation of these scenes is correct, the Maya may have reached a profound level of esoteric wisdom in which they believed that God and human beings, by envisioning each other, made *each other* real.

In a fascinating modern parallel to this ancient wisdom Alfred North Whitehead put forward a theory of divine "process." According to Whitehead's theory, the ongoing creation of the universe occurs through a mutual divine-human interaction. God "lures" the beings of the created world into making "creative advances," as Whitehead calls them. At the same time, every "creative advance" on the part of Its creatures contributes to the further unfolding and development of the Divine Being Itself. In this way, the manifest and unmanifest aspects of God give rise to each other and make each other progressively more real. By becoming the "mothers" of God, the Maya shamans entered into a creative partnership with the Lords of Life in their continuing re-creation and resurrection of the universe.

"Sympathetic magic" was another reason the Maya performed their bloodletting ceremonies. Sympathetic magic expresses the belief that all things mirror each other—so much so that when human beings perform rituals that imitate mythological events in the Dream Time, they reactivate those supernatural events and manifest them on earth. When a shaman-king let his blood to dedicate a new pyramid—itself a model of the universe in all its aspects—he was stimulating the energy fields of *ch'ulel* throughout the cosmos and concentrating them in the temple. When a queen let her blood to conjure Tlaloc/Venus warrior-energy for her husband's military campaigns, she was reactivating the Otherworld triumph of the Twin Gods over the Lords of Death.

The ultimate purpose of bloodletting for the ancient Maya was to achieve enraptured oneness with the God of creation. Through pain to divine passion, through divine passion to transcendence, bloodletting was the way to learn to live forever.

In no religion does ecstatic oneness with God cancel out the dependent relationship between the creature and its Creator that acts of piety, confession, petition, and even conjuring embody. Instead, merger with the Divine goes *beyond* the ego's experience of itself as a finite being to the deep core of the soul where God and the individual are one. This is the part of the soul Hindus have called the "Atman," Buddhists the "Essence of Mind," and Jung the "Self." According to all ancient wisdom traditions, including that of the Maya, this is the infinite and eternal part of us that each ego must engage in a creative, self-transcending relationship if it hopes to survive the death of the body.

The experience of ecstatic oneness with the Divine comes in many forms: quiet contentment, a sense of gentle rapture, a mystical feeling of universal harmony, all-consuming passion, flights of spiritual abandon, and ferocious joy. The quest for ecstasy explains drug addiction and the use of mind-altering substances by the mystics and seers of many religions. It also explains all kinds of sexual behavior, and the human fascination for atrocities as well. But the most powerful experience of ecstasy is a combination of all these feelings, when, in one unforgettable moment, we touch the hidden God—the terrible and wonderful Mystery that has given birth to all things and that makes them glow and dance with Its life force. In those moments we may see what It sees and feel at least an infinitesimal part of what It feels.

The Hindu sages teach that we are all Brahma playing at being us. Brahma plays his parts so well—He has infinite ability—that he "forgets" who he is. It is the human soul's job to remember. When it does, according to the gurus, it loses its individual identity in perfect oneness with Brahma.

The experience of oneness with God reaches exhilarating— and dangerous—heights, dangerous both from the standpoint of the ego, which may be swallowed up in their darker aspects, and dangerous for the well-being of the individual in a society less spiritually advanced than himself or herself. The great Sufi prophet al-Hallāj was condemned to death by the Moslem clerics for proclaiming this mystical oneness of creature and Creator in the depths of the soul. Caught up in the rapture of his insight he spoke the words that ended his life: "If ye do not recognise God, at least recognise His signs. I am that sign, I am the Creative Truth, because through the Truth I am a truth eternally!" Christian mystics have felt a similar identification with the Divine Being in moments of ecstasy, often with the same fatal, or near-fatal, results. Spelling out the powerful implications of his own ecstatic experiences, the medieval Christian mystic Meister Eckhart said:

> It is more worth to God his being brought forth spiritually in the individual virgin or good soul than that he was born of Mary bodily. But this involves the notion of *our* being the only Son whom the Father has eternally begotten. When the Father begat all creatures, he was begetting me; I flowed out with all creatures while remaining within in the Father.

Meister Eckhart came very close to being branded a heretic and executed for statements like these.

The same experience of merger with the Divine appears in the writings of the Jewish kabbalist Abulafia. Speaking of the scholar-mystic who has experienced God directly, he wrote:

> . . . now he is no longer separated from his Master, and behold he is his Master and his Master is he . . . and there is no difference between them, except that his Master has His supreme rank by His own right. . . .

In contrast to the teachings of so many mystical traditions—both of the East and the West—that the goal of ecstatic merger with God is the destruction of the ego, the ancient Maya shamans sought a balance between their impulse for self-annihilation and their fierce desire to keep their individual identities. We can see that they achieved this balance in the way they depicted masks and costumes. When the Maya artists showed masks in X-ray or cutaway views, they were affirming the individual human identity of the wearer at the very moment he or she was transforming into a god. The elaborate costumes that helped their wearers deify, at the same time powerfully reinforced their human personalities. The most dramatic examples of this are the stelae of Eighteen-Rabbit at Copan. On these huge carved limestone slabs the king at first seems almost lost in the overwhelming detail of his elaborate mythological costumes. But the artists made his face such a striking portrait of the *man,* and contrasted his features so forcefully with the welter of imagery that envelopes him, that even after twelve hundred years the power of his personality still leaps from the stones. The enraptured face of Eighteen-Rabbit—not his costumes—is what lingers in the visitor's mind as a haunting memory.

More restrained than the mysticism of most other faiths, Maya spirituality usually represented the God-human merger as a "like-in-kind" relationship rather than as a total absorption of the human by the Divine. This applied to wars, ballgames, sacrifices, building dedications, and other ritual events. Even though they celebrated the experience of oneness with the gods, they also proclaimed the actual historical actions and the individual personalities of the shaman-kings who performed them. And, as is poignantly illustrated at Palenque, the kings sometimes even changed the myths to fit the patterns of their own lives and the histories of their families.

The great scholar of ancient Maya history and spirituality, J. Eric Thompson, said that the Maya always approached the Divine Being in a practical way. He claimed that they never worshiped their gods out of love or even for the sake of the ecstatic experiences they could have. Instead, said Thompson, the Maya always expected something in return—actually, not very different from the attitude most people have today. While we can't really know what these long-dead people felt in their moments of rapture with the great Mystery, it does seem logical that the shamans viewed their experiences as tools, as part of the technology that would help them win their resurrections.

At the same time, we can also see in Maya art, architecture, and

King Eighteen-Rabbit of Copan deep in an Otherworldly trance.

writing what appears to be a great yearning for at least a *near*-abandonment of the individual self in a terrible and wondrous merger with Something far vaster, more permanent, and more real than themselves. For the Maya, as for other Native Americans, the Otherworld was more real than this earthly realm of illusions and dreams. From everything that we can learn about it, the Maya soul hungered to push through the surface of the world and celebrate and test itself in the dimension of nightmare and bliss on the other side. It thirsted to find—or create—the places where the physical world could become transparent to that other, more alive dimension. That was the world in which the drama of death and resurrection was *really* taking place—forever—and with more intensity, more savagery and joy, than its hallucinated replica here.

Some people may feel repulsed by the Mayas' rituals of bloody self-sacrifice and the beliefs about God, the nature of reality, and the hungers of the human soul that lie behind them. But to dismiss the ancient beliefs would be to miss their profound wisdom. More than that, if the Maya were right about the darker aspects of the divine nature and its demand for self-sacrifice, the consequences for this dismissal are potentially catastrophic.

Artists, inventors, and innovators of all kinds know the painful truth that all important creations require an enormous paying out of physical and emotional energy, an investment of the soul so intense and so focused that other areas of their lives must often be sacrificed. We all know that achieving any of our life's significant goals demands our "blood, sweat, and tears." These things may be largely psychological. But they may be literal as well. In a culture that falsely promises instant gratification, it might do us good to face facts about what the universe demands in exchange for our achievements. These facts indicate that authentic achievement and reaching the kind of goals that come out of who we really are and what we really need to be doing with our lives always involves paying our dues to the ferocious underside of life—and the divine forces that give rise to it. According to the Maya shamans, this applies—and with even more urgency—to the greatest goal of all—presiding over the death of death.

CHAPTER 5

The Creations of
the Lightning-Serpent

For those sensitive to spiritual "energy fields," driving through the Yucatan at night during the rainy season can be an awesome experience. The darkness fills the wild landscape like the black waters of Xibalba flooding the earth plane from their mysterious depths. The tropical air hangs heavy with the humidity that rises from the dank vegetation. Thunderheads bloom high in the ion-charged atmosphere, slowly churning like Otherworldly billows of *itz*. Soon the rain begins to fall in patches. One side of the road is left bone dry, still locked in the grip of the past season's drought, while the other is soaked by the night rain.

As the traveler speeds through this undomesticated countryside, what can only be described as a presence—of something magical but also demonic—gently closes in. It tracks the intruder just outside the headlights' narrow beams. One passes tiny villages, some of which go back to pre-Hispanic times, towns with names like Balamcanchen, Kunkunul, and Kanxoc. Almond-eyed children stand in palapa doorways staring out into the humid darkness. Lightning flickers silently in the distance over the rain forest, illuminating a ruined temple's roof comb, rising, a chalky-colored ghost, above the treetops. The traveler feels enveloped by the miraculous, and present at the very moment of creation.

At the end of the 1989 archaeological season at Copan, William

Fash and Ricardo Agurcia made a discovery directly related to just such stormy Yucatan nights. As they tunneled deep inside the Classic Period pyramid archaeologists have named Structure 16, they came upon the remains of a far more ancient temple entombed within the more recent construction. This earlier pyramid was ornately decorated with huge stucco masks of the Principal Bird Deity disgorging the head of Itzam-na.

The ancient temple had originally been painted bright red and had supported a sweeping roof comb of brilliant white. Before the new pyramid was built over it, the old temple had been ritually deactivated and a thick coat of plaster applied to seal in its accumulated power. Fash and Agurcia's discovery of this hidden pyramid was a remarkable event. But there was more to come.

During the 1990 season the archaeologists were digging along the west wall of the ancient temple, racing to complete their survey before the onset of the rainy season. On May 30, the next to the last day of their work, they suddenly struck through a rubble-packed doorway in the side of the inner pyramid and found themselves in a room painted an uncanny bloodred. They knew immediately that they were in an extraordinary ritual space.

On June 1, they made a spectacular find; they opened the very heart of the "living mountain" and beheld the central core of its supernatural power. In a small niche in the red room they found a cache of sacrificial instruments—flint knives, a jade bead, a stingray spine, spiny oyster shells, and shark vertebrae. But far more significant than this bloodletting equipment, they encountered nine of the most dazzling so-called eccentric flints ever discovered, each of them over a foot and a half long. Scraps of the blue-green cloth they had been wrapped in still clung to the mysterious objects. For the Maya, these painstakingly carved flints were the physical embodiments of the ongoing resurrection of the cosmos, concrete evidence that the creation was continuing through the inspired minds and hands of their most gifted shaman-artists.

Eccentric flints are found all over the Maya area. They are large, flat pieces of stone carved into portraits of gods and demons. But the stones Fash and Agurcia discovered are particularly powerful and evocative. Portraits of the nine Lords of the Underworld who manifested the hours of the night, these flat silhouette sculptures are frightening and wonderful fantasies in stone. Created to look like frozen forks of lightning, the reptilian forms curl and jut with razor-sharp notches and spiky, scalelike edges. Four of these flints are truly extraordinary. One wears a headdress that looks like a lightning bolt flaring into two spirit manifes-

One of the eccentric flints discovered by
Ricardo Agurcia and William Fash in
the "mummified" pyramid at Copan.

tations. The first spirit is leaning forward, clutching at the air, seemingly
straining to extract itself from the head of the Underworld Lord. Wearing an elaborate headdress itself, it looks like a monstrous baby squeezing
through its mother's birth canal. The other spirit faces backwards, its
head joined to the first by a thin bridge of soul-stuff. It sits contentedly
on a spiky thronelike object. The Xibalban demon itself has a monkey
face, a tiny tyrannosaur-like arm, a sagging belly armed with sharp
points, and a bushy tail that rises in jagged plumes and ends in a claw.

A second Lord of Darkness wears a headdress that looks like a giant iguana sunning itself. His arms are thrust forward holding what seems
to be a huge contorted baby bird, its long beak open in a silent screech.
This demon has spiked legs and a crocodile tail that lashes upward to
meet the iguana on his head. A third Lord of Death, possibly Itzam-na,
wears a Principal Bird Deity headdress. The monster-bird is ragged and
scrawny. Its feathers are sharp ridges, and it grips Itzam-na's head with
deadly talons. Itzam-na is seated on a throne. He raises a tiny hand to his
mouth as if puffing on an invisible cigar. A fourth Underworld Lord, with
an elongated torso, sports a miniature arm that emerges from his neck,
an ejaculating penis, and a small, mirror-image spirit manifesting from

the back of his head. He is squatting. What appears to be a pungent fart pushes out from between his buttocks and curls in a cascade of solidified gas.

All of these gods are in the process of manifesting or creating something—spirits, monsters, or semen that will seed the earth with life. Before deactivating the ancient pyramid the shaman-priests carefully wrapped these Lords of Night in cloth the color of the Otherworld ocean. Then they placed the demon-gods in the red heart of the pyramid, "mummified" the temple, and sealed these lightning-bolt creations deep within it.

For the Maya shamans, the lightning strikes of the Divine Being were present everywhere, if one had eyes to see the hidden process of creation/awakening/enlightenment taking place at the heart of all things. Creation and enlightenment were ultimately the same wondrous event. Both came from a God who insisted on imparting His wisdom to human beings by splitting their skulls with His lightning bolts and offering them the chance to participate in the cosmic resurrection He Himself was envisioning.

The ancient Maya word for stone—*cauac*—comes from the word for lightning. In the imaginations of the shamans who delighted in paradox and hidden connections, these opposites—one hard, enduring, and seemingly eternal and the other illusive and effervescent—came together in the so-called Cauac Monster. This Monster, the expression of the divine life of lightning/stone, appears in carvings and paintings as a huge skull-like figure with half-closed eyes and ornate earflares. The top of its head is a stepped cleft identical to end-view depictions of ballcourts, the *hom-*

The Cauac Monster as depicted on Stela 1 from Bonampak, showing First Father being reborn through the split in the top of the Monster's head.

"Abyss" portals to the Underworld. Sometimes a corn plant, or even First Father as the Maize-god, rises from the floor of the Monster's cleft head. The Monster appears solid and heavy with the weight of the earth, and represents the limestone of the Yucatan peninsula, as well as flint, obsidian, and other less common stones. At the same time, it shimmers with flowing lines and shapes, with the very life force of First Father's miraculous resurrection. When the Cauac Monster is shown in humanlike form, it appears as a gnarled old man with a huge boa constrictor wrapped around his shoulders or as a young man whose legs have transformed into iguana or crocodile limbs.

The Maya carved the Cauac Monster hieroglyph on boulders and altars to mark them as sacred stones. Sometimes the Monster represented the caves where the Maya believed lightning was born. Sometimes it depicted lightning itself. At other times it depicted the places where lightning struck.

According to the Maya shamans, something wonderful happened at these *ch'ulel*-impacted places: Through the serpent-energy of lightning the gods gave human beings the raw materials for building the portal-opening machinery by which they could pierce the veil of earthly time-space and enter the realm of the gods. These raw materials were the most sacred of all the forms of *cauac*—flint, or chert, and obsidian.

Eccentric flints were the lightning within the stone freed by the hands of artists. In ecstatic states created by the inner lightning strikes that split their skulls these artists could see the gods writhing within the stone, and they chipped away at the flint to reveal their electrified forms. By doing so, the artists, like the shaman-kings in their bloodletting rituals, gave birth to the Divine on the earth plane.

The Maya represented this insight-laden process of "birthing" and creation as the lightning-struck—and striking—god K'awil. In the iconography of Palenque, K'awil was the third-born son of First Mother and First Father. He was the brother of the Twin Gods, and represented the divine life force they used to triumph over death and begin the resurrection of the cosmos. K'awil is always shown in Maya art at the very moment he takes a divine lightning hit. He wears the X-ray vision obsidian mirror on his forehead, and lightning in the form of a smoking celt (or axhead), a burning cigar of hallucinogenic tobacco, or a flaming torch smashes through the mirror and strikes him in the brain.

If K'awil was himself struck by lightning from the Otherworld, his miraculous serpent leg conveyed the shattering power of Divine lightning to the earth plane. It transmitted the creative force of the great Mystery

smoke scrolls

K'awil dancing on his magical serpent foot.

in Its most violent and dramatic form. K'awil usually appears in Maya art as a humanlike figure dancing on this fearful manifestation, or "materialization," leg. In some depictions his leg has just begun to transform into the terrible snake; only his foot has taken on the serpent identity, yet already it has become a thing of horror and wonder. Its mouth gapes open to spit out shimmering blood-lined clouds of *itz*. In other representations his entire leg has "morphed" into the undulating body of the deadly rattlesnake. In still other portrayals K'awil's humanlike form itself is materializing from the bloated coils of a vision serpent.

The Classic Period Maya interpreted K'awil's serpent leg both as a searing bolt of spiritual lightning and as his Vision Serpent *uay*. In fact, from recent progress in decoding K'awil imagery we now know that *the Vision Serpent was the animal familiar of this frightening god of energy transformation, while he himself was the humanlike expression of the cosmic snake.* A Post-Classic Period form of K'awil who appears in the *Popol Vuh* as Cacula Huracan—"Lightning One-Leg"—makes the identification of lightning with the Vision Serpent in the person of K'awil clear.

For the Maya, lightning, like so many other aspects of the cosmos, was the expression of simultaneously death-dealing and life-bearing snake-energy. The fact that K'awil was the god of manifestation and materialization, and that the central symbol of this process was the Vision

Serpent as his lightning-bolt leg, means that the Maya experienced these creative expressions of divine *ch'ulel* penetrating the earth plane as jolting, frightening, and violent events.

Although we have not yet discovered a direct reference to the so-called third eye of Eastern mysticism in Maya writings, the imagery of the lightning strike through the mirror on K'awil's forehead makes it clear the ancient Maya shamans knew this same spirit-releasing phenomenon. It also shows that the Maya believed that the head and brain are the seat of imagination, intelligence, and spirit.

To be struck in the forehead by *ch'ulel*-charged Otherworldly lightning was to experience the sudden rending of the great portals to the spiritual realm within the soul. The emphasis in Maya art on severed heads and skulls, violently cleft and giving birth to new life and creative forces, confirms this conclusion. So does the evidence from the *Popol Vuh* about the vital importance of *ch'ulel*-powered intelligence and ecstatic insight in defeating the forces of destruction and death and winning the resurrection for the individual soul and for the universe as a whole. We now know how First Father's (the Cauac and Waterlily Monsters') and K'awil's heads came to be cleft. They were split open and transformed into life and creation-bearing portals between the worlds by "mind-blowing" assaults of divine lightning.

The modern Maya say that "lightning in the blood" causes the blood to "speak." It "speaks" words of wisdom and truth, and, above all, artistic creation. We ourselves use expressions like "a bolt out of the blue," "struck by lightning," "thunderstruck," and "a flash of insight" to describe sudden transformational events and revelations. As the history of discoveries of all kinds and our own life experiences show, many of the greatest artistic achievements, innovations, inventions, and insights come to us in this way. For the Maya, to be struck by lightning meant that the person was in a state of radical alteration. Being struck by lightning through the third eye, and being awakened to new life and creative action as a result of the Otherworldly revelations imparted by the lightning, was the Maya form of en-*lighten*-ment—both the foundation and the goal of all mystical traditions.

Maya artists depicted the most radical—and violent—transformational and creative events of all—birth and death—as K'awil, or as human beings in their K'awil aspects. As the divine process of manifestation and materialization by which the human soul first dies to its life in paradise and is born into the world of time and space, and also the process of resurrection by which the soul dies to its human life in order to be re-

King Yax Pac of Copan standing in the Underworld with K'awil's flaming torch piercing his forehead.

born as a god, K'awil and his lightning-split third eye smashed the two great portals to and from the Otherworld. It was K'awil's fertilizing and re-creating lightning that blasted open the 01 Portal to allow the souls of babies to enter the earth plane. It was this same serpent-force that tore open the jaws of the White-Bone Snake/Black Transformer Portal of death. And it was K'awil, the brother of First Lord as Chac-Xib-Chac— god of thunderstorms and sacrifice, manifesting as the four rain-bearing *chacob*—who hurled his lightning bolt axes at the Cosmic Turtle Shell and split it open to give birth to First Father.

The shaman-kings showed themselves as infants being born from the mouths of vision serpents with smoking celts through their foreheads. And on his sarcophagus lid Pacal's forehead is smashed by a smoking ax as he falls down the Milky Way "Road of Awe" on his way to the Otherworld. On a powerful portrait stela King Yax Pac of Copan appears in the Underworld as a bald and bearded old man, "thunderstruck" by his own death, and already transformed *by* and *into* K'awil, a flaming torch piercing his bony forehead.

The Maya used the image of K'awil as the so-called Manikin Scepter, along with the double-headed serpent bar—the symbol of his twinned brothers—one of the most powerful embodiments of sacred kingship. When the shaman-kings grasped the K'awil scepter they proclaimed themselves the masters of Vision Serpent portal technology and the process of manifesting the finite things of this world from their Otherworldly sources. By wielding both of these scepters they identified themselves with all three of the creator brothers.

Closely related to his function as the divine process of energy transformation, K'awil also symbolized the physical embodiment of *itz*. In fact, one of the meanings of the ancient word *K'awil* was "sustenance" or "life-giving substance." On the earth plane this sustenance had originally appeared in the form of divine blood and maize dough—the ingredients of the human body. It continued to appear as corn, all other foods, and all forms of abundance—physical and spiritual. Most important, it manifested as the spiritual force that fueled the soul's resurrection, and it materialized itself through all human creative actions and artistic expressions. As these things came into being in the form of material objects and life-engendering events, K'awil filled them with his lightning-struck presence. Like the Christ of the Gnostic Gospel of Thomas who said, "Lift the stone and you shall find me, cleave the wood and I'll be there!" K'awil was the secret inner life of all earthly things—their bloody, electrically charged essence. Ultimately, it was K'awil's lightning-serpent spirit that the ancient sculptors tried to free from the storm-born stones when they created their eccentric flints.

For the Maya, opening the third eye and regaining godlike vision did not come from a gentle unfolding of the soul. Enlightenment did not arise organically after years of quiet meditation. While the shamans, shaman-kings, and artists prepared for their awakenings through fasts and lonely vigils in the dreaming places within the pyramids, when enlightenment came it left them dazed and reeling, their bodies trembling in a state of shock, and their blood sizzling with inner fire. The Maya quest for enlightenment was not the search for pastel-colored bliss. It was the quest for divine passion—the passion First Father felt when Something even deeper and more powerful than he split his skull in order to shake him into the vision of a resurrecting universe.

The God of the Maya had no patience to waste on those who would not join him in the defeat of death and the resurrection of the cosmos. Those who refused his call to be reborn did so at their own peril. The modern poet D. H. Lawrence, who drew much of his inspiration from Mexico, knew this same fierce creator God. In his poem "No Joy in Life" he pointed to the ancient K'awil way of re-creating the human soul. He wrote:

Never, my young men,
you who complain you know no joy in your lives,
never will you know any joy in your lives
till you ask for lightning instead of love
till you pray to the right gods, for the
thunder-bolt instead of pity. . . .

Though the ancient Maya myths about the creation of the world take several tacks and portray somewhat different divine actors (or perhaps the same divine actors under different names), and at least seemingly different sequences of events—so much so that modern scholars have not been able to integrate them into a coherent megamyth—they all do begin, one way or another, with fiery blood or lightning.

At Quirigua, Copan's ancient rival in the mountains of Guatemala, archaeologists have discovered a remarkable monument. Called Stela C, this *te-tun*, or "tree-stone," as the Maya termed these carved slabs, bears one of the rare hieroglyphic accounts that have survived of the first moments of creation. It opens with the word *hal*, which means "to speak," "to make appear," and "to manifest." As in the Hebrew story from the book of Genesis and the later Christian Gospel of John (both based on ancient Egyptian sources), the Maya creation began when the creative aspect of God "spoke" through the lightning-charged haze of his blood-ecstasy. What he spoke "appeared" or "manifested."

The Quirigua inscription says that the Divine Being envisioned and spoke a scene in which three creator gods—the Jaguar and Stingray Paddlers (the Twin Gods in one of their many aspects), and the "Black-House-Red-God," almost certainly Itzam-na—set the three primordial hearthstones of the new creation in the center of "Lying-down-Sky, First-Three-Stone-Place." We know from other inscriptions and carvings that "First-Three-Stone-Place" was in the center of the Otherworldly ocean, "Lying-down-Sky," when it still covered the earth. In the pitch-blackness of those ocean depths, before the birth of the true sun, Xibalba was everything.

Before a world could be made out of the featureless black waters, an absolute center had to be established for the new universe. The Maya shamans, like the mystics of all spiritual traditions, believed that all creations begin from such a center—from a Hearth, a Primal Mountain, a Cosmic Turtle, a World Tree, the heart, phallus, womb, navel, or the head as the blossom of the "tree" of the spinal column—and in modern cosmology, from the infinitely small point from which the universe exploded into being.

Crossing the black waters of the Underworld in the Canoe of Life, the Paddlers brought Itzam-na, the "Water Wizard"—Lord of the Xibalban ocean—to the "First-Three-Stone-Place" that was at one and the same time the center of the earth plane and the sky. Itzam-na and the Paddlers then painted the three hearthstones on "Lying-down-Sky." When First Father later raised the World Tree he separated the images of the stones. One image stayed on the earth as the greatest of all "power points," around which all pyramid-temples and ballcourts would be built. The other image was lifted into the night sky as a triangular pattern of three stars in the constellation Orion. The so-called Orion nebula, a cloud of gas and dust that can still be seen in the middle of this triangle, became the *ch'ulel*-bearing smoke of that first sacrificial fire that rose when the creator gods burned their own sacred blood, the very blood they had used to paint the images of the hearthstones. The Quirigua inscription ends with "It was his action, Raised-up-Sky-Lord." "Raised-up-Sky-Lord" was one of First Father's postresurrection titles.

Fragments of other creation texts have been deciphered, most of them from sites that we can't yet identify. One of them names the first manifestation as the Cosmic Turtle from which First Father was reborn. The stars that marked the split in its shell through which First Father stepped are also in the constellation of Orion. One is the first of the three hearthstones. This means that, for the Maya, the two creation events—the painting or laying of the hearthstones and the resurrection of First Father—were like-in-kind. In the "eternal now" of the Maya "Dream Time" these two events were seen as reenactments of each other. The K'awil-cleft Cosmic Turtle Shell/Primordial Mountain/Ballcourt Abyss/sprouting corn kernel/lightning-struck head appears at the central place in the Otherworld from which all creations erupt in a shower of light and flashing stars.

Another source for our growing knowledge of the ancient Maya creation myths is the so-called Vase of the Seven Gods. This Classic Period funerary ceramic shows seven creator gods meeting in council to plan the resurrection of the universe. The gods glow against the intense black background of the Underworld. Six of them sit facing the seventh, who reclines on a jaguar-hide-covered throne. The hieroglyphic text identifies five of these lesser gods as Holy-Thing-Sky, Holy-Thing-Earth, Holy-Thing-Nine-Footsteps, Holy-Thing-Three-Born-Together, and Holy-Thing-Ha-te-chi—the Jaguar Paddler. The lord on the jaguar

The Vase of the Seven Gods.

throne is the so-called God L, or his double, Itzam-na, the king of the Underworld.

The divine figures depicted on this vase are at one and the same time the demons of Xibalba and the Overworld gods of life. In that far-off epoch before and after earthly space-time, the gods and demons were and will be one and the same, and the Overworld, Underworld, and earth plane are one.

In the scene on the Vase of the Seven Gods, God L/Itzam-na sits inside a house made of mountain-monsters smoking his hallucinogenic cigar as he imagines the world that he and his council are about to make. He is wearing a headdress that features the diabolical Muan-bird, the Underworld aspect of the Principal Bird Deity. A ravenous crocodile—perhaps the Cosmic Monster impatient to take up his position in the sky—bares its teeth and thrashes its tail on the roof of the living mountain house.

The hieroglyphic text says that as the council of god-demons spoke, a place called "Black-Its-Center" was "brought into being." We don't know what this mysterious place was, but it's possible that it was simultaneously the 01 Portal of life and resurrection and the Black Transformer of death.

At Palenque, language experts have deciphered yet another creation story. On the tablet of the Cross we read that First Father, named Hun-Nal-Yeh—"One-Maize-Revealed"—in this inscription, was born on June 16, 3122 B.C. First Mother in her moon aspect first appeared on December 7, 3121 B.C., six years before the creation actually began. Then First Father, with the Paddlers and Itzam-na, painted the hearthstones at "Lying-down-Sky, First-Three-Stone-Place," and the center of the universe-to-be "became visible."

Researchers have found independent confirmation of this Palenque image of First Father as a sky artist. On a carved shell we see First Father emerging from a cleft peccary with a paint pot and brush in his hands. The fact that he emerges from a cleft peccary adds another piece to the puzzle of Maya creation imagery. Since First Father's original form was that of a celestial peccary, his rebirth as the Maize-god/Creator from a peccary describes his rebirth from *himself.* This is the same theme that appears on the tripod plate where he is reborn out of his own split skull. Furthermore, we know that the Celestial Peccary, like the three hearthstones and the Cosmic Turtle, was in the constellation of Orion. This means that, for the Maya astronomers as for the painter of the tripod plate, First Father died and was reborn at the center of the universe where he was himself the drama of death and resurrection at the core of the Divine Being. Returning to the Palenque text, we read that First Father raised the World Tree and "became" the sky on February 5, 3112 B.C.

At the huge, almost completely unexplored site of Coba, several miles inland from the beautiful seaside ruins of Tulum, scholars have found still another reference to the creation. Here, in the steamy, jungle-choked vastness of this greatest of the eastern Yucatan cities, lost in its miles-long meandering pathways and its dark, tree-shaded *sacbeob,* or sacred "white roads," researchers have identified a creation text that records one of the largest finite numbers ever calculated by human beings. This text dates the beginning of the present creation to August 13, 3114 B.C.

The *Popol Vuh* pictures the creation as the work of First Father and First Mother in their Celestial Peccary and Tapir forms, and calls them "The Maker" and "The Modeler." They confer with a council of gods like the one on the Vase of the Seven Gods. Amazingly, the *Popol Vuh* account, like that of modern evolutionary theory, depicts the creation as a series of cosmic epochs in which various living things flourish and then die off in mass extinctions, only to be followed by new, more evolved life-forms in a progressive flowering of Being in time and space. Human beings are even shown as evolving from a primate past.

We don't know enough yet to fit these different creation accounts into a coherent whole. But perhaps there's a more basic problem than our lack of knowledge. It seems increasingly likely that, like the ancient Egyptians, the Maya were not interested in logical consistency. Instead of systematic theology they created a vivid, living, kaleidoscopic rush of images that seems designed to evoke a sense of beauty and wonder. The shamans themselves may have felt overwhelmed by the aesthetic grandeur of the creation stories unfolding in the night sky. They may have exhilarated in the dazzling images that flowed through their paintbrushes and chisels when they felt lightning in their blood.

We can see five basic dynamics of the creation process that the Maya believed the Divine Being was using to manifest the world. Implied in the creation texts from the Classic Period and the *Popol Vuh* and made clear in the scenes on the tripod plate, the Huehuetenango vase, and many other funerary ceramics, the first dynamic was the Divine Being's enraptured visioning. This visioning, like that of the shaman-scribes and artists, was powerfully aesthetic rather than logical. It was what religious scholars call suprarational—"beyond the rational."

The second dynamic, as recorded on Stela C from Quirigua, was the Divine Being's speaking of the creative Word. Many creation stories from various times and places begin with this sacred Word. They do so because by naming things, words define objects and events and make them clearer and more focused—real. While human beings, like other animals, can think in images, spoken language—and later, writing— make images concrete. Through language, things seem to manifest out of the shadowy, dreamlike depths of half-conscious feelings and impressions into the light of conscious awareness and intentions. The ancient Maya understood the power of words and believed that language was a gift from the gods and an ability that we share with them.

The third dynamic of the creation process was that of artistic expression. The creator gods were *itz'atob*—"sages" and "sky artists" who painted the opening phases of the unfolding new world. The word *itz'at* literally means "one who can manifest and manipulate *itz*," in this case as blood-ink/paint. First Mother was also a painter who colored the earth, certain trees and flowers, and other special objects with her favorite hue—the red of her menstrual blood—and wove the cosmos into being on her celestial loom. First Father and First Mother were both sculptors, the Maker and Modeler of the created world. The Maya *itz'atob* themselves celebrated the acts of creation in art rather than in theological treatises.

The fourth dynamic of creation was sexual. It was shown in the Huehuetenango vase and other sources as the creator gods' bloody ejaculations through phallic bloodletting rites, and in the texts and images that depict First Father's raising of the World Tree as his cosmic erection. In this imagery, creation came from the rapture of orgasm with its uprush of life-bearing divine libido.

This phallic creation dynamic appears on almost every available architectural surface at Uxmal in the Puuc Hills of western Yucatan, mostly in the form of carved snakes that cover the elaborate ornamental facades of the buildings. But the most dramatic expression of this sexual creation energy is the gigantic World Tree/Cosmic Phallus, carved from a single immense block of stone, that thrusts up from the ground on the broad terrace in front of the building archaeologists call the Governor's Palace. Above the serpent-festooned central doorway, directly in line with the great phallus of First Father on the terrace below, was a magnificent sculpture of one of Uxmal's shaman-kings. This man must have stood in the doorway of his palace, shimmering with snake-energy, and addressed his subjects as they clustered around the giant erection that had centered

A doorway to the Governor's Palace at Uxmal. The central emblem is framed by seven skeletal serpents.

Three of Eighteen-Rabbit's resurrection stelae from the Great Plaza at Copan through which he imitated the "Dream Time" death and resurrection of First Father/First Lord.

the Cosmos and separated the earth and sky at the dawn of the universe. By placing the great phallus before the portal from which he made his ritual appearances, the king proclaimed that the sexual forces of creation were part of his own divine essence.

The fifth way the ancient Maya had of picturing the process of creation was that of giving birth. As we've seen, First Father's resurrection was often shown as a birth, and he was even represented as a newborn baby carried by one of his sons on a jeweled platter. We've already noted that the word for "birth" was used in those scenes in which the gods appear in placenta clouds during bloodletting rituals. And K'awil was the birthing process itself by which souls entered this world to become human beings and then left it to become gods.

If late Maya sources are accurate guides to Classic Period beliefs, women giving birth were believed to be performing self-sacrificial bloodletting rituals of the most vital kind. They were seen as pouring out their *itz* to bring new life into the world and thereby advance its ongoing re-creation from the abyss of death.

For the Maya, all of the creation dynamics they identified were penetrating, powerfully disruptive, and emotionally violent processes. Ecstatic visioning was a violent invasion of the soul by the Divine Being who entered it in the form of all-engulfing "fire." Speaking in ecstatic trance states, as anyone who has attended Christian revival meetings in which "speaking in tongues" takes place can testify, is also an emotionally violent event. Authentic artistic creation, no matter how refined and disciplined it may seem, is an aggressive act that forces raw materials into entirely new forms and that always arises from experiences of great depth and passion. Orgasm too is an invasive, "violent" experience that shakes the very foundations of our daily-life identities. And childbirth causes the most powerful and painful sensations a human being can know.

As we've seen, the ancient Maya surrounded all of their creations with rituals that imitated the patterns of the gods' actions at the dawn of time. When a Maya farmer sowed his cornfield, he did it according to the events in the night sky that portrayed the Twin Gods' descent into Xibalba. When a child was born it was welcomed according to the formula created by First Mother when she gave birth to K'awil. In these and other ways the Maya stared destruction and death in the face and placed themselves on the side of life.

Many human beings spend considerable amounts of time and energy in creative processes and projects of one kind or another. Most of those who do seldom—if ever—see their creative actions from a cosmic, or spiritual, perspective. Most of us do not recognize the scope or power of our creations, or experience them as vital parts of a divine life-and-death drama. Most people never imagine them—no matter how small or great—as materialized triumphs over the darkness.

Making a home, designing a new computer program, implementing a better system of office management, teaching, making love, and raising children are all the outpourings of Being. What if we were to see these life-affirming actions of ours in the Maya way, as concrete manifestations of the K'awil lightning strikes of an ongoing resurrection? What would happen to us if we believed, as the Maya did, that we are in a fight for our very lives, and that whether we win that fight or not depends on the quantity and quality of our creative actions?

We might begin answering such ultimately fateful questions by thinking about where in our lives we have already taken lightning-serpent hits, felt fire racing through our veins, and—against all odds—created a new world.

CHAPTER 6

God

When they were asked what their gods looked like by the Spanish, the Maya shamans replied that they had no pictures of the Divine Being because they could not depict such a great mystery in physical form. And yet they, like all other peoples, did try to show in carvings, paintings, and myths what in the end cannot be shown. To modern people, raised with the idea of a God of love, what the Maya portrayed can be deeply disquieting.

In the ballcourt at Chichen Itza on that same frieze that depicts the decapitated ballplayer and the eruption of snake blood and water lilies from his neck, there is something else. Between the "terminated one" and his killer is a large round disk dripping with blood. The disk represents the ball used in the ballgame just ended. At its center is a grinning skull, its jaws open in silent "song," the speech of the Otherworld that could only be heard in this world by those who understood the language of the gods. We know the head is "singing" because from its fleshless mouth "song scrolls" are emerging like eddies of wind. It is speaking with the breath of God. Scholars know from the rest of the frieze and from other sources that this death's-head is chanting the words of *ik*—"life."

This magical head hidden in the ball is the living skull of First Father in the Otherworld after his decapitation by the Lords of Death—the

The Singing Skull from the great
ballcourt at Chichen Itza.

same that chokes the White-Bone Snake on the tripod plate and that appears in other scenes as a severed head on a jeweled platter. Having lost the ballgame—and his own head—the terminated one has now *become* First Father through the beautiful terror of blood-ecstasy—and his sacrifice has re-created the world. At one with the Divine Being who embraces the darkness and the light, pain and pleasure, disease and health, and destruction and creation, the sacrificial victim has now merged with the core essence of God.

In the jungled ruins of Yaxchilan archaeologists and language experts have been working to decipher a haunting hieroglyph. It appears three times on the panels of thirteen stairs that lead down from the cosmic temple of the shaman-king Bird-Jaguar. Carved on the risers of these so-called "stairs of death" are scenes from a ballgame Bird-Jaguar played to reenact the fateful ballgames between the gods of life and the Lords of the Underworld. The hieroglyphs that accompany the scenes place the ballgame in the deep past—in the "Dream Time" before creation—and say that the game took place in the *hom*—the "Abyss," or "Black Hole" of Xibalba. Bird-Jaguar designed his game to be like-in-kind to those ancient models in order to reactivate the miraculous events that had led to the first resurrection and the creation of the universe.

The mysteriously repeating hieroglyph shows a grimacing skull with what could be a ballplayer's helmet on its head and a huge knotted ribbon over its bony lips. It seems to be a combination verb-noun that reads *ah Knot-Skull*. Researchers believe *Knot-Skull* was the Maya word for death, or "descent," by decapitation sacrifice. The word *ah* had a rich set of related meanings. *Ah* and the combination word *ahal* meant "to create," "to wake up," "to dawn," and "to appear." These same glyphs also meant "creator" or "creator of holiness," and "the thing created," and reflected the Maya belief that a creator and his or her creation are not separate things, but that, in some mysterious way, the thing created is an expression of the creator's own being.

This eerie inscription seems to be describing three primal decapitation sacrifices—the first of First Father, the second of his sons the Twin Gods, and the third of all later sacrificial victims. The text also seems to be saying that all three descents miraculously changed into "the waking up," "the dawning," and "the creation" of the universe. The hieroglyphs imply that the very *act* of descent-decapitation begins the awakening of the new creation.

An inscription from Palenque makes the identity of the skull in the hieroglyphs clear and brings this wondrous process into focus. The key hieroglyphs in the Palenque text read *u k'ul Knot-Skull*, "It is The Holy Thing Knot-Skull." When interpreted with the rest of the text these words identify Knot-Skull as "The Holy Thing" First Father in the actual process of creating life from death. It affirms that the "place" where life begins is actually the wellspring of death. It is in the Abyss of Mystery at the core of the Divine Being Itself that death turns into life and the resurrection "dawns." Taken together, the complex image expressed by these inscriptions is "The-Holy-First-Father-Decapitated-Dead-Creating-Thing."

This Holy-First-Father-Decapitated-Dead-Creating-Thing is the singing ball of the Maya ballgame. It is the harvested and replanted "little skull" corn kernel that made human life possible. It is the severed head on the Otherworldly platter and the bloody head on the tripod plate that powers the cosmic resurrection. It is also the so-called Cauac and Waterlily Monsters—all manifestations of the ultimate, all-powerful, life-generating head of First Father. Not unlike the gruesome but redeeming image of the crucified Christ, this awesome Maya image is the closest the shamans and artists came to depicting the nameless Mystery of life-death from which all things arise, by which they are sustained, and into which they are drawn back, only to be born again. The Holy Singing Skull Thing was their most profound image of the terrible and wonderful Power they experienced in every aspect of the cosmos.

"God" is not a name. It is a title we use to refer to the nameless supernatural medium in which we find ourselves. The Maya title for God, "The Holy Thing," expressed their experience of the dark essence of God as something that, in the end, cannot be described in human terms. While The Holy Thing had Its humanlike or anthropomorphic manifestations in the form of the many gods, goddesses, and demons, in the Abyss at Its core, human comparisons failed. This Maya image of the hidden essence of the Divine Being is at least as mysterious as the Jewish non-names for God—"the Holy One" and "I-Am-What-I-Am"—and the Hindu term "Bliss."

From the ancient Maya point of view, many modern people have incomplete and shallow beliefs about God. Many believe that God is either the angry moralistic watchdog of their thoughts and feelings or a cosmic Nice Guy who expresses only loving feelings for his creatures. From the Maya perspective, the first group has a stunted understanding of God's darkness, which is far more terrible than mere moralism. The second group cannot make sense of the cruelty and suffering in the world, including in human life. There's a third group the Maya would have found completely ridiculous. For these people God is a cosmic watchmaker who has meticulously crafted the world, wound its spring, and let the lifeless machine tick away its empty existence, far removed from its inventor.

For the ancient Maya, the terrible beauty they experienced in every aspect of their lives was the direct expression of The Holy Thing's integrated mixture of good and evil, creation and destruction, and life and death. The Divine Being demanded that human beings become like It and embody Its own fierce joy. Becoming whole as It was whole was the price the soul paid for its immortality.

The spiritual voyagers of all religions, even those of dualism, have come upon this same God of darkly ecstatic mystery. The eerie tones of Tibetan monks chanting to open the heart chakra re-create the atmosphere of beautiful terror that is always a part of the deepest, most authentic experience of the Divine. Ancient Gnostic Christian meditations captured the sense of awestruck wonder that goes with it. Baffled by the depth of the Mystery they were encountering, the Gnostics could only describe It by saying what It was *not*—"unnameable, inconceivable, invisible, incomprehensible." For the Gnostics, this was "the One in Whom we are." And for them, in the "Abyss of Silence," "Light and darkness, life and death . . . are inseparable . . . nor is life life, nor death death." Sometimes Gnostic hymns broke into ecstatic sounds similar to the mysterious Hindu God-syllable "Om."

In the *Bhagavad Gita*—"The Song of God"—the Hindu Prince Arjuna, about to go into battle, is suddenly overcome by a vision of the great god Krishna who appears to him as the "Personality of Godhead." The *Bhagavad Gita* says:

. . . bewildered and astonished, his hairs standing on end, Arjuna began to pray. . . . Arjuna said: My dear Lord, Krishna, I see in Your body all . . . different kinds of living entities. . . . I see in Your universal body, many, many forms—arms, . . . mouths, eyes—expanding without limit! There is no end, there is no beginning. . . . You are inexhaustible. . . . O all-pervading Vishnu, I am unable to keep the equilibrium of my mind!

The biblical prophet Ezekiel's vision of this dark and awesome aspect of God is equally overpowering. The prophet falls to the ground before a divine revelation that looms in the air above him—a mass of wings, rotating wheels, and lightning flashes that ripple and crack "round about." Terrible eyes glare at him from the middle of the apparition, supercharged with divine power, that has exploded into this dimension from another realm. A humanlike figure speaks to Ezekiel in a thundering voice, like the sound of torrents of water. The vision touches the earth, rises and floats in the air, then touches the earth again, and the figure cries out, "Son of man, stand upon your feet! I would speak with you!"

At the outermost limits of the ability of human language to capture the soul's encounter with the core essence of God, the Sikhs of India throw up their hands and simply call the Divine Being "Oh Wow!" Beyond this, as Joseph Campbell says, words fail.

At this deepest level, all religions agree that experiencing the awefullness of God shakes the soul to its foundations. In those moments, the soul is aware that it is in the presence of Something unimaginably huge and powerful, a gigantic whole of which it is a tiny part. The Christian theologian Paul Tillich called this awareness "God beyond God." Even the common experiences of a ghostly chill, a sense of the uncanny, and of "supernatural dread"—the same feelings people flock to the theater to experience in horror movies—are presentiments of the soul's disturbing encounter with the Divine Presence.

Along with soul-affirming Light, the Black Abyss of the Divine Being's "unmanifest" core yawns open, and the ecstatic voyager is drawn down into the Void of annihilation, of "nonbeing." In the grip of this terrible Presence the soul feels that it is being watched by unseen eyes that are less, and more, than human—and that look at it with the cold indifference of the vacuum of space and, at the same time, with a kind of unimaginably intense love. Then, as the skin stops crawling, as the "portal" closes and the soul remembers its everyday life, it is left with the overwhelming impression of the *reality* of The Holy Thing. As the soul steps back into this world, it knows with a knowing deeper than any other that the Divine Being is *more* Real than any person, thing, or happening in the created world. It is *Reality Itself.*

This experience of the awe-fullness of the Divine Being is what many spiritual traditions call the "Wrath of God." The great religious scholar Rudolf Otto, who spent a lifetime studying this mesmerizing quality of the Divine, wrote:

> . . . it is patent from many passages of the Old Testament that this "wrath" has no concern whatever with moral qualities. There is something very baffling in the way in which it "is kindled" and manifested. It is, as has been well said, "like a hidden force of nature," like stored-up electricity, discharging itself upon anyone who comes too near. . . . Something supra-natural throbs and gleams, palpable and visible, in the "wrath of God," prompting to a sense of "terror". . . .

Otto adds that this "singularly daunting and awe-inspiring character must be gravely disturbing to those . . . who will recognize nothing in the divine nature but goodness, gentleness, love, and a sort of confidential intimacy. . . ."

In the *Bhagavad Gita,* as Arjuna trembles before his vision of supernatural terror, he cries out, "O Lord of lords, so fierce of form, please tell me who You are!" And The Supreme Personality of Godhead says: "Time I am, the destroyer of the worlds, and I have come to engage all people!"

In the Book of Revelation we witness the terrifying consequences of the Cosmic Lamb's wrath, that same lamb who before his bloody sacrifice had been the gentle teacher of love:

> When he opened the sixth seal, I looked, and behold, there was a great earthquake; and the sun became black as sackcloth, the full moon became like blood, and the stars of the sky fell on the earth as the fig tree sheds its winter fruit when shaken by a gale. . . .
> Then . . . every one . . . hid in the caves and among the rocks of

the mountains, calling to the mountains and rocks, "Fall on us
and hide us . . . from the wrath of the Lamb; for the great day
of . . . wrath has come, and who can stand before it?

The Maya explored the "wrathful" side of The Holy Thing with
what can seem to modern people like morbid fascination. Their myths
recounted in almost endless detail the mysterious "kindling" of this terrible aspect of the Divine Being, and the processes—just as terrible—by
which it could be calmed. Their obsession with the darkness made the
Maya specialists in supernatural horror. An atmosphere of deep sadness
and even dread still clings to many ruined Maya cities, twelve hundred
years after the last sacrificial victims were decapitated on the temple terraces and the headless trunks hurled down the "stairs of death" onto the
plaza floors where the demons of Xibalba rose from the ground to snatch
them and drink their blood.

When human beings have tried to picture this terrible Mystery in
physical form they have often found themselves portraying monsters.
Originally the word "monster" meant something strange, marvelous, supernatural, wonderful, and terrifying. Often artists and writers have captured this monstrous quality of God by combining human, animal, and
even plant body parts. These surrealistic portraits of the Divine Being
show what the writer of the *Bhagavad Gita* knew—that the "Godhead" includes all things within Itself.

The ancient Egyptians showed their gods as beings who were part
crocodile, hippopotamus, cow, ibis, baboon, insect, and human. The author of the Hindu *Rāmāyana* depicted the hero of this epic, the incarnated
god Rama, as a wondrous mixture of many animals. Tibetan art shows
gods with bulging bloodshot eyes and huge fangs protruding from the
corners of their mouths, but robed with images of abundance and life.

But it was the Maya, more than any other people, who best captured in their art and myths the monstrousness—the dark wonder and
beauty—of The Holy Thing. The aliveness of that terrible and miraculous Thing gave the Maya universe its enchanted quality. Anything was
possible. Supernatural forces were hidden just beneath the surface of apparently ordinary things, waiting to erupt in displays of magical power.
Pots and pans could speak, grinding stones could complain about the
abuse of their human masters, and tools could attack their owners. The
wings of birds, the surface of water, shells, water lilies, fire, rain, blood-

A "rollout" illustration of a vase painting, showing First Lord attacking Itzam-Yeh with his blowgun. First Jaguar is hiding behind the World Tree with one paw extended.

letting instruments, the ax of decapitation sacrifice—in moments of unearthly "transparency" everything could reveal the monstrous life of God.

A Classic Period funerary vase depicts the Twin Gods creeping toward the World Tree where Itzam-Yeh is perched, ready to begin their attack on the cosmic bird. This vase shows the tree itself as alive with Divine Presence. At its base a frowning cross-eyed Tree-god with a bone through its nose glares at the approaching Twins. The knots and gnarls along the trunk are huge staring eyes, and the fruit of the tree has also sprouted eyes that gaze with fear at First Lord's coming.

The so-called Witz Monster was the living mountain form of The Holy Thing. The Maya believed that it was the inner life of all hills, mountains, and pyramids. When the Maya ritually activated their pyramids the Witz Monster rose up into them from its dark Underworld hiding place. From then on, the Monster's miraculous powers allowed shamans and shaman-kings to open the portals of death and rebirth in the temples at their summits.

Maya artists depicted the Witz Monster as a gigantic skull whose melting flesh was hardening into living rock. Its eyes were blind, and in the Otherworld behind them mysterious figures and hieroglyphs appeared. The top of the Monster's decomposing head was split open, and from this split streams of blood and the leaves of the Cosmic Corn Plant spilled out. As if in time-lapse photography, they raced outward to cover the earth with life-bearing ears of corn. Sometimes the artists showed First Father himself squeezing through the split in the monster's head as a newborn baby emerging from the birth canal.

First Mother was another Maya monster. She was sometimes shown as an elegant lady, bare-breasted, wearing a Buddha-like smile, and kneeling at her cosmic loom. In this form she had a radiant goodness about her and appears as the ideal wife and mother. As we've seen, she was also pictured as a divine artist. In addition, she could appear as a temptress, promising sexual bliss in the life beyond the tomb. But at other times she was shown as a goddess of death and destruction. In these scenes, in place of her hair a snake coils on her birdlike skull, and her hands and feet are the clawed limbs of a crocodile. Her huge breasts— once life-giving—now sag to her waist, and her black skirt, like the Hindu goddess Kali's necklace of skulls, is covered with crossed human thighbones. In a scene from the Dresden codex she is pouring a pitcher of disease-infested water on the earth, ending the present cosmic age with a catastrophic flood.

Vision serpents were also manifestations of the monstrousness of the Divine Being. Sometimes they rose from the smoke of sacrificial fires as life and wisdom-bearing Otherworldly messengers. At other times they appeared in the skies above favored warriors in the heat of battle as Waxaklahun-Ubah-Kan, the terrible War Serpent. Often they were plumed with shimmering quetzal feathers—flashing green, blue, copper, silver, depending on the light—the physical manifestations of the hallucinating God who dwelled behind the ever-changing forms of this world. Maya artists pictured these beasts of wonder and terror with their skins partly flayed, divine *itz* running down their sides and soaking their feathers. Related to the Vision Serpents, snake-footed K'awil danced the miracle of "manifestation" on his writhing snake leg, itself covered with torn and bleeding patches of skin and glowing with iridescent Otherworldly colors.

The Witz Monster from the tablet of the Foliated Cross at Palenque.

First Mother at her loom, weaving the world into being.

Human beings often experience the monstrousness of God as de-monic. Indeed, by itself, without the miracle of life's reemergence and resurrection, divine wrathfulness seems like pure destruction—a divine "death wish." Rudolf Otto says that demons and gods come from the same underlying Source. In all human descriptions of demons—in our scriptures and in our art—we have tried to show what the darkness of God looks like when it is exposed in its raw form: the terrifying fire ser-pents that prowled the corridors of the Egyptian Underworld; the Japa-nese Shinto demons with their wolflike heads and scaly monsters in their

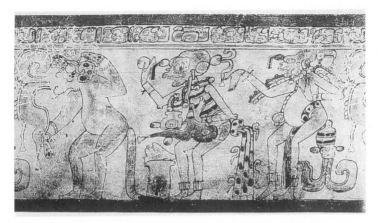

Three Underworld demons as depicted in a vase painting rollout.

hair; the giant scorpions of ancient Sumerian nightmares; and the deformed imps of Hieronymus Bosch's paintings. To this day, Babylonian demon figurines with their scrawny wings and clawed feet send chills through museum visitors.

The demons in our modern movies have the same effect—the Antichrist of *The Omen* and *The Exorcist,* Satan in *Rosemary's Baby,* and *Tyrannosaurus rex* and the velociraptors of *Jurassic Park.* Though our rational minds try to deny their existence, something deeper and more instinctual within us knows that, in some way, demons are real.

In the *Popol Vuh* the most important Maya demons go by names like Blood Gatherer, Pus Master, Skull Scepter, and Stab Master. The king of the Underworld is a twin deity named One/Seven Death. He is almost certainly the Classic Period demon scholars call God L. We know many of the other Classic Period demons from their portraits on funerary ceramics. On one famous vase, painted in oranges, reds, and blacks, we see three Xibalbans. The first is a catlike creature breathing out a toxic cloud of decay and blight. The second figure is gloating over a severed head on an altar. He wears gouged-out eyeballs, their optic nerves still dangling around his deformed head. Two huge streams of blood are pouring from his chest, and he is expelling a stream of blood-spattered diarrhea. The third demon has a painfully swollen stomach, a symptom of the parasitical diseases that were common among the ancient Maya. His fart is so pungent it has taken physical form as a jar protruding from his buttocks, pouring liquid stench onto the ground behind him.

Other Maya demons appear in paintings and carvings as skeletons with bursting bellies, skulls with a single lock of straggly hair still clinging to the naked bone, half-animal/half-human-like beings who are hacking off their own heads with axes and knives, and emaciated old men smoking poisonous cigars.

Maya demons often symbolized various forms of death from natural causes. Others, like the demon of the number zero, were the embodiments of specific kinds of human sacrifice. In the case of the Demon Zero, who was shown with his jaw missing and streams of blood covering his face, sacrifice was performed by removing the living victim's jaw.

The spiritual teachers of many religions have tried to separate the goodness of God from the demonic side of supernatural reality. Christian theologians have tried to do this by promulgating the doctrine of Satan, the great Adversary and Tempter, who acts independently of a wholly good God. But a closer look at the Lord's Prayer shows that the very Being Jesus called *Abba*—literally "Daddy"—is himself the Tempter. Jesus begs his "Daddy" not to lead us into temptation. And a thoughtful reader of the New Testament sooner or later runs into such questions as: If God is completely good and all-powerful at the same time, who is really responsible for the creation of evil? If evil has a source that is independent of God, how can God be omnipotent? Aren't there, then, at least two gods? And what kind of being exactly *is* the God of Love whose terrible "Wrath" against his creatures can only be appeased by the human sacrifice of his son?

The truth is that at a certain point in spiritual experience and thoughtful reflection it becomes hard to tell the difference between gods and demons. In the gray areas between the Overworld-Otherworld and the Underworld-Otherworld, gods and demons merge into one awe-full experience of "holy dread."

The Maya believed that the Divine Being *was* demonic. But they also experienced Its benevolent side. Chac-Xib-Chac defeated an untamed nature and created a life-supporting natural order. Because of his enraptured visioning the black waters of Xibalba that seeped up to the earth's surface changed from deadly poison to life-bearing *itz.* Jaguars were restrained in their nightly attacks and the power of the demons of the Underworld was limited. No longer could they overrun the earth plane, causing disease and death at will.

According to the *Popol Vuh,* First Jaguar was the god who first concentrated the life force so intensely that, against all odds, he was able to resurrect First Lord after he had been decapitated by a Bat-god in the Underworld. Together the Twin Gods had then brought First Father back to life. They had dug up his bones from the floor of the ballcourt of

Xibalba, recovered his head from the fruiting tree, and put his body back together. Through the power of the *ch'ulel* they were able to focus, they reclothed First Father's bones with flesh. Then they put him in the Canoe of Life and took him to the place of rebirth—the Cosmic Turtle Shell/Witz Mountain/Womb of First Mother—his own living Head. And by the miraculous power of their soul-essence this once weak and tragic god became the all-powerful Lord of Life. He burst forth from the womb-tomb of the Underworld with a bag of seeds clasped to his chest, ready to carry the resurrection forward.

J. R. R. Tolkien, who wrote his fairy-tale epic about the hobbits with a mythological point of view strikingly similar to that of the Maya, called the resurrection powered by this brighter side of the Divine Being a *eucatastrophe*—"a sudden joyous turning." For Tolkien, as for the Maya, the great eucatastrophe of the hobbits' triumph over evil took place before the human world came into being.

Like the shamans and mystics of all religions, the Maya believed that all things were born, flourished, and died within the Divine Being as expressions of Its dark-bright essence. The gods were fractal manifestations of the great Mystery that delighted in multiplying and dividing Itself into countless living beings, each with a different—but not so different—set of qualities. This celebration of diversity-in-unity is true of all polytheistic, or multigod, faiths. No matter how many gods are worshiped in these spiritual systems, one ultimate God stands behind them all. These lesser aspects are pictured in the world's mythologies as divine children and grandchildren, hierophanes, archons, angels, and saints. The Hindu Upanishads and great epic poems make this clear. The Brihadaramyaka Upanishad proclaims: "Worship this god! Worship this god! One god after another! The entire world is his creation, and he himself all the gods. . . ."

In ancient Egyptian religion, depending on what priesthood one belonged to, either Ra, Amun, or Ptah was the ultimate Divine Reality from which all the other gods and goddesses were descended and of which they were all specialized expressions. The indigenous spirituality of North America affirmed the reality of Wakan Tanka—the "Great Spirit"—who had created all lesser spirits. African tribal religions also believe in an invisible Creator who has given birth to the other deities. In a similar way, Buddhists worship many local Buddhas who are all aspects of the one true Buddha.

The Christian Trinity expresses the idea that one God manifests as three separate persons who share the same divine substance; and the Virgin and many of the saints appear as localized fractal forms of themselves. In its mystical teachings, even monotheistic Judaism describes the ten *Sefiroth,* or "sacred attributes," of the Holy One. And mystical Islam counts at least one secondary manifestation of Allah—the "Idea of Mohammed." Contrary to what many of us have been taught in our churches or synagogues, the difference between polytheism and monotheism is one of emphasis rather than kind. Polytheistic spiritualities emphasize the many faces of the Divine Being, while monotheistic religions emphasize Its unity.

The polytheistic spirituality of the ancient Maya produced a kaleidoscopic experience of gods and demons who nevertheless maintained their ultimate identity with one another. The mythmakers and artists showed this diversity-in-unity nature of The Holy Thing by mingling the gods' symbols and characteristics, and by depicting relationships such as twinship, father-son, mother-daughter, and male-female as expressions of the Divine Being's complex oneness.

According to the *Popol Vuh,* First Father, known in this text as One One Lord, had a twin himself—Seven Lord. It was this first pair of twins that the Lords of Xibalba sacrificed, and First Lord and First Jaguar brought back to life. The Maya saw the first set of twins and their sons as ultimately one and the same being—the husband-son of First Mother.

In the *Popol Vuh,* One One Lord and Seven Lord confront and are defeated by their archenemies, the demon kings One and Seven Death. We know from the parallels in their names that these two sets of twins were twins themselves—Overworld and Underworld mirror reflections of each other.

Even mothers and sons were aspects of the same Divine Being. First Mother, as the goddess Ix-Chel of the Classic Period and "Blood Woman" of the *Popol Vuh,* was the moon. At the same time, First Jaguar in the Classic Period was also named Balam-U-Xib—"Jaguar Moon Lord." In the later *Popol Vuh,* as Xbalanque, he ascended into the sky after his victory over the Xibalbans as that heavenly body. If we remember that First Jaguar *was* his father, then we can see that First Jaguar and First Mother were really same-generation male and female mirror images of each other, male and female aspects of the same Moon-god/dess.

From the point of view of comparative mythology and depth psychology, the Twin Gods appear in some form in almost *all* the twinship patterns of the Maya universe. In addition, they were the so-called Pad-

A tablet from the Temple of the Cross at Palenque, showing Itzam-na/God L smoking a hallucinogenic cigar.

dler Gods who took First Father in the Canoe of Life to the Cosmic Turtle Shell. As divine shamans, the Twins were also Itzam-na/God L. Ultimately, in fact, they were the Overworld-Underworld itself.

The ancient Maya shamans saw a deep mystery in the complex interplay of characteristics and forces within and between the Twin Gods. The Twin Gods' overlapping but distinct characteristics and myths were, in the end, only the outward expressions of the inner workings of The-Holy-First-Father-Decapitated-Dead-Creating-Thing.

People who have grown up in the Judeo-Christian and Moslem spiritual traditions have usually been taught to believe that the concept of one god is more advanced than the idea of many. But there are advantages to the many-faceted experience of the Divine Being. One is that by celebrating the rich diversity of supernatural forces *within* God, the believer is allowed to realize that the struggle between good and evil, creation and destruction, and life and death is not something that takes place *outside* the Divine Being, between a finite God and an external force like Satan. Not only is this way of looking at the Divine Being more honest, it also helps remind us of Its immensity. Unable to simplify the struggle between life and death to a "Good Guy/Bad Guy" scenario, we are forced to face the truth that the "God beyond God" is far more mysterious than our human comforts and discomforts.

In addition, polytheistic spirituality works against our normal human tendency to reduce God to a cardboard caricature of ourselves, our parents, or our tribes and nations. By maintaining the diversity within The Holy Thing and, at the same time, by recognizing Its ultimate unity, the believer can experience a Being whose very complexity blocks his or her attempts to trivialize, idolatrize, or domesticate It. The soul simply cannot grasp such complexity or shrink It to monoscopic proportions. Instead, it is forced to experience the Divine Being from a dazzling, multiscopic perspective. It is also forced to confront the absolute limits of all human ways of thinking. This can have the same effect on the soul that Buddhist *koans* do. Buddhist *koans* force the mind to imagine the unimaginable—"the sound of one hand clapping"—then to snap and release the soul into an ecstatic experience of oneness with its Source and final Destiny. That was the goal of the ancient Maya shamans and all those who, meditating on the complex unity of The-Holy-First-Father-Decapitated-Dead-Creating-Thing, tried to achieve oneness with the Mystery from which they had come and to which they hoped to return.

CHAPTER 7

The Soul

In a remote valley on the far southwestern fringe of the Maya area lie the ruins of Tonina. In the Classic Period this isolated city, surrounded on all sides by lush rain-forested mountains, commanded the last frontier of the Maya realm. Beyond this remote outpost of civilization the barbarian tribes of Mixtecs and other fierce peoples roamed the misty hills. West and south of Tonina the light of Maya culture flickered out and the perpetual darkness of savagery reigned.

Tonina, like all Maya cities, imagined itself as the center of the universe. To boost the flow of *ch'ulel* its mythologically centered location provided, the builders of Tonina had carved their city out of a Witz Monster mountain at the head of the valley. The Toninans had constructed their palaces and temple-pyramids, their plazas and ball-courts, on a series of terraces and platforms cut into the side of the mountain. In doing so, they had converted the natural mountain into a huge artificial pyramid, and thereby proclaimed that all of Tonina was a living mountain—indeed, the "First True Mountain" from which the creation had begun. In ancient times, the whole city was painted white and red. It sat like a supernatural jewel sparkling in the green vastness that rolled like the waves of the Otherworld ocean toward the awesome realm of the gods and demons. According to the Toninans, the

The Stucco Wall of Tonina, showing the sacrificial scaffold and a Xibalban dancing with a freshly severed head.

barbarians who lived beyond the tiny state's borders were the Underworld demons themselves.

Tonina was a small city by ancient Maya standards, but it was unusually warlike. More than many Maya centers, its public art celebrated the torture and decapitation sacrifice of noble captives. The famous Stucco Wall of Tonina depicts the fearful scaffold on which these tortures and beheadings took place. The scaffold is shown hung with the trophy heads of enemy chiefs, and a gigantic skeleton-demon dances through the wicker supports, swinging the freshly severed head of a famous captive. The head has squeezed its eyes shut and choked up its tongue.

One of the most terrible of Tonina's monuments is the great ballcourt of the shaman-king Baknal-Chac. The inscriptions tell us that Baknal-Chac, as the personification of the World Tree and the Sun, dedicated this ballcourt on July 7, 696 A.D. and named it "Seven-Black-Yellow-Place-Three-Conquest-Ballcourt." Scholars think that "Seven-Black-Yellow-Place" may have been another name for the Cosmic Turtle Shell cleft from which First Father was reborn. "Three-Conquest" referred both to the ritual sacrificial stairs—the "stairs of death" down which sacrificial victims were rolled—and to three mythological descents into the Underworld. Baknal-Chac regarded his ballcourt as a cosmic resurrection generator, as an earthly replica of the Otherworld place where death turned into life.

Under the tangled vegetation of the ballcourt floor, archaeologists made an astounding discovery, one that would change our understanding of ancient Maya beliefs about the origin and the potential destiny of the human soul. As they cleared away the centuries of dirt and plant growth from the center marker of the "Seven-Black-Yellow-Place," they gradually revealed the portrait of a young man cradling a strange object in his arms. Maya experts had never seen this object before and didn't know how to interpret it.

This mysterious center marker was in the form of a carved lime-stone disk set in the earthen floor of the ballcourt. Beneath it was a hollow stone cylinder several feet deep that symbolized the portal to the Underworld. The lid-marker for this portal to the hidden dimension under the earth showed a man whom the hieroglyphs that rimmed the disk identified as Six-Sky-Smoke sitting on a platform depicting a cosmic partition of some kind. The inscription said that Six-Sky-Smoke had died on September 5, 775 A.D. and been entombed on May 22, 776.

Maya ballcourt markers, like the viewing ports of glass-bottomed boats, were "transparent." They offered a view of events occurring in the eternal now of the Underworld-Otherworld. From this and the hieroglyphic inscription the archaeologists knew that Six-Sky-Smoke in his ballcourt portrait was alive somewhere in the Otherworld beyond the gates of death. They were seeing him beneath the ballcourt floor, in effect, being reborn from the cleft Turtle Shell as First Father in the Dream Time of the myths.

In this timeless moment Six-Sky-Smoke is sitting in the cross-legged position of ecstatic trance. He's wearing what appears to be a Principal Bird Deity headdress, and he's clasping the double-headed serpent bar to his chest. But instead of the ecliptic symbol ending in two vision serpent heads, or in the emblems for Venus and the sun, the hieroglyph for "white flower" emerges from either end of the magic bar.

The central ballcourt marker from Tonina, showing Six-Sky-Smoke in the Otherworld, holding his own soul.

What was Six-Sky-Smoke—whoever he might have been—doing pressing this strange "flower bar" to his chest in an attitude of awe and wonder? And what was this previously unknown modification of the traditional badge of shaman-kingship?

While the decoding of the Tonina ballcourt marker was going on, at Yaxchilan scholars were trying to decipher the mysterious phrase *ch'ay sak-nik-nal*. From the rest of the inscription, they knew it was some kind of death phrase. Various readings had been tried, but none seemed to fit until Nikolai Grube and David Stewart, two of the most creative decoders of the ancient hieroglyphs, made an amazing breakthrough. It turned out that the word *ch'ay* was a verb that meant "lost energy," "diminished," or "expired." And *sak-nik-nal* could be translated as the noun the "White Flower Thing." This phrase, therefore, read, "Lost energy the White Flower Thing," or "Expired the White Flower Thing." Since this text was referring to a person and not to a literal flower, and since the white flower was not just a flower but rather a "White Flower *Thing*," scholars realized that in this death phrase they had stumbled upon the central Maya idea-gram for the human soul.

Now Six-Sky-Smoke's Underworld portrait could be decoded. And what an astounding decoding it was! Six-Sky-Smoke had made a successful descent into the land of death, and was sitting in the Underworld-Otherworld clasping his own soul to his chest in rapture. Not only that; by changing the serpent bar from its Vision Serpent/Cosmic Monster/Twin God–ecliptic form into a double-flowered portrait of Six-Sky-Smoke's soul, the artist was showing that the human soul *is* the Vision Serpent and the Cosmic Monster-Twins—the sun and Venus! In other words, according to the artist, the core essence of the soul is God, just as the shamans taught. The end result of ecstatic visioning—beyond conjuring demons and ancestors, even beyond becoming one with the gods—was conjuring one's Self, one's own essence. And there—as that Self, within that Self—one would find the whole universe, including the process of destruction and renewal through self-sacrifice. Here was this long-dead man, still visible in the Underworld, holding his own soul in his arms, a soul that just happened to be the Divine Being Itself! The power and the poignancy of this image immediately strike anyone who sees it, and they haunt the imagination forever after.

From carefully comparing all the evidence researchers have gathered over the last twenty years, we now know that the Maya believed the soul had a life cycle that began in paradise, continued on the earth plane as its participation in the struggle to defeat and absorb the forces of destruction and death, and that was intended to end in an eternal celebration of life and Being. The soul determined its own ultimate fate by how well it constructed a durable "Resurrection Body" during its sojourn on earth.

If our interpretation of the significance of Six-Sky-Smoke's flower bar is correct, the Maya belief that the soul in its essence is all things finds support in the mystical traditions of many religions. The Hermetic faith of the ancient Mediterranean area claimed that the experience of God comes only through embracing this deep truth. The Eleventh Hermetic Tract says:

Become Eternity. . . . Embrace in yourself all sensations of all created things; be simultaneously everywhere; be at once unborn and in the womb, young and old, dead and beyond death; . . . then you can apprehend God.

In his Surangama Sutra, the Buddha said:

. . . is it any wonder that you . . . supposed . . . that all the external things, mountains, rivers, the great open spaces, and the whole world, were outside of the body? Is it any wonder that you failed to realize that everything you have so falsely conceived has its only existence within your own wonderful, enlightening Mind of True Essence . . . ?

This "Mind of True Essence," the Buddha taught, was that core part of the human soul that is immortal and infinite—in Western religious terms, the *Imago Dei,* the "Image of God" within. The Buddha made this point even clearer when he said simply, "In truth I say to you that within this fathom-high body . . . lies the world and the rising of the world and the ceasing of the world."

In order to help their students grasp the idea that all things are within the soul, the Hindu gurus teach them to practice saying "Thou art that!" whenever they are tempted to accept the illusion that they are distinct beings separate from the "external" things of the world. Jung said that everything occurs to us within our imaginations, within, as he put it, the "psyche." The novelist Forrest Reid captured the feeling of wonder that comes from this realization. He wrote:

> . . . it was as if everything that had seemed to be external and around me were suddenly within me. The whole world seemed to be within me. It was within me that the trees waved their green branches, it was within me that the skylark was singing, it was within me that the hot sun shone, and that the shade was cool.

According to the Maya shamans, because the universe is really within us, we are the beings that straddle all the dimensions of reality. One of the ways they dramatized this belief was through the symbolism of a piece of ballplaying equipment called the yoke. The yoke was a horseshoe-shaped wicker tube that went around the waist. Its practical uses were to protect the ballplayer and to hit the ball. Through the palma, a wedge-shaped deflector set into the yoke, the player could control the ball's trajectory. Since, as in modern soccer, players could not hit the ball with their hands, the yoke was the most important part of their equipment.

But the yoke was far more than practical. It symbolized the earth plane and the White-Bone Snake entrance to the Underworld. This symbolism appears in a scene on a Classic Period vase in which First Lord is shown dancing with the White-Bone Snake wrapped around his waist in a position similar to that of a ballplayer's yoke.

The yoke was decorated with the figures of gods and demons, and had a gap on one side that depicted the Black Transformer Portal. Similar to the Hindu chakra system, it divided the player's body into "higher" and "lower" sections. The upper body symbolized the Overworld, while the lower body represented the Underworld. The human torso and head were the centers of feeling and thinking and were like-in-kind to the passion and intelligence of the gods in their Overworld forms. The heart, called ollin—"movement"—was the place of strong emotions, including the ecstatic sense of oneness with the Divine Being, while the head was the location of sight, the vital quality the creator gods had tried to deny human beings in order to keep them from sharing their powers.

The parts of the body below the yoke—in the Underworld—were microcosms of the realm of defecation/decay, and fertility. As funerary ceramics show, the demons of Xibalba were often depicted expelling streams of diarrhea and toxic farts. In fact, one name for "demon" in the ancient Maya languages was *cizin,* which meant "terrible odor." The Maya knew that plants rise from the decay of other organisms and that animals, including human beings, are dependent on plants. They were well aware of the life-giving effects of fertilizer on their fields. So it seemed right to them that the organs of creation were located in the Underworld region of the body.

According to the Maya, as we've seen, the human body was made of corn and blood. Through the symbolism of the ballplayer's yoke the Maya saw the human body as the primary physical manifestation of the Cosmic Corn Plant/World Tree that had its roots in the Underworld, in the form of legs; that rose through the earth plane—the yoke; and that soared upward into the Overworld to end in the vital, life-giving head— the hairy, corn-tasseled fruit of the Cosmic Tree.

Also, with their two arms and two legs, human beings embodied the four cardinal directions. Fingers and toes were concrete manifestations of time, the physical expressions of the twenty days of the Maya months. Intestines were the umbilicals that carried divine *itz* to every part of the universe, and human blood was this *itz* in its purest, most precious form.

In modern Western culture most of us have been taught to believe that the soul—if it exists at all—is a by-product of the body. The Maya believed exactly the opposite. They believed that the body was a manifestation of The White Flower Thing's ecstatic visioning. A depiction of this manifestation process in reverse appears on a carved panel from the Temple of the Foliated Cross at Palenque. On this panel a being symbolizing the humanlike form of The White Flower Thing emerges from the mouth of a huge conch (or snail) shell. Hieroglyphs on the shell identify it as "Precious-Shell-Metawil," the heavenly Otherworld realm where First Father, First Mother, and their sons, the Twin Gods and K'awil, live forever. The White Flower Thing is pulling a gigantic corn plant into the shell. One of the ears of corn is represented as a human head, indicating that, among other things, the corn plant is a human body. This image seems to show the soul gathering its body back into the Otherworld from which it had imagined it into being in the first place.

Since the body was an expression of the soul it was really the soul that spanned the worlds. This soul had both a personal and an infinite, eternal, or transpersonal core. The Maya called the personal part of the soul the *uich*—the "face"—that aspect of each human being that is unique, stamped with the imprint of our own individual personalities and life experiences. This was the part that refused to simply merge with the Divine, that insisted on its own clever and heroic deeds, and that caused the shaman-kings to reshape the stories of the gods for their own purposes. This was also the part that, through a lifetime of growth and seasoning, would lead in the defeat of the Lords of Death on the other side of the grave.

But this earth plane–Overworld aspect of the soul was only one aspect of The White Flower Thing. Below the personal level lay the boundary of the Underworld-Otherworld. Pictured by the Maya as the water-lily-covered surface of pools and canals, this boundary between what modern psychologists might call individual, or "ego," consciousness and the hidden depths of the unconscious was dangerous.

The Maya were careful with boundaries, including the boundaries of their sacred geographies, and they marked them with *ch'ulel*-infused monuments. Ballcourt portals were often built between groups of pyramids and plazas to honor the divisions between noble families within the same city and to bind them together through the death-life ritual of the ballgame. In some areas these cleft Cosmic Turtle Shell/Primordial Mountain/Abysses were constructed at the edges of the kingdoms where they interfaced with the "Underworld demons" of neighboring cities.

Deformity and disease also manifested the boundary with Underworld-Otherworld forces. The Maya believed that sick people, humpbacks, and dwarfs were specially chosen by the gods to manifest their supernatural power. They were human beings who lived on the frontiers between the dimensions of reality. All signs of otherness showed the all-pervasive life force of the gods that was ready to break through to the earth plane at any unguarded moment. First Lord/First Jaguar had carefully ordered the earth plane to prevent such catastrophes; and the cities with their shaman-kings and their customs and rituals tried to manage and direct these upwellings from below. The shaman-priests who sealed Pacal's burial vault had been trying to do this very thing.

The fearful portals to and from the Overworld-Underworld-Otherworld were the most terrible boundaries of all, but by using portal technology the personal aspect of the soul could venture into its own mysterious depths. In the Otherworld within it could keep its identity while, at the same time, it could become the Lords of Death and Life. This is what the artist who created the portrait of Six-Sky-Smoke imaged so powerfully—the individual man in the Underworld-Otherworld, holding his Twin Gods–divine-soul-essence in eternal ecstasy.

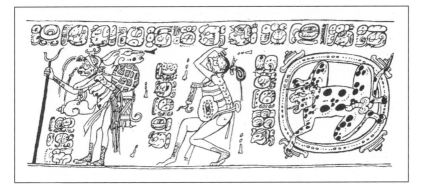

Three *uayob,* including First Jaguar swimming in the Otherworldly ocean.

From a somewhat different point of view, this is also what the figure of the decapitated ballplayer from Chichen Itza shows. In this scene, the victim's neck enforces the boundary between the individual personality and its supernatural ground. Once the personal part of a human being—the head—was removed the Otherworld below exploded upward in a cascade of supernatural wonder and horror.

Like the ancient Egyptians, the Maya believed that every human being had more than one soul. Modern hypnotherapists and specialists in multiple personality disorders—even mainline Freudian and Jungian psychologists—recognize this same truth.

As the Maya shamans entered the White-Bone Snake/Black Transformer through their many portals and crossed the boundary between their conscious minds and the Abyss of the deeper Self, they encountered a host of soul-fragments that became increasingly less concrete and individual the deeper they went. Immediately below the surface they encountered the *uayob.* Similar to the ancient Egyptian Underworld gates with their guardian spirits and the Tibetan *bardo* levels in which the dead soul is confronted by terrifying demons, this dimension of the soul was midway between normal human consciousness and the deeper-dwelling gods and demons.

The *uayob* were intermediaries or transitional soul forms that the spiritual voyager encountered before going on to meet these gods and demons. Shamans, gods, and demons could transform themselves into the same *uayob,* making it impossible at times for modern researchers to tell whether the sources of these *uayob* are human or divine.

Whichever they were, perhaps both at the same time, ancient Maya funerary ceramics are alive with these supernatural beings. On a

Classic Period vase from Seibal, deep in the Usumacinta rain forest, we see three *uayob,* two of them in the form of living skeletons. One appears as a traveler with a staff and backpack. The backpack contains the usual camping gear; but it also reveals the decapitated head of a monster-dog. The other skeleton *uay* has a bulging stomach. The artist has shown the bloated abdomen in X-ray view in order to reveal the terrible growth within it.

The third figure is the jaguar *uay* of a Seibal king. Set in a large oval cartouche that represents the infinite ocean of the Underworld-Otherworld, this jaguar—really First Jaguar—is shown swimming on the surface of the unearthly sea. In a fascinating detail, the painter has depicted First Jaguar from below, as if the artist himself were immersed in the deadly waters, watching the god swim by above him. From this angle we can see his huge testicles and fully erect penis.

Many other *uayob* appear on Maya funerary vases as animals or were-animals—dogs, snakes, crawfish, birds, insects, monkeys, and monstrous combinations of these and other creatures, like the jaguar-dog, the deer-monkey, and the deer-horned dragon called Chi-Chaan. The Vision Serpent itself was a *uay* of the person performing the bloodletting ritual.

The masks, headdresses, and costumes of shamans, shaman-kings, and warriors showed them transforming into the *uayob* of the gods, often those of First Lord and Itzam-na. The magnificent, awe-inspiring battle palanquins of the kings displayed gigantic figures of such supernatural beasts as First Jaguar and the Waxaklahun-Ubah-Kan killer manifestation of the Vision Serpent.

On a carved panel from Tikal we see King Hasaw-Ka'an-K'awil being carried home in victory from the battlefield in one of these terrifying *uay* palanquins. Hasaw-Ka'an-K'awil sits on his portable throne wearing the costume of Tlaloc/Venus warfare, proclaiming to all that he himself has transformed into First Lord/Chac-Xib-Chac, the executioner and bringer of fertility and abundance. Behind him on the palanquin, three times larger than life-size, the immense figure of First Jaguar has materialized. First Jaguar is rearing on his hind legs, slashing the air above Hasaw-Ka'an-K'awil's head with outstretched paws, and roaring the terrible silent roar of the Otherworld.

Scholars had tried for a long time to understand the significance of these frightening supernatural creatures. Though we now know they were *uayob,* for years they had no name and their meaning was unknown. As part of their efforts to determine exactly what these spirits meant to the Maya, scholars puzzled over a hieroglyph that showed the head of a

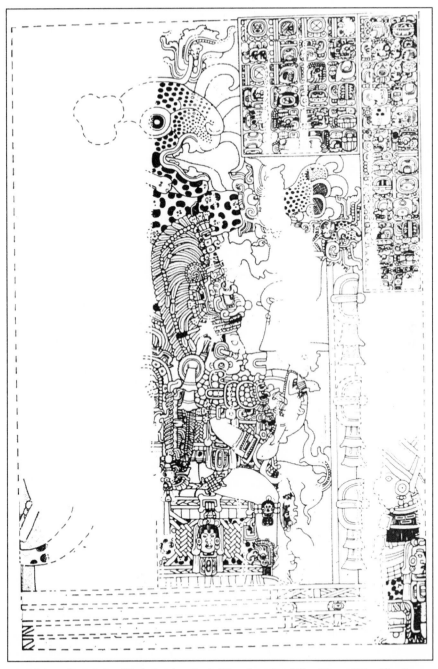

Lintel 3 from Temple I at Tikal, showing the battle palanquin of King Hasaw-Ka'an-K'awil.

sleepy-eyed *ahau*—"lord"—partly covered by a jaguar pelt. They called it the "Jaguar Lord" or "Hidden Lord" glyph. In addition to being a representation of the Twin Gods, researchers also knew that it was the word for "to sleep" and "to dream." It was often found with the words *pib na,* or "underground house," and *kunil,* "bewitching place" or "dreaming place."

Finally, two different language experts, working independently, cracked this "Hidden Lord" glyph and opened the world of the *uayob.* After studying all the glyph's different contexts and consulting with anthropologists who knew modern Maya customs and beliefs, scholars finally realized that what they were seeing in this mysterious symbol was the Classic Period representation of the disturbing idea, common throughout ancient and even modern Mesoamerica, that shamans and sorcerers could transform themselves into animals and prowl the night forests as jaguars.

Scholars now knew that the "Hidden Lord" hieroglyph did not stand for normal sleep states. Instead, it carried the sense of a menacing, subterranean consciousness. They realized that the underground houses and bewitching places were the secret sanctuaries in which the shaman-kings believed they transformed themselves into shadowy monsters halfway between the daylight world of normal human awareness and the abyssal realm of the gods. In addition, they could now grasp the inner meaning of the far more ancient Olmec cult of the were-jaguar with its unsettling implications for rituals of bloodletting and human sacrifice. The symbol for the jaguar that is hidden within the person of the shaman-king could now be read with sobering clarity. It was the verb "to sleep," "to dream," and "to transform into an animal spirit by enchantment." It was also the noun "shaman," "sorcerer," and "animal companion."

This ancient Mesoamerican were-animal tradition could now be placed in the worldwide context of shamanistic religions that affirmed the reality of mystical twins, spiritual doubles, and animal companions. Among these are the African belief that human souls have their doubles in trees, rocks, and other natural features; the ancient Egyptian idea of the hidden spiritual twin of the human personality; and the European tradition of vampires, werewolves, and witches' familiars.

While they could appear, as they often did among the Maya, in humanlike form, more often than not these alter egos manifested as spirit animals. The idea behind these supernatural beings in animal form is that the animal part of us is closer to the Divine than we are. The Maya probings of the layers of Underworld-Otherworld Reality revealed that the *uayob* level of the supernatural realm was the level on which the human dimension first encountered the Divine and the Divine made contact with the human. Many shamanistic spiritual systems never go beyond this, and many modern people who are attracted to such things as spiritualism, channeling, and psychic phenomena often get stuck on this level of the soul as well.

For the Maya who delved deeper into The White Flower Thing, the *uayob* soul fragments gradually faded and gave way to the dimension of the gods, especially the Twin Gods and the Lords of Death. These deeper archetypes were the truly transpersonal aspects of the soul. But, in spite of their increasingly multifaceted, mirror-image mergers with each other, they still appeared as more or less distinct beings. Just as in the scene on the tripod plate, as the spiritual voyager continued to descend, he or she eventually encountered the still more profound realm of The-Holy-First-Father-Decapitated-Dead-Creating-Thing, the roots of the Vision Serpent/World Tree, and the place of the "First True Mountain"/Cosmic Turtle Shell/womb-tomb of First Mother at the very heart of Xibalba, where the Underworld turned into the Overworld.

Probing further, the shamans finally reached the Mystery Itself, the place, as Joseph Campbell describes it, "where words turn back"—the all-embracing Otherworld. Here were the invisible energy fields of divine *ch'ulel*. According to the Maya, the gods themselves were spiritual materializations of this soul-essence, and even they used it to manifest themselves and their creations. It was the Twin Gods' connection to this final Mystery, greater even than themselves, that had allowed them to defeat the Lords of Death and achieve the resurrection for each other, First Father, the cosmos, and, potentially, for all human beings. Those human beings who could embody the Twin Gods in their own lives could become *ch'ul ahauob*—"Lords of Life" or "Lords of the Lifeforce."

The mystics of all religions talk about this most profound transpersonal dimension in similar ways. Hindu sages call it the "Unmanifest Brahma," the "Void," "nonbeing," and "nirvana." The Taoists of China call it the "Way," and say that anyone who thinks he or she can really talk about it has not experienced it. Christian theologians call it the "Ground of Being." For subatomic physicists it is the "matrix," the "quantum field," or the "Planck Era." Here energy dances forever "before" it manifests as matter. Even the *Star Wars* movies dramatized it as "the Force" and portrayed it as the psychic medium by which all things in the universe are interconnected. For modern cosmologists this hyperenergized realm is the source and final destiny of the universe.

Most theologians believe that this Ground of Being is not personal in the ordinary sense. Nor is it less than personal. Instead, it includes the personal dimension of Being, but goes beyond it. In the experience of this ultimate Mystery Tibetan Buddhist chanting, Hindu "Oms," and Sikh "Oh Wows!" fall silent, and the "peace that passes understanding," the energized tranquillity of complete rapture, envelopes the soul.

This is the deepest the ancient Maya shamans penetrated, and the deepest the mystics and seers of any religion have been able to go. Human beings, including modern physicists and cosmologists, simply cannot see further.

According to the *Popol Vuh,* the soul has five enemies—disease, death, stupidity, arrogance, and fear. Of the first two, one is only marginally under human control while the other is completely beyond it. The third, fourth, and fifth are not. The Maya believed that disease was the whisper of death, its first hint. But it was also an invitation from the Lords of Life to engage in the miracle of turning death into resurrection, of changing nonbeing into Being. A soul could accept this challenge by overcoming its stupidity through education, thereby learning to convert fear and arrogance into a specific set of personal qualities, the same qualities the Twin Gods had embodied. These qualities made up the Maya ideal of the human personality. They included intelligence, wisdom, fast thinking, resourcefulness, cleverness, a sense of humor, fierce courage, ruthlessness when necessary, passion, humility, balance, centeredness, and dignified grace.

Stupidity was the greatest vice; its cancerous effects could be seen in all the others. The hallmarks of stupidity were ignorance, a kind of overall dullness of spirit, and a naive incompetence. In Maya experience, it was because of stupidity that human beings were both fearful and arrogant. If they pursued their educations they would naturally become more humble, and they would learn that by practicing oneness with God they have nothing to fear from either life or death.

The Maya believed that fear cripples the virtues of cleverness, resourcefulness, humor, courage, necessary ruthlessness, and passion. It also keeps the soul off balance so that it cannot feel centered or express itself with dignified grace. Arrogance shows up as many secondary evils, including greed, pride, vanity, lying and false pretenses, incompetence, savagery, cold hard-heartedness, and the desire to stay ignorant.

The qualities of the ideal soul were the qualities of life, of *ch'ulel,* of Being Itself, while the characteristics of stupidity, arrogance, and fear were the characteristics of the Lords of Death and nonbeing. It was because of these basic weaknesses on the part of the demons that the Twin Gods were able to conquer them. And it was because of these weaknesses that a mature Maya soul could do the same—both in this life and in the next.

One of the most powerful depictions of the Maya soul in its matured fullness is the magnificent statue of First Father after his resurrection as the Maize-god. This elegant sculpture from Copan is startlingly similar to statues of the Sakyamuni Buddha. First Father stands upright in an attitude of energized tranquillity. His long hair flares around his face like the rays of the sun. He wears a skull pendant around his neck to proclaim his triumph over death. He holds his left hand in the open-palm position exactly like the Buddha's in his "boon-bestowing" gesture. He raises his right hand, palm forward, in exactly the same position as the Buddha's in his "fear not" gesture.

Even the details of the expression on First Father's face are virtually identical to those of the Sakyamuni Buddha. Both show a world-transcending peace. Both gaze downward—or inward—with dreamy, heavy-lidded eyes that seem filled with compassion. In both portraits their foreheads are high, depicting extraordinary intelligence; their cheeks are soft but firm, showing a loving, open-hearted nature; their lips are slightly parted, indicating that they are about to speak words of reassurance and life.

First Father—the Decapitated-Dead-Creating-Thing—like the Buddha, shows the dignified grace that comes from an awareness of his eternal destiny. Manifesting the signs of the resurrection, he is already living the life eternal even as he maintains his presence on the earth plane to nurture and bless it. This is the consciousness the Maya shamans sought by fully engaging the pains and pleasures of this world, fighting the deadly defects of their own stupidity, arrogance, and fear, and embodying life-bearing ch'ulel in their daily lives.

Though lost to us in all its rich detail, we now know the general outlines of the life cycle of The White Flower Thing. By comparing hieroglyphic inscriptions and carved images of the sak-nik-nal, archaeologists and language experts have reconstructed a fragmentary but breathtaking vision of its origin, its tasks on earth and beyond the grave, and its final destiny. Even though we don't have the full picture, the vision of the stages of The White Flower Thing's life cycle that we do have carries a potentially pow-

A Chinese rendition of the Sakyamuni Buddha.

erful message for us about changes we might want to make in our own lives—if we wish to fashion souls capable of surviving our physical deaths.

According to the iconography we've been able to decode, The White Flower Thing was the blossom of the World Tree in its giant ceiba form. It often appears in Maya art as a stylized bell-shaped ceiba flower with a square-nosed snake emerging from its center. This remarkable image tells us that, for the Maya, the soul itself was a portal from Elsewhere and Elsewhen and that snake-energy dwelled at its core. This snake-

First Father as the resurrected Maize-god, from Copan.

energy at the center of the *sak-nik-nal* was always trying to manifest itself through the earthly life of the soul. The sweet nectar of the ceiba flower was the soul's *ch'ulel*-bearing *itz*. Every flower was individual and unique, but each also carried the same transpersonal life substance that rose through the World Tree from the energy fields below.

We now realize that the flower-shaped earflares the ancient shaman-kings wore when they were impersonating the World Tree at the moment First Father raised it to begin the new creation were much more

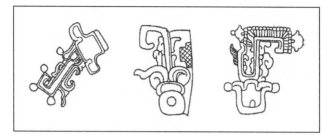

Three depictions of The White Flower Thing.

than simple ornaments. They were images of The White Flower Thing. When the kings dressed as First Father/World Tree, the branches of their costumes were covered with ornamental ceiba blossoms—a detail that hadn't seemed important before the deciphering of White Flower Thing imagery and inscriptions.

The significance of this detail when combined with the fact that the ceiba blossoms around February 5—Creation Day in the ancient Maya myths—is stunning. It seems to suggest that human souls were created at the very moment First Father raised the great Tree and initiated the new universe. Since the ceiba actually begins blooming before February 5, it *could* mean that human souls had actually come into being *before* the birth of the cosmos. An alternative possibility is that since the ceiba often flowers only once every ten years or so, new souls are created in clusters, or crops, at intermittent cosmic intervals.

Whichever soul-creation scheme the ancient Maya may have believed in, it's certain that what we're seeing in White Flower Thing symbolism, as in many of the world's spiritual traditions, is an ancient Maya doctrine of the preexistence of the soul, a soul that is far more ancient and enduring than the brief span of our lifetimes on earth.

But there's more. The ceiba blossoms high up in its topmost branches, so high up that the flowers are hard to see from the ground. Translating this biological fact into Maya myth shows us that the shamans believed that the human soul began in the same place from which all creation arose—in the "Raised-up-Sky" branches of the newly erected World Tree. In addition, the ceiba flowers only at night. When the heat of the day begins to rise, the flowers fold. The fact that in the ancient myths night was the Underworld made visible suggests that the Maya believed that The White Flower Thing actually came into being in Xibalba—the place of *death*—at the very point where the Overworld branches of the World Tree became its *roots* in the Underworld.

There are at least two other important insights about the life cycle of the human soul we can glean from White Flower Thing/World Tree imagery. The first is that since the purpose of flowers is to make other plants of their species, The White Flower Thing's primary role and essence was sexual. It was regenerative to the core. When we put this insight together with the image of the phallic serpent that dwelled at the very center of the *sak-nik-nal,* as well as with the fertilizing World Tree conjuring of the shaman-kings, we can see that The White Flower Thing's fundamental task during its earthly life was to create more "World Trees." All World Tree creations the shamans brought into being through their ecstatic raptures were fractal versions—made present and immediate—of that one miraculous Tree—the life-giving center that was everywhere and from which their own flower-souls had first blossomed. And since the World Tree was also the Cosmic Corn Plant, and human beings were made of corn, The White Flower Thing's ultimate purpose was to regenerate *itself.*

The other insight we can gain from this imagery is equally significant. Since all flowers receive life and nurturing from their parent plant, and since The White Flower Thing began its life cycle in the Overworldly branches of the World Tree in a condition of effortless dependence upon it, the Maya shamans may have believed that the soul has its origins in a paradise similar to the "breast-tree" paradise of ancient Egyptian mythology. Perhaps it is the memory of this preexistence in paradise, shared by so many religions, that awakens our hunger for heaven. Perhaps, more than wishful thinking, the Gardens of Eden, Golden Ages, and Isles of the Blest that appear in all the mythologies of the world are genuine echoes of that blissful dimension from which, say the myths, we have all come.

As we've noted, that blissful Overworldly realm for the Maya was also in some mysterious and paradoxical way the Underworld. Here then, as in every other aspect of Maya mythology, we see an expression of the shamanic belief that all the forms of darkness and death and all the forms of light and life arise from and return to the same mysterious unity of the Divine Life Itself.

The White Flower Thing was eventually called from its state of dreaming innocence into this world of pain, suffering, and cruelty where it became incarnated in a Maya woman. In the womb it took on a body of maize and blood and formed as a human being. The maize of its flesh also came from the World Tree—this time in its this-worldly Cosmic Corn Plant aspect. The blood in its veins came from the bloodletting sacrifice of the gods, as depicted on the Huehuetenango vase.

We know the Maya believed that the soul manifested from its Otherworldly paradise through the 01 Portal jaws of the great Vision Serpent, and that they saw the human mother's birth canal as the earthly embodiment of this snake-energy portal. An inscription from Palenque says that Pacal's son, K'an-Hok-Chitam, was born from the "heart of the center [01] of the Primordial Sea [the Otherworld]," and that his *sak-nik-nal* manifested on earth through the mouth of a vision serpent. Likewise, on a lintel from Yaxchilan Bird-Jaguar's newborn son emerges from the Vision Serpent that is twining around his parents' arms.

Once on the earth plane, the embodied soul had a rude awakening. It was immediately attacked by the Underworld demons. As in the biblical fall of Adam and Eve, the Maya soul was cast out of paradise and hurled into the heat of battle between the forces of creation and destruction. It would have to face the outer evils of disease and death and the inner evils of stupidity, arrogance, and fear that were the toxic effects of the Lords of Death within The White Flower Thing itself.

The soul could make its contribution to the ongoing creation in many ways, through governing, warfare, healing, farming, parenting, educating, and creating objects of truth and beauty. Fundamentally it added to the ongoing triumph of expanding *ch'ulel* by growing *itself* through education and ecstatic bonding with the gods. If it was persevering and diligent it produced a wondrous blossom whose primary characteristic was dignified grace in the face of both triumph and disaster.

This matured flower-soul of the Maya teachings bears a striking resemblance to the "Golden Flower" and "subtle body" of Eastern mysticism and the "Resurrection Body" of Christianity. With this Maya Resurrection Body fully developed, not only had the soul contributed richly to the creation and re-creation of this world; it was now ready to re-create itself beyond the portal of death. If it had succeeded in growing into its divine potential, it rose as First Father and the Twin Gods—but wearing its own individual "face." It danced forever on the surface of the infinite Otherworldly sea. But if it had failed in its earthly task, its life cycle was cut short. It was sacrificed by the Lords of Death, dismembered, and buried under the ballcourt of Xibalba, its life-bearing promise extinguished forever.

CHAPTER 8

The Shaman's
Secret

A series of magnificent carved lintels from the Chiapas jungles depict the shamanic bloodletting rituals of the royal family of Yaxchilan. The scenes portray various ceremonies that took place over a period of years, many of them carried out by the wives of the great king Bird-Jaguar. A number of them were carved by the shaman-artist known to archaeologists as the Cookie-cutter Artist because of the depth of his cuts and their clean edges. These sculptures show the fine details of Maya weaving techniques and the delicate patterned designs of their garments.

One of the most remarkable scenes unfolds on Lintel 15. There we see Lady Six-Tun caught up in the vision she has conjured by her just completed bloodletting rite. She kneels in a darkened room, cradling a woven basket in her arms. The basket holds her bloodletting instruments, along with strips of bloody paper. The rope that she drew through her tongue moments before lies draped over her forearm. She is wearing an elegant *huipil*—a long, flowing robe with cross designs on it—earrings, a pendant, elaborately worked bracelets of jade, and the special collar used for bloodletting rituals.

Her sleek black hair is tied back with strips of blood-spattered paper—except for three proud locks, two of which arc above her forehead,

Lintel 15 from Yaxchilan, showing Lady Six-Tun's bloodletting ritual.

held in place by tubular ornaments. Lady Six-Tun's disheveled but proud coiffeur conveys a combination of careful sophistication and frenzied abandon—no doubt the product of the ritual she's just completed.

Her face is a picture of Maya beauty. Jutting forward across her forehead a third lock of hair conveys a sense of haughty if bedraggled dignity. She tilts her head slightly upward, showing her large, fleshy, aristocratic Indian nose and her long, slightly receding chin. Her almond eyes gaze upward at the vision that has materialized before her. Her powerful jaw hangs slack from exhaustion and perhaps to protect her wounded tongue. Her full lips are just barely parted, showing her prominent front teeth—a mark of feminine beauty in the eyes of the ancient Maya.

Before her on the floor is an offering plate, piled high with blood-saturated strips of paper. She has already set the paper on fire and clouds of smoke billow upward. Twined in the billows of smoke, the coils of an enormous Vision Serpent rise to the ceiling. The huge snake bears the markings of the diamond-backed rattler, and is sprinkled with the drops of Lady Six-Tun's blood that have brought it onto the earth plane from its Otherworldly lair. It throws its head back and spreads its jaws wide, revealing razor-sharp teeth and venomous fangs, and choking up the vision the queen had sought.

The vision itself is a huge male figure whose head and right hand are emerging from the serpent's jaws. His hair is bound in a rakish, almost "punk" style, and waves above his head like the tail feathers of a tropical bird. He wears long, forward-thrusting pendant earrings. His eyes look down at Lady Six-Tun far below, and his heavy lower lip drops as he opens his mouth to speak. His hand gestures with casual authority, its index finger pointing as if explaining something.

The oracular nature of the vision shows us that the purpose of Lady Six-Tun's bloodletting was to call a dead ancestor from the Otherworld to bring her supernatural knowledge. The vision's features are so similar to hers that we could easily imagine him as her father.

This dramatic scene is the most naturalistic depiction of a Vision Serpent that has come down to us. It is also the most powerful portrayal of the oracular function of many of the bloodletting rites. We know that one of the most important responsibilities of the souls that had won their resurrections through the terrifying trials at the hands of the Lords of Death was to come back to this world when their descendants called and give them the benefit of their advice and world-making wisdom, as eternal souls who had now become gods. Like the Buddhist bodhisattvas, Maya souls who had survived the death of the soul apparently could not pass fully into the realm of bliss until they had saved others. This counseling responsibility on the part of deified ancestors was the reason the shamans of Palenque had fitted Pacal's tomb with its spirit tube.

We can only hope that Lady Six-Tun received the wisdom she was seeking in her shamanic ritual, and that her resurrected "father," as a Lord of Life, found his enhanced creator role pleasing.

Shamanism—the powerful psychological and spiritual process for re-creating the cosmos and turning death into life in all the dimensions of Reality—was the driving force behind every aspect of ancient Maya life. It always required that the shaman-creator sacrifice himself or herself, allow himself or herself to be struck by the terrible lightning of the gods, descend into the Abyss, and die in the Black Hole at its center. Death in its many forms—emotional, spiritual, and physical—was the price all creative individuals paid to become "Lords of Life."

"Dying" and achieving ecstatic oneness with the creator gods led the shamans to create what they believed were divinely authentic things. Creating divinely authentic things made one a *halach uinic*—an evolved personality that displayed his or her developed character.

According to the Maya, all authentic human beings were shaman-creators in one way or another. Becoming a shaman-creator required educating oneself, developing one's skills and natural talents, and being willing to undergo the painful deprivations and self-sacrifices that all creative projects demanded. For the Maya, becoming a shaman-creator was not a luxury—not for those who wished to survive their physical deaths. In return for their sacrifices, shaman-creators built their Resurrection Bodies and achieved an intensity of Being that assured them of eternal life.

Ah tz'ibob ("scribes") and *itz'atob* ("artists") were the most authentic human beings. To a lesser extent, the shaman-warriors who went into battle in an Otherworldly frenzy, manifesting their *uayob* ahead of them, were also considered to be members of this exclusive class. The shaman-queens were also creators. A few of them ruled in their own right as *k'in ahauob*—"Sun Lords." But most of them practiced the shamanic arts to conjure divine forces their royal husbands would need to successfully complete whatever world-making tasks were before them—initiating new irrigation projects, dedicating *ch'ulel*-generating pyramids and ball-courts, and making war in order to secure victims for human sacrifice.

For the Classic Period Maya, the shaman-king was the most authentic *halach uinic* because he stood at the life-bearing center of all the worlds and embodied most fully the gods and demons. The shaman-king was the World Tree/Cosmic Phallus. He was the Twin Gods. He was Itzam-na, the Creator and world-making scribe-artist. He was the supreme *itzer*. And he was The-Holy-First-Father-Decapitated-Dead-Creating-Thing—"One Maize Precious," the miraculous Cosmic Corn Plant. When he wore his First Father/Maize-god masks and costumes and grasped the ecliptic serpent bar and the K'awil scepter, he declared himself master of the spirit world. Like Jesus, the Buddha, the Hindu gurus, and the sacred kings of all high civilizations, he was fully human and fully divine at one and the same time.

The other reason the shaman-king was the most authentic of the "true human beings" was that he was the most complete. Above all else, he was the great provider and procreator. He brought abundance and prosperity to his people through his ecstatic visions, his personal blood-letting rituals, and his rites of sympathetic magic. In the most awesome of the fertility dramas, he was the divine executioner, First Lord as Chac-Xib-Chac. It was he who severed the heads of noble captives and sent them in the guise of First Father, the Twin Gods, or the Lords of Xibalba to the Abyss of death—there, in the case of First Father and the Twins, to be reborn as a source of new life for the kingdom and the universe. At times, the shaman-king himself was destined to make the supreme sacrifice. His blood would fertilize the earth of another's kingdom.

A rollout of a vase painting, showing the Monkey Scribe-Artisans painting in their jaguar-pelt codices.

Along with Itzam-na and his *uay* the Principal Bird Deity, the so-called Monkey Scribe-Artisans, ancient gods of the arts of civilization, were important deities of wizardry and creation. They were shown in art as gargoyle-faced monkeys with human bodies, beards made of seashells, and the ears of deer. They often wore jaguar-hide skirts and the star-spangled turbans characteristic of scribes, and had a long scroll, marked with numbers, rolling out from under their armpits like a computer printout.

At Izapa, an early proto-Maya city on the fertile Pacific coast of Chiapas, researchers have discovered a remarkable stela that portrays these divine shaman-creators as the authors of human life. On this stela we see a depiction of the World Tree. A mysterious figure drills a hole in the Tree, and from this hole the bodies of partially formed human beings tumble out. Nearby an old couple—probably the Creator Couple of the *Popol Vuh*—perform a divination rite. To the right of the main scene a small figure, dressed in the turban of the Monkey Scribe-Artisans, finishes shaping the bodies that emerge from the Tree.

As powerful a position as these manifestations of the creative life force within The Holy Thing held in the spirituality of the Classic Period Maya, by *Popol Vuh* times the Monkey Scribe-Artisans had become clown-like figures, at least in the popular imagination. Perhaps their demotion was the result of the peasant revolutions that almost certainly toppled many of the royal families, destroyed many of their books, changed their "elitist" myths about divine scribes and artists, and debunked the importance of education. Even so, throughout the Post-Classic Period and even into Spanish colonial times, those sages who had survived the upheavals of revolutions and wars continued to revere the Monkey Scribe-Artisans as the patrons of all that was sacred and true.

In spite of the setbacks they may have experienced as the era of city-state warfare heated up and peasant revolutions broke out, we now know that it was the Maya sages who played the central role in creating and maintaining the wisdom of Maya spirituality. These shaman-scribes and shaman-artists were the inventors of writing, the mythmakers, the astronomers and astrologers, the curers, the seers, the spiritual explorers, the innovators, the architects, the keepers of the ancient wisdom, and the creators of beauty. And it was they who developed and became the guardians of the secret resurrection technology.

Little physical evidence has survived of the shamanic schools—mostly graffiti scrawled on temple walls and palace compounds by students. But based on the products of Maya civilization—the few surviving books, the astounding architecture and sculptures, the magnificent paintings, the flood of figurines, ceramics, jewelry, masks, and art objects of all kinds—we know such schools existed. We can guess the kind of education the *ah tz'ibob* and *itz'atob* must have received. The classes must have covered fields such as myth, history, festivals and calendrics, ritual practices, reading and writing, calligraphy, literature, artistic techniques and mediums, trancing and spiritual experience, sacred geography, astronomy, mathematics, architecture, mask and costume fabrication, and many others. Through these fields of study the children of the Maya elite were taught the virtues of self-discipline and courage, a balance between patience and passion, and the techniques for recovering divine sight. The highest value of Maya learning was the cultivation of the soul, the processes for growing it into a deeper, more durable version of itself than it had been when it had entered this world.

Before scholars knew how powerful a role shamanism played in ancient Maya religion, they believed that the scribes had a social standing not much higher than that of the peasant farmers. Two archaeological discoveries—both at Copan—completely changed this picture.

The first discovery focused on the Sepulturas compound located some distance from the center of the ancient city. Here, vast interconnected quadrangles of sleeping rooms, bathhouses, and open-air kitchens formed the living quarters of the extended family clans of Copan's nobility. The main building of the compound has an audience chamber at the top of a high staircase that was built to imitate the stairs of the great temple-pyramids of Copan's acropolis. Interestingly, the building's facade is carved with scenes of scribes holding conch-shell inkwells and calligrapher's brushes. At the summit stands a carved bench on which scholars believe scribal patriarchs held semiroyal audiences. From this dais, carved with figures of the scribal gods, these mighty chief *ah tz'ibob* handed down their judgments in interfamily quarrels, made and enforced the rules of the community, and performed public bloodletting rituals. We even know the name of one of these powerful scribes—Mac Chaanal.

The other discovery that changed our view of the scribes' standing in Maya society was that of a tomb within the main pyramid on Copan's Great Plaza. The stairway and balustrade of this temple are elaborately sculpted into the figures of vision serpents manifesting the most powerful kings of the Copan dynasty. These carvings celebrate the awesome unfolding of the Divine Presence throughout the history of the city. The stairs that surround these unearthly stone "hierophanies" are covered with hieroglyphs. In fact, as the visitor gazes up in wonder at this hieroglyphic stairway, it seems to come alive. So energetically yet gracefully carved are the symbols, and so concentrated, that the whole stairway seems to move, slithering and undulating with lightning-serpent energy.

The tomb inside this temple to the miracle of writing held the body of a great man. Originally, archaeologists thought he must have been a king; he was even accompanied in death by a sacrificed child. But when they took a closer look at the objects buried with him—ten paint pots, a decayed codex, and a bowl depicting a shaman-scribe—they reached an arresting conclusion: This man had been buried within a living mountain like the great Maya kings; but he wasn't a king—he was a scribe! Scholars now believe that he was the brother of one of Copan's shaman-kings. It is no accident that he was entombed within the very pyramid that celebrated the divine power of writing.

Judging by the volume of artifacts, by the fact that writing usually provided commentary on visual imagery, and from the accounts of creation that emphasize the divine power of painting and sculpting, we know that the Maya held art in even higher esteem than written language. Throughout most of Maya history, those who could create works of art were people to be admired—and feared. They could reveal the K'awil soul at the heart of all things, make the invisible visible, and the infinite concrete and physical. For the Maya, more than for any other people in the history of the world, art created reality rather than the other way around.

As with the scribes, researchers underestimated the status of the shaman-artists until they could read the texts on the funerary ceramics.

The Hieroglyphic Stairs at Copan as reconstructed by Tatiana Proskouriakoff.

Now we know that, like the scribes, artists were members of the nobility, and received the best education the Maya schools could provide. An important step toward this new understanding of the place of artists in Maya society came from the deciphering of a white-background cylinder vase from Naranjo in the Classic Period Maya heartland. In a hieroglyphic band near the bottom of the vase the word *u tz'ib*—"his painting"—appears, followed by a personal name accompanied by the title *itz'at*. Although we can't read the artist's name, we know that he was the son of a powerful shaman-king of Naranjo. After the hieroglyph for "artist" comes the emblem for the painter's hometown, then the symbol for his mother's city—Yaxha—and the title of his royal father.

Some shaman-artist nobles won reputations throughout the Maya area as especially gifted *itzers*. A great shaman-artist named K'in Chaac signed his name on a stela at Piedras Negras, along with seven other *itz'atob* who had helped him create the stela. Researchers have found his signature at other sites in the Usumacinta River basin as well.

Artists were so vital to the process of giving birth to the Divine on the earth plane that capturing them in warfare and bringing them back to the victorious city was a major reason for conflicts between the Classic Period kingdoms, second only to gaining victims for human sacrifice. Researchers had wondered why the tortured captives in so many Maya murals and sculptures were usually portrayed with far more sensitivity and power than their captors. Now they believe it was because the artists who created these victory memorials for the conquering lords were depicting the suffering of their own fellow shamans, men they knew personally, some of whom may have been their relatives.

From Bishop Landa's eyewitness accounts and other sources we know that the process of artistic creation was a shamanic journey of the highest order. Artists secluded themselves, fasted, performed bloodletting sacrifices, drank *balche*—a fermented drink made from honey and the bark of the balche tree—smoked hallucinogenic cigars, and took mind-altering drugs. They opened themselves to the power of the gods and demons within their own souls and entered the portal of death and transformation—the very place of "dawning" and "creating."

These divinely—or demonically—possessed creators left telltale signs of the ecstatic emotional states they were in when they carved and painted: a large number of glaring errors—in drawing preliminary plans for paintings and sculptures, in the details of the final versions, and in the rendering of hieroglyphs for time sequences. Art specialists know these errors are not due to a lack of skill in workmanship, and certainly not to carelessness, because they appear in art objects of great power and precision. The question is, when the artists came down from their drug-induced highs, why did they let their mistakes stand? The most likely explanation is that they believed the mistakes they made while under the power of the gods were divine interventions. Perhaps like many artists today, the Maya believed these inspired errors added new interpretative possibilities to their creations.

Once an object was finished, its creator or creators gave it a personal name in order to formally announce its birth as a living being. At least in the larger cities every stela, altar, and temple had its own birth name, just as human children had.

When we add up the clues from all the evidence that has survived—from inscriptions, ceramics, codices, sculptures, and sacred architecture—a cryptic pattern begins to emerge like an undiscovered continent rising from the mist. We can now see enough of this hidden world of shamanic symbolism to know that there was a method to the madness of the Maya *ah tz'ibob.* Encoded just beneath the surface of their mythology of death and dawning, their bloody vision rites, their monstrous depictions of the gods, and the creation and resurrection imagery they painted on funerary vases and carved on temple walls was their scheme for building the Resurrection Body, that Body of intensified Being that would guarantee their survival after death. For the ancient sages, greater Being—or the failure to achieve it—was the ultimate factor in determining the final destiny of the soul. As harsh as it may seem, the Maya believed that human beings who failed to achieve the creative lives that were the fruit of divine ecstasy were cut off from any hope of surviving their physical deaths and gaining the eternal life of the Otherworld.

The twentieth-century Christian theologian Paul Tillich proposed a remarkably similar belief in his doctrine of, as he called it, the "essentialization" of the soul "above history." Based on his interpretation of Christian Scriptures, he issued a stern warning to those who are too lazy to become centers of creation and resurrection during their lifetimes:

> The *telos* [the fate] of man as an individual is determined by the decisions he makes in existence on the basis of the potentialities given to him by destiny. He can waste his potentialities, though not completely, and he can fulfill them, though not totally. Thus, the symbol of ultimate judgment receives a particular seriousness. The exposure of the negative as negative in a person [at the judgment] may not leave much positive for Eternal Life.

Tillich claimed that the consequences of not achieving greater Being and creativity—the "positive"—and of staying trapped in the vices of laziness, destructiveness, and inauthenticity—the "negative"—are "eternal death."

This combination of words—["eternal death"]—means death "away" from eternity, a failure to reach eternity. . . . As such eternal death is a personal threat against everyone who is bound to temporality and unable to transcend it. For him Eternal Life is a meaningless symbol because he is lacking in anticipatory experience [resurrection experiences in this life] of the eternal. In the symbolism of the resurrection, one could say that he dies but does not participate in resurrection.

It now seems clear that what the Maya shaman-scribes and artists were doing was cultivating "anticipatory experience of the eternal." They tried to become real in a way that this world of dreaming and superficial living is not, and to prepare to face the trials of the Lords of Death.

This account of how we win eternal life is dramatically opposed to that of the "cheap salvation" put forward by some versions of Christianity and some new-age religions. In these spiritual systems the individual soul hardly has to lift a finger to gain its eternal reward. These religions require such relatively minor efforts as "accepting Jesus Christ as your personal Lord and Savior" or engaging in deep breathing exercises in order to feel "embraced by the Light." But what kind of souls do we build as a result of these simple, mostly mindless, processes? The ancient Maya would say: None at all. And they would add that when we ask an external savior to do all the suffering, dying, and creating for us we will remain the underdeveloped, vulnerable White Flower Things we were when we first blossomed into the effortless realm of the World Tree paradise.

The ancient shamans of Palenque built a resurrection generator to one side of the center of the city in a small recess surrounded by jungle-covered hills. Archaeologists call this ch'ulel "power plant" the Group of the Cross. It is made up of three pyramid-temples arranged in a triangular pattern, each of which has a dreaming place at the top.

The shaman-architects who designed the Group of the Cross believed they had discovered the earthly site of the three hearthstones of creation. They built each of the three temples over one of the invisible but supernaturally detectable stones. They placed the Temple of the Cross at the northern apex of the Cosmic Hearth. On the central, magically charged back wall of its pib na they installed a huge sculpted panel depicting the World Tree at the moment First Father lifted it into the sky.

The Temple of the Cross at Palenque as seen from the Palace.

At the western corner of the triangle they constructed the Temple of the Sun and erected a panel portraying war and human sacrifice. At the eastern corner of the Hearth—the direction of dawning—they built the Temple of the Foliated Cross and placed within it a panel showing the World Tree as the Cosmic Corn Plant.

The shamans arranged the pyramids so that as the night sky wheeled through its yearly cycle to reenact the events of creation, the three temples would engage this celestial pattern and reactivate the Dream Time of that first awakening. When the Milky Way/World Tree rose in the heavens in its "Raised-up-Sky-Tree" position, the constellation Scorpio glittered over the southern mountains, and the Xibal Be flowed in ghostly splendor toward the Black Transformer, the temple complex came alive with Otherworldly forces.

In the dark dreaming-place chamber in the Temple of the Foliated Cross the mysterious image of the Cosmic Corn Plant looms, flanked by depictions of the "First True Mountain," the conch-shell entrance to the Metawil paradise, the dead king Pacal, and his heir Chan-Bahlum. The "First True Mountain" is split open to reveal First Father emerging as the Cosmic Corn Plant. Pacal, wrapped in his death shroud, represents First Father in the Underworld. Chan-Bahlum, as the Twin Gods, has made the fearful journey to Xibalba to bring his father back to life.

The shamans who designed and carved this powerful image believed that when the stars and constellations took up their creation-resurrection positions, the panel glowed with *ch'ulel,* and the Corn Plant

miraculously shone forth as the supernatural image of the Resurrection
Body. To the eyes of the enraptured shaman-king, when the panel of the
Foliated Cross came alive with K'awil energy, Pacal rose from the Un-
derworld.

Because of our progress in understanding the symbols of ancient
Maya shamanism—and with some help from comparative religion and
depth psychology—we can now decode this magnificent icon of the resurrected soul. At the anthropological level of interpretation, the Cosmic
Corn Plant stands for cultivated nature, nature made safe for human habi-
tation by the Twin Gods, and subjected to a domestication regimen that
produces material abundance. Translated into the language of spiritual
symbols, it means that when the soul's own nature is cultivated and made
habitable for the human part of us—when it is tamed, domesticated, and
subjected to the discipline of education and civilized life—it produces

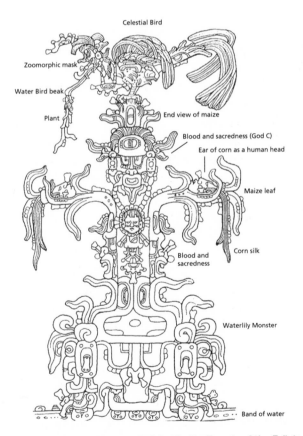

The World Tree as the Cosmic Corn Plant as depicted in the Temple of the Foliated Cross at
Palenque.

spiritual abundance and the fruits of greater Being in soul form. In this human soul form it nurtures the Divine Being and the world, just as maize nurtures the human body.

At the base of the sculpture we see the fetid waters of Xibalba. Floating on these waters and giving rise to the Cosmic Corn Plant is the gigantic severed head of the so-called Waterlily Monster. It has crossed eyes, a bone through its nose, and earflares that end in the shoots and tendrils of the water lily. In Maya spirituality this plant symbolized all the standing bodies of water that manifested the entrance to the world of decay and abundance below the earth's surface. In this sense, the Waterlily Monster was the principal mediator between the Underworld and the earth plane. The Waterlily Monster was a transitional god who embodied the supernatural process by which death transformed itself into life and life sank back into the darkness and mystery of its origins.

If we place the imagery from the tripod plate over this Foliated Cross icon like a transparent overlay, we see dramatic parallels between these two portrayals of the miracle of re-creation. The Waterlily Monster's head is a perfect match for First Father's, and the World Tree/Cosmic Corn Plant that rises from its skull takes the place of the Vision Serpent/World Tree that erupts onto the earth plane from The-Decapitated-Dead-Creating-Thing on the plate.

On the Palenque panel the Monster is wearing the so-called K'an-cross sign on its forehead—a symbol that depicted its split forehead/third eye and marked the absolute center where the wondrous death-life transformation took place. It is here in the Monster's lightning-struck brain—the seat of its intelligence and imagination—that the miracle happens. Using the Maya belief that the human body is a fractal version of the cosmos, and plotting the form of the body on the Cosmic Corn Plant, we see that the Monster's head is located in the area of the genitals. In fact, the genitals do have a mind of their own, as most of us have discovered; and through the death of the ego in sexual rapture and orgasm they create new life. For human beings as for corn plants, this life surges up from shadowy, unknown, and finally unknowable depths.

Translated into the symbolism of the Resurrection Body, the Waterlily Monster stands for the place in the soul where the rebirth begins—the most primitive and unconscious part of us—Jung's collective unconscious. We are, in a sense, plantlike in this aspect of our souls because it is here that the psychological and spiritual processes disappear into the biological functions of cellular death and reproduction. These forms of energy transformation are forever below the threshold of human awareness and beyond our psychological or emotional control. The image of the Waterlily Monster also reminds us that the roots of our souls—which are not shown in the carving—are in the realm of death and nonbeing.

The Corn Plant soars upward, marked with signs of blood and sacredness. In the symbolism of the Resurrection Body the blood that gushes from the main stalk tells us, once again, that we gain the re-creation of our souls and the sanctification of our lives only through painful self-sacrifice. This portrayal of bloodletting on the icon of the Foliated Cross directly parallels the self-sacrificial flow of *itz* on the tripod plate. On the plate, First Father's head, the Vision Serpent/World Tree, and Itzam-Yeh are all gushing blood. Most important, First Lord is achieving his vision of the resurrection of the world through the bloody sacrifice of his hand.

Near the top of the Maize Tree the face of the so-called God C appears. He is always shown in Maya art as a monkey, and he either wears or himself stands for the *ch'ul*—"holy thing"—glyph. Here, he marks the whole Corn Plant as a "holy thing." Probably related to the Monkey Scribe-Artisans, he represents a mind and imagination that is higher than that of the Waterlily Monster's vegetable intelligence. The Monkey-god wears a severed head pendant, symbolizing his victory over death. He also wears a mirror sign on his forehead—the shaman's visionary mirror and the sign for divine brightness. In Maya iconography this brightness symbol depicts the aftermath of supernatural lightning strikes from the Otherworld deep within the soul's own mysterious depths.

The Monkey-god appears on the Corn Plant image at the *uayob* level of the soul; and he implies that it is our animal natures that give us our brightness and divine sight. God C is located where the heart is in the human body. Using the Resurrection Body interpretation, we could say that the ecstatic heart of the transformed soul is the animal part of us. The Monkey-god who marks the whole Corn Plant and its growth process as a "holy thing" symbolizes the ancient Maya belief that as we re-create the core essence of ourselves we become gods.

The Waterbird of the Underworld—who lived in the swamps and canals of the earth plane—perches on the topmost corn stalk of the Maize Tree, wearing the mask of Itzam-Yeh. His long tail feathers are blowing in the winds of the Overworld where the star fields whirl around the 01 Portal of birth. He is flapping his wings to steady himself and grasping a sacred plant in his long beak. Because the Waterbird was the Underworld *uay* of First Lord, and because he is wearing the costume of

Itzam-Yeh, the *uay* of Itzam-na, we know that First Lord has assumed the identity—and the place—of the Water Wizard of Xibalba as the Lord of the universe. Also, since First Lord was really First Father, we realize that this image depicts First Father's entering or becoming the sky and inaugurating space and time as we know them. This perching image directly parallels the scene on the tripod plate where Itzam-Yeh is hovering above the World Tree. But in the Palenque scene First Lord/First Father has already replaced the defeated monster-bird and completed the resurrection of the world.

In the fractal symbolism of the human body, First Lord/First Father represents the head. The shamanic powers of the creator gods, which they have won by assuming the identity of Itzam-na, are symbols of the divine intelligence and imagination that the Maya knew dwell in this highest region of our bodies. In Resurrection Body symbolism, the fact that the gods of resurrection have ascended into the Overworld means that the soul achieves its fully divine identity only when, like First Lord/First Father, it has finally entered and become the Overworld— only when it has reached what other religions call "Christ Consciousness," "Buddha Consciousness," or "Cosmic Consciousness." As we've seen, gaining this transcendent level of awareness was the shamans' ultimate goal.

Sprouting as arms from the body of the Cosmic Corn Plant, two stalks with fully developed ears of corn, luxuriating leaves, and flowing corn tassels miraculously appear. The ears of corn are shown as human heads, the corn tassels as their hair. Again, in the language of Resurrection Body symbolism we can see that the fruits of this life-creating higher consciousness are living things with their own identities, intelligence, imagination, and creativity. These products of the transformed soul, like physical ears of corn, nurture and sustain human—and divine—life.

Finally, we can see that the World Tree/Corn Plant is both a depiction of the fully resurrected soul and a portrayal of the process by which the shaman won his personal transformation. Beginning in the hidden realm of death, and rising through the genitals, the soul finds itself materializing on the earth plane. Through self-sacrifice, and the cultivation, discipline, and energy channeling of education and shamanic instruction, the divine potential of the soul reaches the heart level of animal passion. Still surging upward through the defeat and integration of its own wildness and destructive forces, symbolized by the fall of Itzam-Yeh, it at last achieves Overworldly Cosmic Consciousness. During the process of growth it was a god; but through final union with First

Lord/First Father as the Cosmic Shaman/Creator, it has itself become The Holy Thing.

According to the Maya, as with the corn plant, so with the soul— success is not guaranteed. Many things can happen to stunt the soul's growth or kill it at any point along the way. But if it is allowed to reach its full potential and itself become a source of abundance and sustenance both for the gods and other human beings, it has achieved its purpose on earth. Strengthened by this secret shamanic vision of its task, and made *cauac*-hard through its exercises in self-discipline and ecstatic trance, the Maya soul was now prepared to make its final descent into the Mystery from which it had come, face the terrible trials of the Lords of Death, and win its eternal reward—a resurrection that was far more than metaphoric or psychological. For the Maya, it was literal, palpable, and undeniably real.

CHAPTER 9

Death

Death is the great black wall against which all of our lives shatter. It is the end toward which each of us is racing with our achievements, our hopes and disappointments, our loves and hates, our cherished identities. And when we hit that unyielding wall of impenetrable silence we break apart, we dissipate; we, as we have known ourselves, cease to be.

All of us live under a death sentence. How we deal with it is the most defining thing about us. Death is the great stumbling block, and the beginning and end of all our myths and religions.

In death we must leave all our earthly possessions in the world of the living, and face the Black Transformer alone, naked before the darkness. If any part of us survives this terrible denuding, if we take anything with us into the Void, surely it can only be the spiritual qualities we've developed, the characteristics of soul we've internalized through our earthly experiences.

As the wisdom teachings of all religions proclaim, far more serious than physical death is the death of the soul that all too often destroys human lives long before our bodies fail. The Maya shamans believed that soul-death is so seductive and diabolically clever that, without our knowledge or conscious consent, it often gains our fullest cooperation. It uses our personal weaknesses to attack our own souls and those of the people

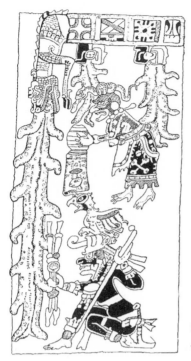

First Mother as a demon pouring poisoned water on the earth, as depicted in the Dresden codex.

around us. In the end, the most subtle of death's strategies for killing the soul is to persuade us that death itself does not exist. If death can hide in the shadows while we are distracted by the daylight world of our earthly concerns, it can ambush us. But if we can learn to see death—its reality, its lies, the seriousness of its threat, as well as its potential life-generating boon—it becomes the great awakener of a more vital and whole earthly existence and of a blissful eternal life.

The Maya feared death—physical and spiritual. Like the ancient Egyptians with their elaborate mummification practices, their morbid Underworld fantasies, and their books of incantations and spells, the Maya were fascinated by the darkness. But their morbidity, like that of the ascetics, warriors, and sages of other religions, had a purpose. It helped them to stay awake to death. When it was no longer invisible, it could be faced; and if it could be faced, it could be overcome. Seeing in this way helped the Maya shamans unmask death's crafty, tricksterish ways and expose its life-imitating pretensions. When they could see as the gods saw, false suns could be destroyed, the demons of Xibalba could be defeated, and severed heads could erupt in torrents of *ch'ulel*.

In contrast to our culture's flight from the darkness, the Maya embraced death and its attacks on both the body and the soul. Death informed every aspect and shaped every moment of their earthly lives and gave them their urgent intensity, their vividness and color, and their quality of terrible beauty.

The Maya forced themselves to stay constantly aware of death through bloodletting, the torture of captives taken in battle, and human sacrifice. They maintained that the only authentic salvation lies in facing the worst head-on, honestly, directly, without flinching. If there is a real basis for hope, they believed, it can only be found at the darkest, most sinister core of the cosmic Abyss. Like the Buddha confronting the archdemon Mara under the Bo tree and Jesus "setting his face toward Jerusalem" to embrace the terror of God's Wrath through his crucifixion, the Maya shamans sought to experience the dark ecstasy at the core of The Holy Thing's dream of Itself and the world. If divine light could not be found there, it could not be found at all.

Many clues exist that point to the connection the ancient Maya made between the awareness of death's reality and a heightened sense of aliveness on earth and in the spiritual realm. The images of K'awil's lightning strikes that bring transformed life at the very moment of death, cleft heads that flow with images of life, sexual icons entombed with decaying corpses, depictions of divine self-sacrifice and the burgeoning of the created world, and the wordplays of the Yaxchilan descent/decapitation/creation hieroglyphs are all portrayals of the awesome beauty the Maya knew throughout their lives. Those awe-full moments in which they achieved their ecstatic mergers with the great Mystery, their monster gods, the cryptic messages of the Cosmic Corn Plant/Resurrection Body from the Temple of the Foliated Cross at Palenque—all these things and more illustrate the Maya wisdom about the life-enhancing power of the awareness of death.

Still, these images and tantalizing texts are only clues. No treatises have survived to make explicit this connection between death and intensified aliveness. But other peoples have made such a connection. Research into Native American spirituality in general and ancient Aztec religion in particular, a religion whose spiritual treatises and metaphysical poems have survived, strengthens the conclusion that the Maya too used their awareness of death to give birth to renewed life.

One of the most powerful statements of this life-from-death spirituality the ancient Maya espoused comes from the anthropologist Carlos Castaneda's accounts of his conversations with a present-day Yaqui Indian shaman from northern Mexico, Don Juan. Though the Yaquis never developed a high civilization like that of the Maya, they still share the general outlook and mythology of the ancient Mesoamerican heritage from which their own spirituality is descended. For the Yaquis as for the ancient Maya, authentic human life is lived as part of the cosmic drama between the forces of life and death. This ongoing battle has powerful implications for how authentic human beings ought to live their lives today.

Strikingly similar to the themes, images, and tone of the *Popol Vuh,* Castaneda's account of his climactic conversation with Don Juan rings with the same urgency about the need to live life fully and purposefully that the ancient Maya must also have embraced. Don Juan, like the Maya shamans, insists that facing our deaths directly makes us more powerful and more energetically alive. The old Yaqui *brujo* uses the imagery of hunting and warfare, images the Maya also used in their art and hieroglyphic inscriptions, to make his point. In Chapter 9 of Castaneda's *Journey to Ixtlan,* Don Juan says:

> This, whatever you're doing now, may be your last act on earth. It may very well be your last battle. . . . Focus your attention on the link between you and your death, without remorse or sadness or worrying. Focus your attention on the fact you don't have time and let your acts flow accordingly. Let each of your acts be your last battle on earth. Only under those conditions will your acts have their rightful power. Otherwise they will be, for as long as you live, the acts of a timid man. . . . A hunter gives his last battle its due respect. . . . It's pleasurable that way. It dulls the edge of his fright. . . .

In this last line, Don Juan seems to be saying, as the Maya through their nightmarish images of death certainly were, that human beings ought not delude themselves into pretending they're not afraid to die. Instead, we should accept our fear and use it to act courageously to gain our creative goals and to achieve a sense of quiet dignity, like that shown in First Father's Buddha-like portrait as the Maize-god. We can live in this more vital way only by engaging our daily encounters with death—physical and spiritual—as if they were our "last battle." This was certainly the attitude Shield-Jaguar carried with him when he took his mask from his wife, kissed her bloodstained cheek, and marched out of Yaxchilan to an uncertain fate.

In the Maya's death-haunted world, sleep, dreaming, trance, and ecstatic visioning were all manifestations of the death-state. Death with its K'awil lightning bolt through the third eye was the fundamental condition of transformation. As we've seen, the dreaming places of the shamans were places of blood sacrifice and awesome communication with the Underworld-Otherworld. The fact that the Maya never clearly distinguished between these two realms—one of eternal death and the other of eternal life—shows the intimate relationship they believed existed between them.

Often in the hieroglyphic texts that describe these transformational journeys to the Black Dreaming Place/Black Transformer, the scribes substituted the symbol of "death" for the so-called *uay* glyph. According to the shamans, all ecstatic experiences of the sacred were brushes with the eternal life that awaited prepared souls in the timeless realm of death-life. In this sense, death was not the end but rather the true beginning—at least for those who could grasp its soul-awakening potential.

The ancient Maya association of dreaming and death finds strong confirmation in the theories of Carl Jung. He believed that in dreams the ego travels down into the collective unconscious to confront not only the repressed fragments of the individual soul but ultimately the gods and demons that haunt this universal—and deathly—Underworld.

The Maya shamans believed that all deaths, but especially those of authentic human beings, are, in their essence, "sacrificial" deaths. In these sacrificial deaths human beings give back to the gods what the gods, through their own sacrifices, have given them—blood for blood, tears for rain, flesh for corn, substance for substance, life for life, Being for Being. Our own English words "sacred" and "sacrifice" are related, and show that we too once knew the intimate connection between death and God.

The actual moment of physical death was the subject of some of the most powerful artistic creations the ancient Maya ever produced: the bloodsnakes and water lilies bursting from the neck of the decapitated ballplayer at Chichen Itza; Pacal's meteorlike fall down the Milky Way/ Xibal Be/World Tree into the Black Transformer, his forehead in flames from K'awil's lightning-serpent blow; Yax Pac standing in stunned amazement in the maw of the Underworld.

Another powerful image of the moment of death, one that appears on four incised bones found in the tomb of the so-called Ruler A at Tikal and again on an eccentric flint from an unknown Classic Period site, depicts death as the sudden sinking of the Canoe of Life. In this imagery, human life is a canoe journey across the surface of the abyssal depths of the Otherworldly ocean. Modeled on the seagoing vessels of the Maya merchants, the Canoe and its passengers symbolize the Maya idea that we are all merchants of life, getting and giving all our days. Our trading partners are the gods.

The Canoe of Life is powered by the two Paddlers, aspects of the Twin Gods, and is itself the Cosmic Monster/Milky Way/Venus-sun ecliptic manifestation of these divinities. It carries the human soul to the climax of its life, to the heights of its development and achievements. In astronomical terms, the Canoe bears First Father to the Cosmic Turtle Shell and the K'an Cross center of the night sky. Then, in the same impossible instant that K'awil blasts open the Turtle Shell to release First Father and begin the rebirth of the cosmos the human soul is struck down, and the Canoe of Life begins to sink. Once again, we see that for the Maya the very act and instant of rebirth is the moment of death, and the call to the Underworld is the moment of resurrection. If the place of death is the place of dawning, awakening, and creation, then, by the same token, dawning, awakening, and creation are also the heralds of the death-state. And death is oneness with The-Holy-First-Father-Decapitated-Dead-Creating-Thing.

The Tikal bones are poignant and powerful. The first two bones show the Canoe of Life hurtling across the waters, bearing Ruler A on his life's journey. In the Canoe with him are an iguana, a spider monkey, a parrot, and a dog. The aged Jaguar Paddler in the bow lashes the water with his paddle, gasping with the effort. In the stern the old Stingray Paddler is also bending to his task. The king in the center of the Canoe wears the headdress of his office, including a leaf that proclaims him the embodiment of the World Tree. He and what may be his animal familiars all press their wrists to their foreheads—in Maya art, a gesture of despair that showed that the moment of death was fast approaching. The hieroglyphs that accompany this journey scene read, "Ruler A canoed four *katunob* [eighty years] to his passing."

On the other two bones we see the stern of the Canoe thrown high into the air as the craft begins its fatal plunge beneath the dark billows. On the first bone the iguana and spider monkey are already thrashing in the water as the suction of the sinking Canoe pulls them under. On the second bone, the catastrophe has advanced. The Canoe has all but disappeared into the Otherworldly Abyss. The dog has

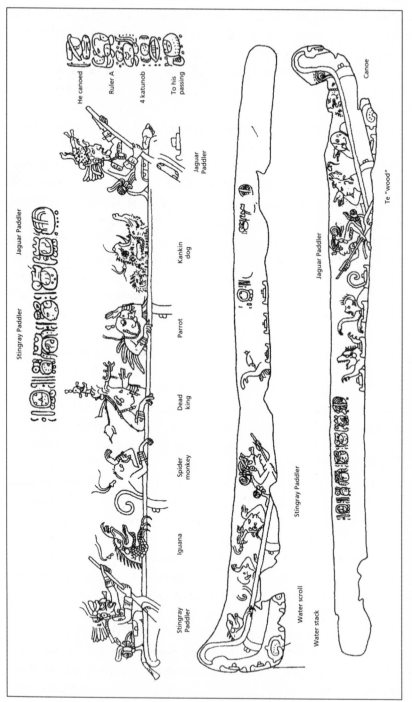

The incised bones of Ruler A from Tikal, showing the sinking Canoe of Life.

slipped from view and only one flailing wing of the parrot remains above the waves, signaling his desperate attempt to regain the earth plane. In both of these scenes the king, still pressing his wrist to his forehead, gazes in fear and astonishment as his own final moment— now just seconds away—rises to engulf him. The hieroglyphic text names this terrifying scene as a First Lord/Venus event—almost certainly a death from natural causes idealized as sacrificial death.

If the Tikal bones are moving, the eccentric flint is overwhelming. The master itz'at who crafted this flint carved the Canoe in the form of the Cosmic Monster. Its prow is the crocodile head of First Lord/Venus. The stern portrays the humanlike aspect of First Jaguar, the flaming ax of K'awil piercing his forehead. These symbols of the Twin Gods are repeated in the form of the Paddlers who here serve as spirit guides to the soul of the unknown lord. No paddles appear, and the Canoe seems to be self-propelled. The king in the center wears a quetzal-feather headdress whose plumes swirl in the wind of the Canoe's sudden downward lunge. Like the sacrificed sun at the stern, he too has been struck by K'awil's deadly celt. The moment of his en-lighten-ment is the last flicker of his earthly life.

The parallel the artist drew between First Jaguar's image and that of the dying king—both of them with flaming celts in their foreheads— shows that they are both, mythologically speaking, the sacrificial victims of First Lord/Chac-Xib-Chac. The identification of the king at the moment of his death with the sacrifice of the Jaguar Sun reflects the belief that in death the divine ahauob—and by extension all other authentic human beings—became First Father in his First Jaguar form. This image expressed the Maya hope that by merging with First Father at the moment of death, they could repeat his "passion" as him, and thereby guarantee their resurrections—like-in-kind to his.

The creator of this magnificent eccentric flint carved the bottom of the Canoe to show the waves of the Underworld ocean crashing against its sides. The waves are the notches the artist cut into the body of the Canoe. Represented in the negative, they are as invisible as the Otherworld, and depict the nonbeing of the Void into which the soul is falling.

This alone is a powerful touch. But the artist went further, and portrayed the terrible g-forces on the Canoe and its occupants as they dive beneath the surface. The Canoe's hull arcs, bending like a bow, and the king and his Paddler companions are hurled backwards as the vessel's

An eccentric flint depicting the moment of death.

plunge accelerates. The viewer watches in fascination as the Canoe of Life becomes the Canoe of Death hurtling into the bottomless Otherworldly sea.

This Maya version of the terrifying descent into the all-consuming Void recalls images of similar descents from the myths of other religions. In ancient Babylonian mythology the goddess Ishtar descended to the Underworld to rescue her slain lover. She was stopped at each of seven infernal gates as she moved deeper and deeper into the earth. At each gate she was forced to remove a piece of her clothing until at last she stood naked before her dark sister, Ereshkigal, the queen of death. Ishtar was sacrificed and her body impaled on a stake. She was destined to rise again, but only after she had internalized the destructive qualities of her sister. Most of the myths of the ancient Mediterranean and Near East were created around the descents of dying/resurrecting male gods, among them Baal, Tammuz, Osiris, Dionysus—and Christ.

A direct parallel to the Maya descent into the bloody waters of Xibalba appears in the ancient images of baptism by blood. For many ancient peoples, baptism, like the ritual of anointing, was a symbolic form of descent, death, and rebirth. In Persian Mithraism the candidate for initiation climbed into a pit beneath an altar on which a bull had been tied. When the bull was sacrificed, its blood poured down onto the would-be initiate, bathing him in its divine life force. Then the initiate ascended from the pit as a new being, cleansed and renewed. Early Christians, who adopted many of the beliefs and practices of Mithraism, believed that in order to be reborn they had to be baptized in Christ's blood.

Another image of blood, descent, and rebirth that scholars of comparative religion and mythology have discovered is the universal idea of the so-called womb-tomb. This idea, which appears in the myths of all ancient agricultural peoples, sees the Underworld as the womb of the earth. The dead body is placed in the tomb, often in a fetal position, and painted red to symbolize the blood of the womb with its life-generating power. When the time is ripe, the soul is reborn from the womb-tomb and rises as a godlike spirit into eternal life.

Jung interpreted this image in a psychological way. He noticed that when many of his clients dreamed of being immersed in large bodies of water they participated in symbolic dramas of death and regeneration. He realized that their unconsciouses were spontaneously using images of the watery prenatal womb on the one hand and symbols of the womb-tomb of ancient mythology on the other. Often, as in the ancient Sumerian myth of Gilgamesh's descent to retrieve the plant of eternal life at the bottom of the sea, his clients imagined the realm of death and rebirth in their dreams as a supernatural place beneath the waves of an infinite ocean. In light of what we now know about these and other myths and dream images of descent, we can see that the Maya depiction of the moment of death was one instance of a universal pattern of fear and hope for the future of the departed soul.

Researchers first discovered the core structure of the ancient Maya resurrection technology on Bird-Jaguar's "stairs of death" at Yaxchilan with their *ah/ahal* Knot-Skull "three descents" formula. The hieroglyphic text is a simple but elegant poem. When we compare it with other inscriptions and the wealth of Maya death and resurrection imagery we can now interpret, this brief passage reveals a world of hidden wisdom and offers us a blueprint for how to overcome the power of death and win eternal life. The poem reads:

It happened at the Black Hole,
It happened at the Abyss—
The first decapitation (descent / awakening)
u na ??? ahal
the second decapitation (descent / awakening)
u cha ??? ahal
the third decapitation (descent / awakening)
ox ahal
—the ballgame of death.

As we've noted, by carefully analyzing the various related meanings of the ancient Maya words—especially the *ah/ahal* Knot-Skull glyph—and comparing other texts that use the same or similar hieroglyphs, researchers realized that these "decapitations" referred to three "descents" into the Land of Death and to the three "dawnings," "awakenings," and "creations" that resulted.

The first two of these "decapitation-creations" appear in detailed form in the *Popol Vuh*. Both in the *Popol Vuh* and at Yaxchilan, they are depicted as taking place in the deep mythological past. If the use of the *Popol Vuh* stories to flesh out the Yaxchilan text is right, we can interpret the poem's first descent as that of First Father. The second is that of his sons the Twin Gods. The third descent is that of every sacrificial victim since. Because the Maya believed that all human deaths were at least potentially sacrificial descent/decapitation/death/awakenings, the meaning of the third descent can be extended to include every human being's confrontation with the forces of destruction and death.

Scholars believe that in this descent mythology the Maya shamans tried to confront and defeat death two different times and in two very different ways. In the myth of the first descent they tried naïveté and denial. But denying the reality and power of death ended in First Father's soul-death. Like Adam, who reached for the fruit of eternal life and was cast out of the Garden of Eden and condemned to physical and spiritual death, First Father met catastrophic defeat instead of victory and eternal life. The shamans learned from this failure. On the second try they were successful. Using the myth of First Lord and First Jaguar's adventures in the Underworld they showed how when the soul moves beyond naïveté and innocence, learns to embody some of death's own cunning ruthlessness, and uses this quality against it, life triumphs.

We don't know the Classic Period explanation for First Father's descent. The hieroglyphs and images give us no clues. But in spite of this lack of narrative detail comparative religion specialists and the psychiatrist Sigmund Freud offer some interesting theories about the probable early motivations for the story. Most ancient peoples believed in a primal king who had been sacrificed and resurrected in order to initiate the birth of higher civilization. This idea parallels the belief in the divine blood sacrifice that began the creation of the universe. The primal king's sacrifice was a reenactment of that original divine "passion." For the Maya, First Father, as both The Holy Thing *and* the first human king, was the link between the Divine Being's inner life-and-death drama and the creation of higher civilization.

Freud explained the universal presence in the world's myths of the dying-resurrecting god-king by his now-famous theory of the murder of the "primal father" by his sons in the "primal horde." It's easy to see how the worship of deified ancestors, mostly sacred kings, arose from the unconscious memory of the sons' guilt-ridden deification of the father they had killed.

In the Maya imagination, First Father's role as the founder of civilization was closely related to his mystical identity with the basis of that civilization—maize. Whatever the original Freudian motives for his myth might have been, once the ancient farmers began the process of domesticating corn, First Father's descent, death, and resurrection were linked to the life cycle of the corn plant. As Hun-Nal-Yeh—"One Maize Revealed"—he had to be "decapitated" and then "buried" in order to sprout again; and, like the corn plant, he could only be "resurrected" by his "sons," the Maya farmers.

But the shamans sought a far deeper meaning in the myth of First Father (and his Twin God aspect) than its connection to agricultural cycles. From the raw material of Freudian guilt and the life cycle of corn they created a symbolic drama about the individual soul's confrontation with death and its hoped-for eternal destiny. Although First Father's descent was catastrophic, by making the Twin Gods aspects of a saved part of himself, and the Lords of Death manifestations of both, the *ah tz'ibob* ultimately located the mystery of life's regeneration from death in one single Divine Being.

The Post-Classic Period *Popol Vuh* tells the story of First Father's original descent in the form of a morality play about the deadliness of naïveté and innocence to the soul's quest for eternal life. It offers an explanation for why First Father was called down into the Land of Death and why he failed in his confrontation with the demons. Essentially, says the *Popol Vuh,* First Father was condemned to soul-death because he was too good and because his naïveté was no match for the crafty forces of destruction ranged against him. By not being able to see death and uncover its lies, First Father fell into death's hands like the ripe fruit his severed head became. Whatever the Classic Period account was, by Post-Classic Period times the Maya shamans had turned First Father's descent into a set of teachings about what *not* to do in the confrontation with death—either in this life or in the life to come.

In the *Popol Vuh* First Father is called One Hunahpu. He, like most of the other characters in the story, is a mixture of divine and human elements. He has a twin aspect who rarely appears in the Classic Period texts and depictions called Seven Hunahpu. Seven Hunahpu is one of First Father's *uayob,* while the character Seven Death, who also appears in the narrative, is a *uay* of First Death, First Father's Underworld Twin. The account of First Father's descent and subsequent soul-death appears in Part Three of the *Popol Vuh.*

In this passage we learn that One Hunahpu and his wife, Xbanquiyalo (another name for First Mother), have twin sons, called One Monkey and One Artisan. These are the divine Monkey Scribe-Artisans of the Classic Period. The *Popol Vuh* says that One Hunahpu and Seven Hunahpu are

> the great thinkers and great is their knowledge. They are the midmost seers, here on the face of the earth. There is only good in their being and their birthright. They taught skills to One Monkey and One Artisan, the sons of One Hunahpu. One Monkey and One Artisan became flautists, singers, and writers; carvers, jewelers, metalworkers, as well.

Interestingly, this passage identifies First Father as the Cosmic Shaman/Creator—"the midmost seer," and portrays the Monkey Scribe-Artisans as the elaborators of Maya civilization—the "singers," "writers," "carvers," "jewelers," and "metalworkers."

One and Seven Hunahpu spend much of their time playing the ritual ballgame "on the road to Xibalba," near the southern horizon where the Black Transformer/Black Dreaming Place leads down into the land of death. The Lords of the Underworld hear them playing above their heads and take offense at One and Seven Hunahpu's casual disregard for

A macaw from the Underworld flying over the great ball court at Copan.

the power of death. The fact that this first pair of Twin Gods/First Father plays so near the dangerous portal of death is evidence of First Father's naïveté—his foolish denial of the power of Xibalba.

Under the false pretense of admiring the Twins' skill, the Lords of Death invite One and Seven Hunahpu to Xibalba to play a ballgame. What the demons really intend is to demoralize and then sacrifice them. They also want One and Seven Hunahpu's ballgame equipment. The Lords of Death send their messengers, a flock of monster-owls, to the ballcourt of One/Seven Hunahpu to trick them into making this first descent into the death-state.

. . . The owls, arriving in a flurry over the ball court, now repeated their words, reciting the exact words of One Death, Seven Death. . . .

"Don't the lords One and Seven Death speak truly!" [exclaimed One and Seven Hunahpu].

"Truly indeed," the owls replied. "We'll accompany you . . ."

"Very well, but wait for us while we notify our mother," they replied. . . .

"We're going, our dear mother. . . . The messengers of the lord have come to get us." . . .

Their grandmother Xmucane sobbed, she had to weep.

"We're going, we're not dying. Don't be sad," said One and Seven Hunahpu, then they left.

First Father successfully negotiates the fearful passage to the Underworld and arrives at the central plaza of Xibalba. Here he encounters two manikins, dressed to look like One and Seven Death. He is fooled by these imitations of living beings, and greets them: "Morning, One Death . . . Morning, Seven Death." One/Seven Hunahpu is defeated because he cannot see through death's lies. "The Lords of Xibalba shouted out with laughter over this."

Then the demons invite First Father to sit on a bench to rest after his long journey. But the bench is really a red-hot tortilla griddle. One and Seven Hunahpu jump up, as the text says, "having burned their butts. At this the Xibalbans laughed again, then began to shriek with laughter, the laughter rose up like a serpent in their very cores. . . ."

One and Seven Death arrange the ballgame for the next day with One and Seven Hunahpu, and then command them to spend the night in a building called Dark House. Once the Twins are inside, "cowering, here in the dark," the messengers of the Lords of Death bring them a flaming torch and two lit cigars and tell them to return the torch and cigars to One/Seven Death in the morning "as they look now . . . intact." But, says the text, "they were defeated. They finished the torch and . . . the cigars that had been brought to them. . . ."

The next day One/Seven Hunahpu were summoned before One/Seven Death. The demon lord asks them:

"Where are my cigars? What of my torch? They were brought to you last night!"

"We finished them, your lordship."

One/Seven Death replies ominously:

"Very well. This very day, your day is finished, you will die, you will disappear, and we shall break you off. Here you will hide your faces: you are to be sacrificed!" . . .

And then they were sacrificed and buried. They were buried at the Place of Ball Game Sacrifice, as it is called. The head of One Hunahpu was cut off; only his body was buried with his younger brother.

"Put his head in the fork of the tree that stands by the road," said One and Seven Death. . . .

Three of death's most important characteristics stand out in this *Popol Vuh* passage—its tricksterish lying, its stupidity, and its cruel hard-heartedness. The Lords of Death lie to One/Seven Hunahpu about their motives for calling them down to Xibalba to play. The demons have their messengers say that they long to play with the Twins because they "are truly amazed" at their ability, and the contest would be exciting, while their *real* motives are a mixture of greed, envy, offended arrogance, and, as we discover, simple bloodthirstiness. As we see symbolized by One and Seven Death's desire to take possession of First Father's gaming equipment, death envies life its fullness of Being and greedily seeks to claim life's characteristics as its own. Death's arrogance and bloodthirstiness are based on its inherent sense of inferiority to life.

The Lords of Death lie again by playing cruel tricks on One/Seven Hunahpu with the manikins, the hot seat, and the torch and cigars. Along with the tortilla griddle image, the bench represents the Classic Period king's throne where sacrificial victims were bound before their executions during the accession rituals of the *ahauob*. The manikins teach a powerful lesson about death's attempts to disguise itself as life. By One/Seven Death's portraying himself as a wooden dummy he is showing his ineptness at creation and his missing human—and godlike—qualities.

The manikins were as stupid and hard-hearted as their builders, and recall the *Popol Vuh*'s account of the gods' failed second attempt to create authentic human beings. Part One, in which the stories of the three failed creations appear, says that the manikinlike humans the gods had made failed because "there was nothing in their hearts and nothing in their minds" and "no memory of their mason and builder." In other words, they were mechanical imitations of living human beings; they had no soul, no spiritual sense, and no memory of God. The fact that the Xibalbans could make only such inferior beings shows their stupidity. The Maya shamans believed death is "behind the times"—caught in a previous and less advanced era. Its supposed creativity is stuck at primitive levels; it does not have the true knowledge of life, of how to make something out of nothing.

From the Maya perspective, to the extent that human beings are still this way, they are the wooden expressions of death—and doomed just as the manikins of the second creation had been. Technical cleverness is no substitute for creative passion. Unfortunately for One/Seven Hunahpu, death's imitation of life was convincing. He was unable to tell the difference between the creations of life, and death's automatons. Judging by much of our own behavior, this is a vital skill many of us may also lack, and one that brings with it the same deadly results.

In a strange way, the trick of the torch and cigars shows that for the Maya shamans death is ultimately in the service of Divine Life. Like the "trials and tribulations" of Satan—the trickster and adversary in Western spiritual traditions—First/Seven Death's tricks are tests of First Father's spiritual maturity. Mysteriously, death is ultimately a collaborator in life's goal of creating intensified Being.

The flaming torch and lit cigars are symbols of K'awil's transforming spiritual consciousness, the consciousness that empowers human beings to change death into life in whatever dire circumstances they may find themselves. In their lying, tricksterish way, the Lords of Death offer First/Seven Lord the opportunity to escape eternal soul-death. If he can keep his spiritual consciousness alive through his dark night of the soul, he will win the opportunity to confront death in the final contest—the sacred ballgame—and win eternal life.

In this *Popol Vuh* passage the Lords of Death speak three fundamental lies to One/Seven Hunahpu. The first is that there is no danger in their invitation to the Underworld ballgame; death is not real. The second, related lie, conveyed through the manikin trick, is that death is really life. Then death speaks a third lie, which at the moment of First Father's sacrifice is completely convincing. One/Seven Death says, "This very day, your day is finished, you will die, you will disappear, and we shall break you off. Here you will hide your faces. . . ." In other words, there is no resurrection.

The Maya belief that death is dishonest in its core essence finds parallels in the teachings of many religions and in modern psychology. Jesus called Satan the "Father of Lies." Hindu and Buddhist scriptures describe the illusion-generating demons who appear to the ego the moment it steps into the inner world. Psychologists say that neuroses are the products of false suffering, a suffering that comes from not facing the real sources of our pain—of our "deaths" in life. From the ancient Maya point of view, neurotic people, like those described by M. Scott Peck, are indeed "people of the lie." Lying, in turn, is itself a symptom of a cold detachment from empathic feeling, a condition psychologists call schizoid. In the *Popol Vuh,* death's lies and imitations of life reveal its empty, hard-hearted essence, its "schizoid" core.

This *Popol Vuh* text also shows what the Maya shamans believed about the nature of the last judgment. Unlike the ancient Egyptian, Jewish, Christian, and Moslem judgments in which departed souls are evaluated on the basis of their moral behavior during their earthly lives, the Maya judgment decided the soul's fate according to the degree of wholeness it had been able to achieve—its K'awil substance and the level of intelligence, wisdom, and maturity it had developed.

Judged by this aesthetic morality of ancient Maya duality First Father failed the test of wholeness and spiritual maturity. An important clue about First Father's spiritual immaturity comes in the statement that "there is only good in [his] being." The authors of the *Popol Vuh* wanted their students to understand that it was exactly this fault that was First

Father's primary undoing. In response to the message of the owls from the Lords of Death, First Father exclaims, "Don't the lords One and Seven Death speak truly!" The owls, no doubt hiding their amazement at his credulity and exchanging snide glances, say, "Truly indeed!" When First Father runs home to tell his wife/mother, who already knows what's coming and begins to cry, he says, "[I'm] going, [I'm] not dying. Don't be sad." His naïveté blinds him to every one of One/Seven Death's tricks. Once he's imprisoned in Dark House, however, the terrible truth begins to sink in. The text says that when the torch and cigars were brought to him he was "cowering, here in the dark."

In fact, First Father as he is portrayed in the *Popol Vuh* embodies all three of the primary weaknesses of the soul that the Maya believed were inflicted by the Underworld demons during our earthly lives. His innocence and naïveté are symptoms of his emotional stupidity and show that his "great knowledge" is only, as we say, head knowledge. He certainly does not have the wisdom of heart knowledge that comes from a rich life experience. In a strange way, he is also arrogant. He doesn't believe he will die. Finally, when First Father's stupidity and arrogance have been brought to light, and his true defenselessness before death has been revealed, his third major weakness of soul appears—his fear. For this sin, as Paul Tillich would put it, he was "exposed in [his] negativity" and "left to annihilation."

The Maya said that before its final approach death attacks us in the forms of suffering and cruelty. Death comes to the body as disease, disfiguring, handicaps, reduced resources of energy and concentration, growing aches and pains—failing biological and mental systems. It whispers to the soul through all the deaths we die in life—our emotional pain, our griefs, our losses, our regrets, our defeats, our failures. What human beings do with these assaults from the Void during their lifetimes determines the significance of their earthly lives. It also determines whether their own third descents to the land of death will be modeled on First Father's failed first descent or on his sons' triumphant second descent.

CHAPTER 10

The Trials of Xibalba

There is no way to understand the ancient Maya resurrection technology or benefit from its wisdom without making the second de-
capitation/descent with the Twin Gods, entering Xibalba with them, and
joining their search for the life-restoring light they believed was hidden
there. As dark as the practice of bloodletting and the self-mutilation it involved were, the darkness deepens as we enter the subterranean realm of
all the suffering they themselves endured and the cruelty they inflicted on
others, especially noble captives taken in battle.

According to the Maya, suffering is an inevitable part of life, and
cruelty is an inherent aspect of every soul. Suffering is far more than
mere misfortune and cruelty more than a symptom of childhood trauma.
Instead, both suffering and cruelty are vital, if regrettable, aspects of human life. Through the process of actively engaging suffering and cruelty,
the soul learns to approach its own third descent the way the Twin Gods
approached their second descent. The soul learns to channel its necessary
suffering and its appropriate cruelty into creative actions and resurrection events.

One of the most powerful depictions of both suffering and cruelty
to come down to us from the ancient Maya is a Classic Period figurine
from Campeche in western Yucatan. This figurine was originally a reli-

A reliquary from Campeche, showing a
tortured and disemboweled war captive.

quary that once contained a war trophy of some kind. It is made in the
form of a hideously tortured captive. The once noble warrior squats with
arms bent back at the elbows, and knees thrust wide apart. His chest has
been forced forward and a row of kindling wood tied across his back. His
face is beaten and swollen. His scalp has been cut away—but not completely; it hangs by a flap of skin from the nape of his neck. His hands and
feet have been twisted out of joint. As the final act of savagery, he has just
been disemboweled, his stomach ripped out along with his intestines.
The captive's head cranes back, his mouth gaping in a howl of agony. The
man who served as the model for this terrifying portrait of pain probably did not live long enough to feel the flames burning into his back as the
wood was set on fire.

    This agony symbolized all the kinds of suffering—natural and
man-made—that a cruel world inflicted on every human being. In spite
of the efforts of First Father in his Twin Gods aspect to drive back the
forces of destruction, the created universe continued to manifest the
power of death through the diseases that made so many human lives little more than sojourns of misery, the starvation and natural disasters that
often threatened in the form of droughts, floods, hurricanes, failed crops,
volcanic eruptions, and earthquakes, and the short life spans that were

the lot of most Maya. In addition to suffering from natural causes, Xibalba made its presence felt through acts of *human* cruelty. The Maya saw these human acts of brutality not as morally flawed exceptions to the norm of an otherwise benevolent nature, but instead as specialized forms of the natural cruelty they endured every day of their earthly lives.

Evidence from the bones of ordinary Maya shows that chronic malnutrition ran rampant through the poorer classes of various cities, especially toward the end of the Classic Period. Rio Azul and Kalak'mul are dramatic examples of this. And in the tombs of eighth-century Copan researchers have discovered skeletons—of rich and poor alike—that show signs of starvation and sickness on a massive scale.

Originally enormously successful at its location in the fertile Copan Valley, Copan's maize fields stretched for miles in every direction, along with vast plantations of squashes, peppers, and beans. The surrounding mountains were covered with thick forests of oak and pine, and in the Valley itself ceibas and other tropical trees flourished. But as the population grew, due in part to a huge influx of immigrants from the non-Maya east, the city expanded in a process we would call today urban sprawl. It began gobbling up rich agricultural land as the subdivisions of all classes, but especially the wealthy, fanned out from the acropolis area. In addition to its encroachment on valuable farmlands, the mushrooming population began stripping the mountains of trees. Enormous amounts of wood were needed for cooking fires as well as for the lime ovens in which plaster for the ever-intensifying building projects was made.

By the late eighth century the consequences of this urban expansion were all too clear. The diseases, including those related to undernourishment, from which the Copanecos and other Maya in similar circumstances suffered appear in Maya art as the demons of the Underworld. Lung diseases from the smoke of cooking fires are depicted as streams of blood flowing from emaciated chests; intestinal parasites are shown in X-ray views of bloated stomachs, in torrents of bloody diarrhea, and liquidy farts; and skin blotches and hair loss portray an often toxic and vitamin-deficient world. The *Popol Vuh* pictures six Lords of Death in the form of these and similar diseases. There is Pus Master and Jaundice Master who cause lockjaw and "make pus come out of [people's] legs," Bone Scepter and Skull Scepter who bring on fatal edema and "reduce people to bones . . . until they die from emaciation," and Wing and Packstrap who cause "sudden death" "on the road" "from vomiting blood."

In addition to physical suffering from diseases, starvation, and other natural causes, the ancient Maya, like all human beings, were prey to psychological suffering. Fear and the other weaknesses of the soul that resulted from the demons' attacks on The White Flower Thing were sources of enormous emotional pain. As we've seen, if left untreated, these defects of the soul would cause the greatest suffering of all—eternal soul-death at the Place of the Ball Game Sacrifice.

Along with this personal dimension of suffering, the Maya endured what we might call "institutional cruelty." The Classic Period Maya lived with an increasingly oppressive class system, malevolent sorcerers, and intensifying warfare. The upper classes expanded far more rapidly than the peasants, as kings and lesser *ahauob,* thanks to their large harems, reproduced at an accelerating rate. This growing horde of nobles put an enormous strain on farmers and laborers just at the time when resources were beginning to dwindle as a result of both prolonged drought and man-made ecological catastrophes like that at Copan. The nobility ate better, grew larger, and lived longer than the increasingly squeezed peasants who supported them.

The massive Classic and Post-Classic Period building projects taxed the average Maya even further. More and more palaces, pyramids, and ballcourts had to be constructed for the pleasure and ritual use of growing numbers of "authentic human beings." But perhaps the greatest cruelty imposed by this rampant classism was the growing rift between the educated *itz'atob* who knew the secret of eternal life and the peasants who did not. No doubt the lower classes had their own hopes for immortality, but, deprived of the education vital to the shamans' resurrection technology, the peasants may have seen themselves at a crippling disadvantage when they faced their own "moments of truth."

Minor nobles may have turned to sorcery and witchcraft to support themselves economically and reinforce their power over the lower classes. Even today the Yucatan is known as a center of witchcraft. It is believed that for a fee, *brujos* can bring on terminal diseases, cause miscarriages, and dispose of unwanted lovers. Maya peasants living in small towns in the interior of Yucatan, Guatemala, and Honduras fear the sorcerers in their midst—men and women who they believe are able to transform themselves into were-animals and prowl the countryside at night, mutilating sheep, destroying property, and kidnapping babies.

For the Classic Period Maya, warfare became more and more a matter of territorial and material conquest. The Tlaloc/Venus warfare introduced at Tikal in the fourth century gradually got out of hand. By

The Bonampak battle scene.

the ninth century intercity fighting had reduced once great cities of higher learning and elegant art to illiterate, increasingly barbaric fortress compounds. By the time the Spanish arrived in the early 1500s only a few sizable cities remained, and the Maya were locked in a nightmare of mutual assured destruction.

The suffering from both natural and man-made causes—both believed to be the work of increasingly hostile gods—was so great in the end that by the late Post-Classic Period suicide was honored as the supreme act of self-sacrifice, one that guaranteed the soul's immediate entry into the Otherworldly paradise.

But even before the disintegration of the late Classic and the Post-Classic Periods, the Maya knew that they—and all human beings—lived in a dangerous universe. Faced with either denying the danger and running from it into the pure goodness of First Father before his sacrificial death *or* confronting it head-on, the shamans chose to face the cruel forces ranged against them honestly.

In addition to the rituals of bloodletting, painful as they were, the ascetic practices that accompanied them—seclusion, fasting, sexual abstinence, lonely vigils, the toxic levels of balche and hallucinogenic substances consumed, and the terrible hangovers that followed—all of these painful things concentrated and dramatized for the questing soul the strangely exhilarating darkness of the Divine Being. These practices allowed the *itz'atob* to enter the death-state and learn to deal with the ultimate terror that dwelled in that Abyss.

On those same murals at Bonampak with the blue Underworld background we see some of the most gruesomely realistic depictions of warfare ever created. King Chaan Muan of Bonampak leads his warriors into battle against a jungle tribe. Set in the emotional Xibalba that all human atrocities are, the scene is charged with the desperate energy of men who know that if they are defeated or captured a fate worse than death awaits them. In this brilliantly colored painting we see images of brutality rendered with careful attention to detail: severed heads and hands, gushing blood, and the crazed expressions of warriors caught up in a demonic battle frenzy, the whites of their eyes flashing fiercely against the dark brown of their faces.

King Chaan Muan lunges forward, grabbing an enemy chief by his hair—the Maya ritual gesture of formal capture acknowledged by both victor and victim. The enemy chief has already been stripped of his finery and dressed in a skirt of paper or cloth strips to signify his war captive status and the mutilation and sacrifice that will be his lot. The doomed king is pulled off his feet by Chaan Muan's grip. As he falls, his arms and legs flail and his spear breaks in half.

Chaan Muan wears a jaguar pelt jerkin, a gigantic jaguar mask headdress, jade bracelets and collar, and a shrunken head emblem suspended upside down by a cord around his neck. His scraggly chin beard accents his raptorlike nose and his glaring eyes, which dart across the battlefield searching for more captives. One of his captains stands beside him wearing a snarling Baby Jaguar headdress and a freshly severed head around his neck, and grasping another fallen warrior by his hair. The battle rages around these central figures as the Bonampak lords, in fantastic costumes, hack their way through the enemy ranks. A warrior dressed as a crocodile brandishes his spear as he leaps into the melee from the right. Below the capture scene an *ahau* wearing a Cosmic Monster–deer-head mask strikes an opponent in the forehead with his lance. The victim's mouth drops open in a gasp of pain and disbelief.

We know all too well what became of the captured warriors in this scene from their portraits of pain in the Bonampak "Judgment" mural. Their fingers were twisted out of joint and their nails pulled. They were beaten and cut with razor-sharp flint or obsidian knives. Finally, they were sacrificed.

They were not alone. The facades of the enclosure buildings in the ballcourt at Tonina are decorated with bound and tortured war captives, and many are the funerary ceramics that depict those destined to become terminated ones. On these ceramics we see captives whose faces have been beaten to a pulp engaged in acts of self-mutilation. In one case, the victim, no doubt plied with drugs and tortured beyond endurance, is cutting off his own head.

Carved stelae and panels from all over the Maya area show simi-

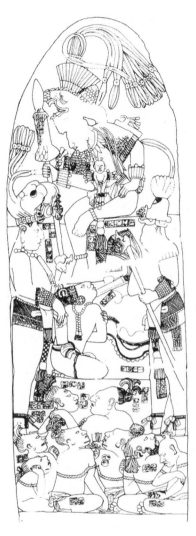

Stela 12 from Piedras Negras, depicting
tortured captives at the feet of a Lord of Life.

larly horrific scenes. At Dos Pilas in Guatemala we see the likeness of
the so-called Ruler Three dressed in his magnificent Tlaloc/Venus warfare costume, standing on a platform carved with hieroglyphs. Bent
double beneath the platform, and supporting the weight of both Ruler
Three and the platform, a war captive grimaces under the strain of his
burden.

At Piedras Negras, also in Guatemala, an unknown *ahau* sits on a
dais high above two standing attendants. His proud quetzal headdress arcs
above his head. He holds his battle spear with one hand and clasps his
knee with the other. He sits with one leg folded on the dais and the other
dangling over the side in a relaxed pose. He wears a shrunken human

body on his chest as a pectoral. At his feet eight captives are tightly bound together. Each shows signs of having been tortured. One of them, an old man, studies his hands with an expression of despair. A well-dressed captive crouches on the platform step just below the lord, his neck stretched back to look into the eyes of his executioner. In contrast to the despair and pain of the captives the ruler and his attendants seem without emotion. Through his pose on the dais and his impassive face as he gazes down at his war trophies, the ruler himself shows casual indifference to the plight of his victims.

After torture and sacrifice, the heads of the victims were often impaled on *tzompantlis,* or "skull-racks," where they joined the rotting skulls of previous victims. While the name of each of the terminated ones was recorded and celebrated, the mounting of the head on the skull-rack alongside so many others dramatized the impersonal nature of the humiliation, suffering, and cruelty captive torture and human sacrifice embodied. There could be no illusion of individual specialness in the face of that monument to the cold indifference of death—of nature itself—to human personality. Like Hamlet contemplating the fate of Yorik, the skull-rack reminded those who stood before it of the frailty of their personal identities and inspired them to intensify their efforts to build durable Resurrection Bodies.

Although it may be hard for most modern people to understand, torturer and tortured shared the same beliefs about the necessity of these terrifying dramatizations of suffering and cruelty. Both victim and victimizer accepted the idea that, at least under certain circumstances, cold indifference to the ruination of others was a necessary lesson every Lord of Life had to learn. The acceptance of cruelty, like that of suffering, drove home the point that there is finally no way around these harsh realities, and that "authentic human beings" have to face them, feel them with every fiber of their beings, internalize their lessons, and transform them into a greater good—for themselves, their communities, and the world.

Suffering and cruelty opened for the Maya the possibility of redemption and salvation. In addition to feeding the gods, acting out the brutality of life allowed them to stay aware of death's presence. The merciless indifference of the victors toward their victims taught them to integrate the hard-hearted quality of the Underworld. Similar to the goal of the passionless transcendence of suffering and cruelty taught by Eastern religions, but achieved for the most part in a dramatically different way, the Maya practice of indifference allowed the torturer to transcend and so be free from this dreamlike world in which success and pleasure, even life itself, could be snatched away in the blink of an eye. By wading knee-deep in this underside of life and participating fully in its horror, the shaman achieved personal empowerment and liberation.

The most mature souls among the tortured—those who had steeled themselves through years of bloodletting, deprivation, and ecstatic visions, and who had also accepted and practiced their own cruelties on others—endured their torments believing that their sacrifices were the necessary reversal of fortune every human being had to undergo sooner or later. Through the haze of their pain the tortured captives sought K'awil's transforming ax blow and the fire in their blood that would deliver them into eternity.

The Maya believed that the purpose of death's assaults in this life is to test the strength of the developing White Flower Thing. While this testing theme is implied in the Classic Period iconography, the Post-Classic Period *Popol Vuh* makes it explicit. In so doing, it links the salvation potential of the ancient Maya "road of trials" with those of other Native American peoples and of ancient religions in general. The *Popol Vuh* pictures these tests as taking place in the Underworld on the other side of the grave. But the trials of Xibalba, whatever else they are, also depict the soul's *earthly* struggles against the forces of death. In this sense, the three mythological descents, in addition to being journeys to the Land of Death, were descents from the paradise of the World Tree into the "vale of tears" that so much of earthly life is.

Called down to the Underworld by the Lords of Death like their father, the Twin Gods turned the second descent into the permanent Dream Time victory of life over death. The second descent appears in Part Three of the *Popol Vuh*. In this second descent, the tests of Xibalba take the form of the manikin, hot seat, and torch and cigar tricks—as far, we recall, as First Father got—plus three rigged ballgames and six houses of torture: Dark House, Razor House, Cold House, Jaguar House, the House of Fire, and Bat House.

First Lord and First Jaguar begin their fearful descent by successfully crossing all the barriers on the road to the Underworld and arriving at Xibalba's central plaza. They come before the manikins and the hot seat as First Father had. But this time the outcome is very different.

"Bid the lords good day," said someone who was seated there. . . .

"These aren't lords! These are manikins, woodcarvings!" they said as they came up.

And after that, they bid them good morning:

"Morning, One Death. Morning, Seven Death. Morning, House Corner. Morning, Blood Gatherer.

"Morning, Pus Master. Morning, Jaundice Master. Morning, Bone Scepter. Morning, Skull Scepter.

"Morning, Wing. Morning, Packstrap. Morning, Bloody Teeth. Morning, Bloody Claws," they said when they arrived, and all of their identities were accounted for. They named every one of their names. . . .

The Twins are offered the bench, but they refuse it:

"This bench isn't for us! It's just a stone slab for cooking."

Then they enter Dark House where they are given the same flaming torch and lit cigars that First Father had wasted so disastrously. The Twins place macaw feathers on the end of the torch and fireflies on the tips of the cigars to simulate fire. When they appear before One/Seven Death the next morning, the torch and cigars are still burning. The Lords of Death are frightened:

"What's happening? Where did they come from? Who begot them and bore them? . . . They're different in looks and different in their very being," they said among themselves. . . . "Where might you have come from? Please name it," Xibalba said to them.

"Well, wherever did we come from? We don't know," was all they said. They didn't name it.

Having passed the test of Dark House, the Twins play the first of three ballgames with One and Seven Death. They soon discover that the ball of Xibalba is the skull of a sacrificial victim with a flint knife inside.

As soon as the Twins receive the Xibalbans' punt, the dagger leaps from the skull and goes "clattering, twisting all over the floor of the court." In mock indignation, the Twins charge the demons with trickery. The game then continues with a real ball. First Lord and First Jaguar allow themselves to be defeated in order to lure the Xibalbans into a false sense of security and to win the opportunity to pass another test, and further demoralize the forces of death.

That night they enter Razor House, a place filled with living knives. The knives slither over the walls and floor, seeking to rip the Twin Gods to pieces. But:

> . . . they spoke to the knives then, they instructed them:
> "This is yours: the flesh of all the animals," they told the knives, and they no longer moved—rather, each and every knife put down its point.
> And this is how they stayed there overnight, in Razor House. . . .

The next morning, when the Lords of Death see the Twins alive and well, they are overcome with fear. Still, they propose a second ballgame. This one ends in a tie.

That night the Twins enter Cold House. Here:

> There are countless drafts, thick-falling hail inside the house, the home of cold. They diminished the cold right away by shutting it out. The cold dissipated because of the boys. They did not die, but were alive when it dawned.

The following night they enter Jaguar House:

> . . . the jaguar-packed home of jaguars:
> "Don't eat *us*. There *is* something that should be yours," the jaguars were told.
> With that, they scattered bones before the animals.
> After that, the jaguars were wrestling around there, over the bones.

Again, to the astonishment of the Xibalbans, First Lord and First Jaguar emerge from Jaguar House unscathed. The demons ask in bewilderment: "What sort of people are they? Where did they come from?" That night the Twins enter

a house of fire with only fire alone inside. They weren't burned by it, just toasted, just simmered, so they were well when it dawned . . . the Xibalbans . . . lost heart over this.

The text moves to a climax as First Lord and First Jaguar enter the last of the torture houses, Bat House.

Now they were put inside Bat House, with bats alone inside the house, a house of snatch-bats, monstrous beasts, their snouts like knives, the instruments of death. To come before these is to be finished off at once. [The snatch-bat was one of the manifestations of the god of decapitation sacrifice.]

When they were inside they just slept in their blowgun; they were not bitten by the members of the household. But this is where they gave one of themselves up because of a snatch-bat that came down; he came along just as one of them showed himself. They did it because it was actually what they were asking for, what they had in mind.

And all night the bats are making noise. . . .

Then it lets up a little. The bats were no longer moving around. So there, one of the boys crawled to the end of the blowgun, since Xbalanque said:

"Hunahpu? Can you see how long it is till dawn?"

"Well, perhaps I should look to see how long it is," he replied. So he kept trying to look out the muzzle of the blowgun, he tried to see the dawn.

And then his head was taken off by a snatch-bat, leaving Hunahpu's body still stuffed inside.

"What's going on? Hasn't it dawned?" said Xbalanque. No longer is there any movement from Hunahpu. "What's this . . ."

He no longer moves; now there is only heavy breathing.

After that, Xbalanque despaired:

"Alas! We've given it all up!" he said. And elsewhere, the head meanwhile went rolling onto the court . . . and all the Xibalbans were happy over the head of Hunahpu. . . .

In these passages we see the shamans' secret resurrection technology swing into action as one after another of death's attempts to destroy the Lords of Life fails. The single most important line in this passage comes toward the end, just before First Lord's decapitation by the Bat-god. The author makes clear that despite its accidental appearance First Lord's sacrificial death is *not* an accident. He says that the "snatch-bat . . . came along just as one of them showed himself. They did it because it was actually what they were asking for, what they had in mind." Hunahpu's sacrifice is, in fact, the riskiest but potentially the most transforming part of the resurrection technology the Twins have implemented so far. It carries the aspect of genuine despair with it, as Xbalanque says, "Alas! We've given it all up!" But this act of voluntary defeat—along with everything else the Twin Gods have done, and will do—is part of their elaborate hoax, the series of lies they use in order to lure the Lords of Death to their own destruction.

Like the Christian ransom theory of salvation in which God tricked the Devil into submission by dangling His Son as bait on the hook of the cross until Satan snapped at him and was caught like a fish, the Maya resurrection technology defeated death by using its own trickster-ish strategies against it. Everything First Lord/First Jaguar do in these passages and those that follow are part of their foreordained plan to resurrect the universe and the human soul.

Unlike First Father, the Twin Gods bring to their descent a powerful spiritual consciousness that includes insight, wisdom, flexibility, and the integration of death's own lying and hard-heartedness. Similar to the therapeutic techniques modern psychologists recommend for overcoming nightmares, First Lord and First Jaguar reenter the horror of Xibalba to this time "get it right" and force a happy outcome.

The Twin Gods make their descent armed with insight—seeing as the gods see. They are not fooled by death's pretense at life. They immediately identify the manikins as wooden imitations of the Xibalban lords; they call each of the principal demons by its proper name, until "all of their identities were accounted for." This naming of the demons gives the Twins power over them. According to an ancient and universal belief found in all the religions of the world, because of their dishonest natures demons must hide themselves in shadows and subterfuges in order to survive. As soon as their names—their true natures—are known, their power is neutralized.

The Twin Gods' insight also allows them to see the hidden connections between seemingly unrelated things: between macaw feathers and fireflies and K'awil's enlightening consciousness; between dawn and decapitation/death—*hal/ahal;* and between all living things. This insight empowers the Twins to draw upon the underlying energy fields of *ch'ulel* that bind all things together into one infinite Reality and that have the power to transform death into life anywhere, anytime, a spiritually mature soul calls upon them.

Through a flexibly applied wisdom the Twins know when to appear weak, when to pretend to be defeated, when to negotiate, and when to make a stand. By losing arguments and ballgames with the demons the Twins show that they know when to "lose a battle in order to win the war."

In fact, First Lord/First Jaguar show all the characteristics of the fully developed Maya soul. All of these qualities are the fruits of their one most vital attribute—a mature spiritual consciousness. It is this consciousness that enables them to keep K'awil's torch and cigars burning. And it is this ongoing connection to the *ch'ulel*-charged forces of light, life, and transformation—of appearance into reality, of reality into appearance, of defeat into victory—that allows them to work their magic in the annihilating darkness of the Abyss.

After the initial tests of their ability to see through death's lies, the Twins move to Dark House and the evaluation of their overall level of spiritual development. They pass this test, in part, by lying as death lies, thereby showing that they have integrated death's weaknesses, which, in the context of their own mature spirituality, are transformed into strengths. In Razor House the Twins negotiate with the sacrificial knives by granting them the flesh of animals in place of their own. The Twins redirect suffering and cruelty away from themselves, but recognize that these inevitable parts of life must be satisfied in some way. In Cold House they defeat the drafts and hail by keeping the inner glow of their fiery K'awil passion alive throughout the bitter night. In Jaguar House they again deflect death by letting destruction destroy itself. They distance themselves from the forces of death and simply watch them "eat each other alive." In the House of Fire they "keep cool" while the flames rage round them. And in Bat House they defeat death by "giving the Devil his due," his "pound of flesh," as we say—in this case, Hunahpu's head.

When we interpret these coded messages in a modern psychological way we can see the ancient Maya blueprint for how every human soul can turn the suffering and cruelty it experiences into "anticipations of resurrection." We learn that in our Razor House times we need to negotiate with whatever or whomever is threatening us. We need to accept that suffering and cruelty must be given some kind of outlet. We turn these assaults of death away from us by giving them an alternate target. In Cold House moments—perhaps periods of depression, anger, or emotional withdrawal—we need to keep the fires of our true passions burning. We need to hold on to a spiritual perspective that keeps our hopes and our faith alive. In House of Fire moments—when everyone around us is "inflamed" with emotion, when everything we've worked for "goes up in smoke," when we ourselves are overwrought, or when we feel ourselves "under fire"—we need to stay cool, calm, centered, and passionless. That way, like the Twins, we become more powerful by being "toasted" and "simmered."

In Jaguar House times we may need to stand back and watch the forces of death feed on their own destructiveness. Jesus advised his would-be followers to "let the dead bury their dead," and psychologists teach a technique called "objectification" by which their clients can learn to separate themselves from their destructive emotions, but without losing sight of—or repressing—them. The Twin Gods watch the jaguars devour each other while they themselves keep a safe distance. In Bat House moments we may have to sacrifice our present well-being for a greater good.

As soon as the Twins arrive in Xibalba, the Lords of Death realize they have something very different on their hands than their first victim—the naive, all-good First Father. They say, "They're different in looks and different in their very being," and they wonder, "What's happening? Where did they come from? Who begot and bore them?" The Xibalbans realize that First Lord/First Jaguar do not act like run-of-the-mill good souls. Instead, they act disturbingly like the Underworld demons themselves. The authors of the *Popol Vuh* maintained that this is precisely the secret of the Twins' life-generating power.

The answer to the Xibalbans' questions lies in the Twin Gods' dual nature. As the authors of the *Popol Vuh* show, the Twin Gods are fully integrated mixtures of the Overworld and the Underworld. Their father came from the ultimate source of life and goodness—the "God beyond God" on the other side of the 01 Portal. Their mother—Blood Woman—was the daughter of the Blood Gatherer aspect of First/Seven

Death. So the Twins were half Xibalban and half divine. They were a combination of the forces of life and death, integrated in a way that produced a fuller, more intense level of Being.

According to the shamans, as the "saved remnant" of First Father that caused the Underworld calabash tree to fruit and impregnated First Mother in her Blood Woman manifestation, the Twins were that part of every soul that, having learned the lessons of suffering and cruelty and internalized the necessity of both, could rise in empowered fulfillment of its divine-demonic potential. The fierce goodness depicted on the Classic Period tripod plate where we see First Father—decapitated, dead—envisioning his wiser and more whole sons defeating Itzam-Yeh finds a powerful parallel in the *Popol Vuh* account of the Twin Gods' victorious sojourn in the Underworld. Together, these two visions of the triumphant soul portray the ancient Maya ideal of human Being in its fullness, a fullness that embodies all of who we are, and in such a way that we become creators, rather than destroyers, of life.

Understandably, most people spend much of their lives trying to avoid suffering. The problem with this naive approach to suffering, as the Maya shamans discovered, is that it leads to psychological and spiritual paralysis and fear. In the end, if we don't face the fact that suffering is an inescapable part of our lives, we will be forced to become its victims. To some degree, the victim mentality that is so much a part of contemporary Western culture can be seen as a product of our neurotic refusal to accept the inevitability of suffering and cruelty.

The only real question is: Do we believe that our suffering is meaningful, or do we believe it is accidental—something that we can either ignore or eventually do away with through social programs or modern medicine? The answer to this question has powerful emotional and spiritual consequences for the way we live our lives. If we believe that suffering is meaningful, as the Maya did, we can transform it into a joyful triumph of Being. But if we believe it is meaningless, we will find ourselves teetering on the brink of despair. For each of us is forced sooner or later to make the third descent into the dimension of death-in-life.

The cultural historian Thomas Berry says that "Pathos is suffering that is not creative." In this sense, Maya suffering, at least on the part of those shamans who followed the road of soul-growth laid out by the Twin Gods, was anything but pathetic. Like all the ascetic traditions of the world's great spiritual systems, the Maya's embracing of physical and emotional pain led to greater aliveness, intensified creativity, and soul-growth.

Using suffering to grow our souls is one thing. But what do we do with cruelty? The ritual cruelty of the Maya justly invites our sense of horror and revulsion. The atrocities they committed seem unthinkable to modern people. And yet we too have our mass murderers, our teenage assassins, warfare on an unprecedented scale, and—when we are un-flinchingly honest with ourselves—our own fantasies of cruel acts against those we believe have wronged us. Mass murder almost always includes an element of captive torture. Gang conflicts are forms of ritualized slaughter. And do we really believe that the horrors of modern warfare are any less savage than the far more limited warfare practiced by the ancient Maya?

If there really *is* something terrible and bloody at the core of every human soul, something sadistic that demands satisfaction, then if we try to wish it away, ignore it, or demonize it, we must still encounter it—but in more dishonest ways. Trying to repress instead of integrate our own cruel urges may even lead to more violent and devastating outbreaks of them. Carl Jung believed that there is no choice for civilized human beings but to acknowledge their own darkness and integrate it in a controlled way into their conscious personalities. In the process of integrating this shadow, our personal darkness becomes transformed—just as the Maya sages said it would. For the shamans, integrating the characteristics of death made The White Flower Thing more powerful and grew its capacities for love and creative achievement.

As the Maya shamans saw and modern psychologists confirm, the trick to integrating this deadly part of us is to do it in such a way that the soul does not become overwhelmed by it. We need to allow ourselves to be honest about our destructive feelings without acting them out in rageful and sadistic ways. In the *Popol Vuh* the Lords of Xibalba are possessed by their shadows, while the Twin Gods have transformed theirs into powerful forces in the service of a greater good. Perhaps, as in the second descent of First Lord/First Jaguar, we need to learn to channel our own cruelty into powerful actions that advance our own legitimate agendas as well as the creative unfolding of a world in search of greater intensity of Being.

The dignity and transcendence the Maya sought in suffering—and torture—appears on the faces of many of the captives depicted on sculpted panels and stelae, painted murals and ceramics, and figurines. One figurine in particular is unusually powerful. Recovered from Jaina,

A portrait figurine from Jaina, showing an old man awaiting his sacrificial death.

the ancient Maya burial island off the west coast of Campeche, Yucatan, scholars believe this statuette is the portrait of a real man. The features of his face are treated with sensitivity, and his potbelly with its realistic navel has been rendered with a naturalness that could only have come from seeing the man in person. The artist has shown him stripped naked with his arms tied behind his back at the elbows, but standing proudly with just a hint of casual disregard for his situation. His receding hairline, gaunt cheeks, chin beard, and belly show that he has reached late middle age.

The striking thing about him is his presence. He has been beaten bloody. His nose is swollen where his captors have broken it. He grimaces slightly and his lips are barely parted in what looks like an effort to bypass his ruined nose and breathe through his mouth. His brows are slightly knit and there are bags of exhaustion under his eyes. And yet in his moment of total humiliation he looks into the eyes of the artist who is sketching him with what seems to be a kind of ironic amusement about his impending doom. He radiates strength and wisdom. He may even be talking to the artist as he waits, probably with a group of other captives, for the next, more painful stage of his ordeal. Shorn of his family, his friends, and his beloved home city, he faces a lonely and terrible death. He has fallen from a lofty position of wealth and privilege to the status of a "terminated one." Yet he seems to be saying, "Well, I've had a rich life! Now it's my time to suffer."

While the Maya teachings about cruelty are difficult for people brought up in a turn-the-other-cheek spirituality to accept, many psychologists believe that the problem for most of us is not that we are *too* cruel—although some of us certainly are; instead, the problem for most of us is that we aren't "cruel" enough. This is especially true when it comes to getting our own needs met, maintaining our rightful psychological boundaries, pursuing our real loves and passions, standing up for ourselves against the subtle manipulations of others, and living the lives we want.

To admit the legitimate savagery within our own souls would certainly demand that we see ourselves and others in a new and perhaps more disturbing light. But by making the third descent we all must make anyway—consciously, intentionally—and taking responsibility for our own terrible beauty, we can know the victory of life over death. For the Maya, only those sacrifices made by and at the hands of such spiritually mature, empowered human beings are effective. Only these souls can generate the resurrection.

The Maya believed that beyond the torture houses every one of us must enter in life—and at our deaths—the culminating "moment of truth" waits for us at the Place of the Ball Game Sacrifice in the Underworld of our darkest imaginings. What we do at this inner "Place of Fright" when the time comes depends on the qualities of soul we bring to it.

▼▲▼▲▼▲▼▲
• • • • • • • • • • • • •

CHAPTER 11

The Ballgame
and Human
Sacrifice

On a cloudy afternoon, the East Court of Copan seems haunted. A heavy atmosphere of sadness and pain seems to rise like a mist from the damp, leaf-strewn ground. From a distance the melancholy lowing of cattle drifts across the still air like a voice from another world. At the same time there is a strange lightness about the place that has nothing to do with the occasional breaks in the clouds. The humid tropical smells of decaying ceiba leaves and palm fronds mix with the scent of dry stone. The leaden sky, pregnant with rain, mutes the vivid green of the surrounding jungle with its exulting trees and its tangle of vines and thornbushes. But the forest is alive with the hum of bees and the songs of birds.

Standing at the top of the court's east platform the visitor looks down the sheer drop of the acropolis bluff across a pasture to the band of trees that mark the course of the Copan River as it snakes its way through the forest, glinting silver between the trees. Turning back to the court the visitor sees King Yax Pac's magnificently carved temple-tomb to the south and the back side of the pyramid-within-a-pyramid in which the famous eccentric flints were found. Along the west platform he or she sees a statue of Chac-Xib-Chac, flanked by two rampant jaguars, rising from the jaws of the ecliptic Vision Serpent. At the

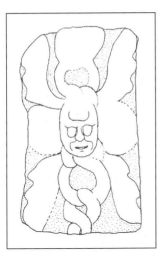

First Father's severed head peering up from
the Underworld calabash tree as depicted on
the center marker of the East Court at Copan.

north end of the court, at the summit of the platform, stand the roof-less remains of Eighteen-Rabbit's great temple, its doorway framed by the toothed jaws of the Cosmic Monster/Vision Serpent. Here too stands the *popol na*—the "Council House"—of the kings of Copan. Great public spectacles that included the sacred pronouncements of the divine *ahauob,* ecstatic dancing, and magical reenactments of the creation took place on the terrace in front of these temples and on the stepped platforms around the court.

On the east side, now partly eroded by the Copan River that used to flow just under the acropolis cliff, stands a row of badly ruined temples. Researchers have identified one of these temples as Copan's Bat House, the earthly counterpart of the torture house described in the *Popol Vuh* in which Hunahpu lost his head. In the imaginations of the ancient Copanecos, it was from the doorway of this replica temple of death that the god's head had rolled, bumped down the stone steps of the platform, and come to rest in the center of the court below.

In fact, the whole of Copan's East Court may have been built as the this-worldly embodiment of the central plaza of Xibalba, which the Copanecos believed lay just beneath their feet. The river below the bluff was the earthly counterpart of the Underworld river in which the resurrection of the Twin Gods had begun. It could be that, along with Bat House, the row of small temples on the east side of the court, as well as the jaguar platform to the west, may have re-created the testing places of Xibalba in the very heart of Copan.

The plaza floor itself was built as a false or ceremonial ballcourt,

The great ballcourt at Copan.

complete with three center markers set into the ground to separate the various zones of play. These markers survive. In the spiritual imaginations of Copan's inhabitants, it was to the central marker, the holiest and most terrifying of these monuments, that Hunahpu's head had rolled. Made even more unearthly by the centuries-long weathering of wind and rain, the stone slab shows the blurred outlines of the Dream Time instant in which the miracle of death's transformation into life began. Peering up at us through a tangle of branches and broad leaves, from the Place of the Ball Game Sacrifice, First Father's severed head appears, in the very act of changing itself into a calabash and making the tree alive. The fact that First Lord's head rolled to this central place of absolute darkness proclaims First Father and First Lord to be the same Decapitated-Dead-Creating-Thing, and their two descents to be the same miraculous event.

It could be that, as in the *Popol Vuh,* war captives were forced to endure nights of torture and testing in the temples of the East Court and then play a series of games in the real ballcourt just beyond the East Court's platform. Scholars now believe that after playing in this real ballcourt, the exhausted captives were brought here for the "last play" of the game—to make their own third descents and join First Father at the center marker to become full participants in his cosmic drama. The last thing these doomed men saw as First Lord/Chac-Xib-Chac's ax fell was the terrible beauty of The-Holy-Decapitated-Dead-Creating-Thing staring up at them. Then their spirits rushed downward into the earth through the center marker and became one with the Mystery that awaited them below. Head after head, spirit after spirit, the eyes gazing up from this "holy of holies" are now those of all the god-men who died here to make the world alive.

For the Maya, the ballgame and the sacrificial act by which it ended were a model for how human beings ought to live their lives. The Maya believed that we ought to look forward to the fearful and transformative moment when the executioner's ax falls on our own necks. And if, knowing they are inevitable anyway, we can actually will our own deaths and leap with courage into the Void, then, incredibly, we will be part of the transformation of death itself. We will take death with us to our—and its—origins in the Divine Life, and we and death together will become the pure Being of God.

When played in earnest, the Maya ballgame—called *pitz*—was the climax of the divine "passion play" of which suffering, cruelty, bloodletting, warfare, and captive torture were the preludes. And the *ah pitz-lawalob*—the "ballplayers"—were the ultimate representatives of the Divine Being's beautiful terror to a universe hungry for its own continued unfolding.

So central was the ballgame in determining not only the fate of the universe but, even more important, that of the individual soul that the Maya buried ballgame equipment and trophies with their dead. Unlike the ancient Egyptians who thought they could take their earthly possessions with them into the next life and for whom material wealth was paramount, the Maya believed their eternal destinies would be decided by one thing only—how well they played the final *pitz* against the demons of destruction and death. Along with their funerary ceramic "Books of the Dead," almost the only other things the deceased took with them were their yokes, palmas, and knee and forearm guards. With nothing but cryptic vases and offering plates, their ballgame equipment, and their personal qualities, generations of Maya souls stepped into the center of the Underworld plaza to challenge the power of the forces that had attacked them in life.

A ring marker from the ballcourt at Uxmal.

Ballcourts on the earth plane were built as like-in-kind replicas of the universe and of the central Cleft/Abyss/Cosmic Turtle Shell/Peccary/Head/First True Mountain/Womb-Tomb from which First Father and the created world had been reborn.

From the dank, forest-shaded ruins of Coba's ballcourt with its cavernous, moss-covered walls, and the windswept hilltop courts of the Guatemala highlands, to the imperial, light-filled arena of Chichen Itza, the Maya ballcourts all followed the same basic pattern. They did so because, in the end, they were all the *same* ballcourt, the Cosmic Court at the center of Xibalba and the night sky. Although there were local variations in architectural details, all of the Maya ballcourts mirrored the structures of the universe and the human body. They were open-ended, I-shaped gashes in the earth. The cross bars of the "I" depicted the four quarters of the cosmos and human arms and legs. The stepped walls of the court represented the Cosmic Cleft itself. Illustrations of ballcourts seen in cross section look exactly like the stepped-cleft splits in the Cosmic Turtle Shell, the "First True Mountain," and the heads of the Witz Monster, Cauac Monster, and First Father.

Ballcourts were usually built along a north-south axis to reflect the path of the "Road of Awe" that led to the 01 and Black Transformer Portals, and the Overworld and Underworld. The walls of the courts bore sculpted markers in series on both sides—at Copan, macaw heads; at Tonina, bound captives; and in the northern Yucatan, rings carved in the form of entwined feathered serpents. Researchers still don't fully understand the complicated symbolism of ballcourt architecture or the spiritual significance of the wall markers.

In addition to the yokes, palmas, and padding, ballgame equipment included elaborate masks and costumes by which the players took on the identities of the most important gods and demons. In these fearful games—most if not all of them rigged—the king-athlete-executioners usually wore the costumes of the Lords of Life and dressed their condemned opponents in the trappings of the Underworld demons, or Itzam-Yeh. At Yaxchilan Bird-Jaguar dressed for his games in the net skirt of First Father and wore an image on his back of the magical fish the Twin Gods became at the moment of their resurrection. The Dos Pilas kings also wore fish emblem backracks as part of their ballgame costumes. Often, along with their demon costumes, the opposing players wore cloth strips to show their sacrificial victim status. The victors often covered their bodies, except for their faces, in black paint to show that they, like the Twin Gods, had integrated the characteristics of the Lords of Death who dwelled under the "black waters" and in the eternal darkness of the midnight sky and the lightless tomb.

On a carved panel from an unknown city, possibly Kalak'mul in the Peten area of what is now modern Guatemala, we see the victorious

A ballgame scene on a carved panel from an unknown site (possibly Kalak'mul), showing a victorious king defeating his exhausted captive.

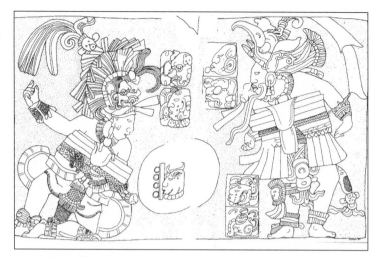

A carved panel from an unknown site (possibly Kalak'mul), showing First Jaguar playing ball with the Underworld demon, God L.

king dressed as First Jaguar in Tlaloc/Venus warfare regalia. He wears a jaguar-hide balloon turban, a skull pendant, Tlaloc-faced kneepads, and a right forearm guard with jaguar claws embedded in it. He hits the ball towards his captive who has fallen to the ground in exhaustion. The soon-to-be terminated one is wearing an Itzam-Yeh headdress and cloth strips with holes punched in them to show that his end is fast approaching. The sculpted panels of the great Chichen Itza ballcourt show this same First Jaguar–Itzam-Yeh struggle. The ballplayers dressed as Itzam-Yeh are doomed to die.

A less obvious winner-loser scenario in the cosmic game between the Twin Gods and the demons of Xibalba appears on a series of three carved panels from an unknown site. Here we see players dressed as First Lord and First Jaguar in magnificent array—proud jade cuffs and collars, jaguar pelts, and flashing quetzal-feather headdresses—facing a sinister-looking opponent costumed as God L/Itzam-na. The player representing First Jaguar kneels to catch the ball on his hip and send it hurtling toward the "demon king" who waits to receive it on his yoke. The God L impersonator is a massive figure with snarling, downturned lips and a shrieking Muan-bird headdress that frames his brutal face. The outcome of this game at least *appears* to be in doubt, although it too was almost certainly prearranged.

We know from the many ballgame carvings and paintings that have survived that the *ah pitzlawalob* wore many other types of costumes.

Those of the players who impersonated the Lords of Death were terrifying. Fanged, goggle-eyed, beaked, and bearded monsters appear in ballgame battles with the First Father and Twin Gods players.

In addition to the human games, depictions of the divine ballgames between First Lord and First Jaguar and the Xibalbans have also survived from the Classic Period. They demonstrate the overall faithfulness of the Post-Classic *Popol Vuh* to its more ancient sources. In the quadrafoil-framed ballcourt markers from the real ballcourt at Copan, the figures of First Lord and the Demon Zero square off against each other before, during, and after the game. First Lord's plumed headdress waves in the breeze caused by his energetic plays while the lumbering Demon Zero, a disembodied hand clasping his jaw, ready to rip it off in the jaw-removal sacrifice, thunders forward to receive First Lord's powerful hit. Again, on a ballcourt marker from the ruined city of La Esperanza we see an eager Demon Zero kneeling on a richly ornamented knee guard to make a hip shot with First Lord's head as the ball.

Unfortunately, we don't know how the *pitz* was actually played. Many of the specific resurrection technology teachings encoded in its complex symbolism are lost forever. But from the fragmentary clues that still do exist researchers have been able to piece together the general outlines of the ancient game. We know the ball itself was twelve to eighteen

A ballcourt marker from La Esperanza, showing the
Demon Zero striking First Lord's head as the ball.

inches in diameter, and that it was often—if not always—formed around the skull of a sacrificed victim. It was made of *chicle* from rubber plantations on the Veracruz coast and weighed around eight pounds. We also know that shamans, sometimes women, performed the opening ceremonies that caused the White-Bone Snake/Black Transformer to gape open and transform the earthly ballcourt into the Place of the Ball Game Sacrifice at the Underworld-Otherworld center of the universe.

Play began in one of two ways: Either a queen, a dwarf, or the captain of one of the teams hit the ball in the direction of the opposing players; or the ball, suspended from a scaffold that symbolized the rafters of the Twin Gods' house, was cut down and dropped into play between the opposing captains. Similar to a jump ball in modern basketball, these captains may then have struggled for possession.

Mirroring the descent myths of First Father and the Twin Gods, earthly teams were made up of either a single player each—like medieval champion knights—or two players on each side. By studying the Maya iconography and comparing later forms of the ballgame, especially as it was played by the Aztecs, researchers believe that the Maya *ah pitzlawalob* were not allowed to use their hands. Only their shoulders, forearms, hips, and knees could contact the ball. Whenever possible players tried to hit the ball at the markers set in the walls of the enclosure buildings. But we have no idea how the Maya kept score.

Some games were not games at all. At Yaxchilan and elsewhere the "ball" is depicted as a captive, tightly bound in a spherical position. The victim is shown hurtling down a flight of stairs to be struck by the king who is waiting below to make either a hip or shoulder shot with the human ball. In these scenes we see the Three-Conquest Stair and Six-Stair Place false ballcourts in action. Some scholars believe that hurling a bound captive down the sacrificial stairs sometimes took the place of decapitation sacrifice as the final play of the game.

From the masks and costumes the players wore, and from what we know about captive torture with its forced ingestion of hallucinogenic drugs, researchers believe that many—if not all—of the games were played in an altered state of consciousness. This altered state of consciousness made the three descents of the cosmic life-death-resurrection drama seem immediate and real. Once the *hom* portal had been opened, the Maya could experience the earthly ballcourt as the Cosmic Court. Players and audience alike could really believe they were watching events that took place before the creation of the world.

The ecstatic Reality in which the Maya believed they lived and which they dramatized in the ballgame appears in the *Popol Vuh* as the gradually intensifying dreamlike quality of the Twin Gods' exploits in Xibalba. The *Popol Vuh*'s magical atmosphere thickens as the shaman-authors describe the third, and final, ballgame between First Lord/First Jaguar and First/Seven Death.

Xbalanque restored Hunahpu's head in the form of a squash or pumpkin after his decapitation by the snatch-bat. Then the Twins rigged the final ballgame to frighten and demoralize death by confronting the demons with a revelation of unconquerable life. The key player in this strategy to turn the tables on death was a rabbit. Xbalanque tells this rabbit to stay above the sunken playing field at ground level "in the oaks." At his signal the rabbit will hop off into the forest, imitating the bouncing ball.

The ball itself, dropped into play by the Xibalbans, is the head of Hunahpu. The Lords of Death punt Hunahpu's head toward Xbalanque, who stops it with his yoke and hits it high into the air so that it lands near the rabbit. The rabbit bounds into the woods with the Xibalbans in hot pursuit.

While the demons are chasing the rabbit, Xbalanque quickly seizes Hunahpu's head and puts it back on his shoulders. Then the Twins place the squash where the severed head had landed and call to the Xibalbans, "Come back! Here's the ball! We've found it!"

The Lords of Death straggle back from the forest, confused by the Twins' deception. The decisive moment of death's undoing has come. Xbalanque punts the squash:

> . . . The squash was wearing out; it fell on the court, bringing to light its light-colored seeds, as plain as day right in front of them. . . .
>
> With this, the masters of Xibalba were defeated by Hunahpu and Xbalanque. . . .

Tantalizing remnants of Classic Period ballgame symbolism fill this final ballgame passage. We see the ball-as-severed-head—First Father/First Lord's—depicted in Classic Period art. We also see the Classic Period theme of head "harvesting" and its imagined connection with the harvesting of corn, squash, and other crops. The harvested squash in this passage is cleft like the Classic Period divine heads, the Primal Mountain, the Cosmic Turtle and Peccary, and the ballcourt itself.

Once the squash is broken it reveals its life-bearing seeds with their promise of resurrection just as the Classic Period Primal Mountain and Witz Monster break open to reveal corn plants exploding onto the earth plane, and the K'awil-blasted Cosmic Turtle Shell splits to allow First Father to emerge and begin the new creation.

When faced with the miracle of life's reemergence from death, the Lords of Xibalba fall back in shock and fear. They know they have been defeated by a life force they now realize is far stronger, more clever, and resourceful than they. The fact that the broken squash "bring[s] to light its light-colored seeds" links it to the Classic Period dawnings that follow the three descent/decapitation/deaths.

The Maya ballgame had its roots in the distant prehistoric past, at least as far back as the beginning of the domestication of corn (between 7000 and 5000 B.C.), perhaps even as early as the cultivation of squash and other vegetables. Stones that may once have marked the playing area of a primitive ballcourt have been found at an ancient site called Gheo Shih in Oaxaca, Mexico, and are dated to about 4500 B.C.

The first concrete evidence for the ballgame comes from the Olmec cities. Gigantic heads of Olmec shaman-kings seem to be wearing ballgame helmets, and the main plaza in the Olmec ruins of La Venta near the steamy Tabasco coast may have contained a ballcourt that could be magically activated by the feet of the doomed players.

Part of an almost universal Native American tradition that extended from what is now the southwestern United States to the heart of South America, the shamans and seers of different Indian peoples imagined a variety of meanings into the game. The Maya ballgame itself expressed at least three levels of meaning.

The most ancient of these was astronomical-agricultural. Originating in this most basic level of symbolism two great games were played each year. They were timed to resonate with the complex relationships between the positions of the stars, planets, and sun, the dry and rainy seasons, and the growth cycles of crops, especially corn. The first game took place at the spring equinox, during the dry season, when the Maya farmers planted their maize fields. Because the corn kernels—First Father's head—were buried in the ground at this time, the players portraying First Father and the Twin Gods lost this game to those who represented the Lords of Death. The second game was played at the fall equinox, at the beginning of the rainy season, when the corn was ripening toward the harvest. This time, the players identified with First Father and the Twin Gods defeated their opponents from Xibalba.

In the ancient Maya world in which everything becomes everything else, the picture was actually more complicated than this. Some evidence suggests the *spring* victory of the Twin Gods and their defeat in the *fall.* At both equinoxes, every day, and on the deepest, most spiritual level, in every moment, life became death and death became life.

The daily expression of the cosmic drama's great climax also contributed to the richness of ballgame symbols. According to the shamans, First Lord/Chac-Xib-Chac/Venus—the "death star"—sacrificed his brother, the Jaguar Sun, in Xibalba every night. Then, after midnight, First Jaguar rose from the dead. He ascended at dawn into the topmost branches of the World Tree to overthrow Itzam-Yeh. In fact, said the Maya mythmakers, First Lord sacrificed his brother because his sacrificial death was the only way he could truly awaken and begin his resurrection and dawning.

We know that the ball of the sacred *pitz* carried a number of symbolic meanings for the Maya, one of which identified it with both the physical and the spiritual sun. Like the maize kernel that created new life from its "decapitation" and "burial" in Xibalba, the sun, through *its* decapitation sacrifice at the hands of Venus, also rose again to create and sustain all living things. In the end, the sun and the maize-kernel head of First Father/First Lord were one and the same Holy Thing.

The coming of each new day, like the coming of spring, meant that the Overworld had once again triumphed over the Underworld. Yet, even though the Light was triumphant, it was so only because it had "suffered, died, been buried," and "descended into hell." Like Christ who could claim his cosmic throne as Christ Pantocrator—the "All-Ruler"—only after his Crucifixion, the Maya gods of resurrection could become the lords of the new creation only through their annihilation in the Abyss of Xibalba.

At this most ancient level of ballgame symbolism the true identities of the *ah pitzlawalob* who portrayed First Father/Lord/Jaguar and those who played the Lords of Death are a surrealistic tangle. If the Lords of Life lost the spring equinox game and were sacrificed, in at least some of the Classic Period scenes, were the players dressed as demons really the victorious *ahauob,* and those dressed as First Father/First Lord/First Jaguar the tortured captives? Was the opposite true for the games played at the fall equinox? Or, consistent with the belief that, in the end, the demons of Xibalba were really aspects of the gods of life, were the players portraying First Father/Lord/Jaguar also the Lords of Death, depending on the season in which the game was played? And were the captives both the defeated Lords of Life *and* the Lords of Death?

Perhaps the truth in these confusing ambiguities that seem to have been built into the ballplayers' identities is that, in the end, *everyone* won. The first team won by winning, the other by losing. If this was indeed the case, a profound theology underlay the Maya ballgame myths and rituals. That theology proclaimed the universal victory of life over death—under all circumstances, even those in which death appeared to have triumphed.

Beyond this nature-based symbol system, the second layer of meaning the Maya discerned in their sacred game was political. The Maya kings changed the astronomical-agricultural emphasis into a triumphant celebration of their power over the enemy *ahauob* of neighboring cities. By late Classic Period times, probably influenced by the spirituality of central Mexico, victorious kings thought of themselves as warriors of the sun; their rivals became the benighted inhabitants of the Underworld. In the hands of the shaman-kings the ballgame became political theater.

But the Classic Period shamans, even the shaman-kings with their political agendas, saw a third meaning in this holiest of all ritual enactments, a meaning far more gripping than the others. For those who had eyes to see, the deepest meaning of the *pitz* was its actualization of the last judgment and the hoped-for triumph of the individual soul in its quest for immortality. By rigging the games so that their victories were guaranteed, the shaman-kings and lesser lords hoped to gain the experience they would need in order to win the final game beyond the grave. They also hoped that by predetermining the outcome, and so winning—over and over again—these reenactments of life's triumph over death, they were generating a charge of *ch'ulel* that would ensure their postdeath victories. At the same time, the losers—themselves Lords of Life and "authentic human beings"—believed that through their sacrificial deaths either as First Father/Lord/Jaguar in their Overworld manifestations or as these same gods in their demonic Lords-of-Xibalba aspects, they too would win their quest for ecstatic eternal Being.

As we've seen, decapitation sacrifice was usually the last act in these terrible dramas of death and resurrection. In human sacrifice the darkness of the Divine Mystery gaped open to swallow the souls of sacrificed, sacrificer, and witnesses alike. The greatest *ch'ulel* generator of all, it was the climactic spiritual journey, the ultimate penetration of the great Mystery at the very center of sacred Reality, where forces of unimaginable malice and inconceivable life-giving power dwelt in a ferocious union beyond the grasp of human imagination. This terrifying and yet strangely exhilarating ritual was the Black Hole of absolute nonbeing toward which all other beliefs and rituals flowed and in which they reached their soul-transforming conclusion. The place in the utmost depths of the soul where First Father's bloody head gazed into nothingness yet envisioned everything, this was the destination of all those who wished to live again. Annihilation at the hands of the Divine Executioner was the price all such souls paid for their rebirth into the realm of infinite aliveness.

Half a world away, the founder of Christianity, Saint Paul, wrote:

> Do you not know that all of us who have been baptized into Christ Jesus were baptized into his death? We were buried therefore with him by baptism into death, so that as Christ was raised from the dead by the glory of the Father, we too might walk in newness of life.
>
> For if we have been united with him in a death like his, we shall certainly be united with him in a resurrection like his. . . .

The Maya would have agreed—but literally, not metaphorically. They would also have understood Jesus' saying "Greater love hath no man than this, that he lay down his life for his friends," for they themselves experienced something similar in their own myths of the three descents. But the Maya would have broadened the definition of "friends" to include the whole of the created cosmos. As the ultimate transforming act of a mature soul, the embracing of its own sacrificial death made both the re-creation of the individual and ongoing resurrection of the universe possible.

So powerful and potentially soul-transforming was human sacrifice for the Maya that, as we've seen, they idealized all deaths as manifestations of it. Forensics experts believe that Pacal died of natural causes. Yet his sarcophagus lid portrays him with K'awil's torch piercing his forehead, and he falls back onto the severed head of the so-called Quadripartite Monster/First Lord in the exact pose of a sacrificial victim lying on an altar, waiting for the ax to fall.

The emphasis on sacrificial death as the climactic act of human life gave an emotional force to Maya spirituality that few of us today can imagine. Based on its portrayal in art and writing, we know that human sacrifice evoked intense feelings of shock, fear, and awe. These feelings must have been even more vivid than those of present-day Christians on Good Friday for whom the myth of the tortured and sacrificed savior is still immediate and palpable. There are still those who seek, through flogging and mock crucifixion, something approaching the Maya experience of bloodletting, torture, and sacrificial death.

The anthropologist Inga Clendinnen has tried to understand what human sacrifice might have meant to the Aztecs. The Maya certainly experienced the same feelings about their own fearful rites. Clendinnen says that almost unimaginably powerful emotions must have been stirred in the Aztec sacrificers and their audiences by these "extravagant and enforced intimacies with death," as she puts it. But she adds that there is no evidence of pity or grief for the victims. This is exactly what we see in the Maya depictions—the cold, almost casual indifference to the fear and pain of others. Clendinnen believes that the tortures—both physical and emotional—that led up to the final act brought all involved "closer to the sacred state."

She notices what few other researchers have—that "a high degree . . . of cooperation" on the part of the Aztec victims "was essential" to the elaborate rituals in which they were forced to take part in dances and mock battles, and then voluntarily climb the pyramid steps to the waiting altars. The degree of cooperation necessary for the Maya rites was even greater. At times, the Maya required *self*-inflicted bloodletting from their victims, and, even more difficult for most modern people to understand, their energetic participation in the long, complicated, and predetermined ballgames.

Clendinnen wonders, as we might as well, how this degree of cooperation was possible. She answers by suggesting a number of probable contributing factors. First, she says, both sacrificed and sacrificers shared the same beliefs about the necessity of the ritual. Second, the victims were often forced to take hallucinogenic drugs that, in themselves, caused dancing, singing, and other fantastic behavior. Third, the guardians of the captives—the lords who had taken them in battle—fawned over them, called them "brothers" and "sons," and, as Clendinnen says, "cosseted" them. In addition, the Aztecs hired women who played the part of mother figures, soothing and reassuring the victims and urging them to be strong and courageous in their last moments of life. The Aztecs also exhausted their captives through physical and emotional torture to the point that they may have begun to look forward to death as the only way out of their intolerable misery. There was also the promise that sacrificial death would mean the immediate transformation of the victim into a divine being in the Otherworldly paradise. In addition, the victims' own pride, their sense of dignity, their determination to be courageous and to "make their last act on earth" an act of power—especially in front of so many people—may also have played a part. Like the martyrs of other religions, they may also have wanted to be faithful to their religious beliefs. Finally, Clendinnen says that the pageantry of the whole process, "infused" as it was "with the transcendent reality of the aesthetic," drew everyone present into an altered state of consciousness in which death seemed not only inevitable but spiritually "right" and desirable.

We don't know if the Maya cosseted their captives or not, and there is no evidence of professional mother figures from the Classic Period. But Clendinnen's other factors for encouraging the cooperation of the Aztec victims certainly applied to the Maya as well. In Maya art we see the "radically detached quality" on the faces of many of those fated to make the premature journey to Xibalba.

In the Classic Period the Maya victims were almost always noble lords and warriors from outside the conquering cities. Sometimes, as in the case of the unfortunate Eighteen-Rabbit, they were enemy shaman-kings themselves. As we see depicted on a ceramic vase from the Peten area of the Yucatan, infants were also occasionally sacrificed. By late Post-Classic times the Maya had begun to sacrifice women as well. For the Maya the fact that these people were foreign and "other" meant that they carried a greater charge of dangerous—and life-generating—supernatural energy. They were sacred vessels that contained an unusual concentration of *ch'ulel,* and their sacrifices increased the potency of the divine force in the victorious cities.

The most common and most important form human sacrifice took in the Classic Period was decapitation; but jaw removal and disemboweling were also practiced. Decapitation symbolized the detachment of the consciousness and the transformation of the victim into a disembodied, visioning god. In decapitation sacrifice, the human soul fell into First Father's head at the center of cosmos, merged with him, and became the Source of Being Itself.

Disemboweling symbolized making the World Tree within external and visible: The victim's intestines became the branches of the sacred Tree. They were also the supernatural umbilicals that carried *ch'ulel* to the three dimensions of the manifested world. When the intestines were

A rollout of the Fat Cacique Vase.

looped in ritual patterns on a lattice, they depicted and stimulated this *ch'ulel*-bearing system of energy exchange. We don't know what the jaw-removal sacrifice meant; but the horror of it must have made a lasting impression on all those who witnessed it.

By late Classic Period and Post-Classic Period times other forms of sacrifice had become important. These variations on the already grizzly practices of the Maya probably came from central Mexico. In the heart sacrifice the victim was spread-eagled faceup on a convex altar that arched his back and thrust his chest upward. Four assistants, called *chacob,* held each of his arms and legs while the shaman-priest made an incision with a flint or obsidian knife between his ribs and then tore the still-beating heart from its roots of veins and arteries. In the arrow sacrifice the victim was painted blue—the color of Xibalba—tied to a stake, and his or her heart shot full of arrows. In the fire sacrifice the "terminated one" was bound and thrown into a fire to be "toasted." Then, still alive, he was pulled from the flames and sacrificed by the removal of his heart.

The heart sacrifice symbolized the giving of one's central essence, the core of the soul, that which made human beings alive—the organ richest in *ch'ulel* because it moved. Since the arrow sacrifice also targeted the heart, it must have had a similar meaning. The fire sacrifice symbolized giving the entire body back to the gods who had made it of maize and blood.

The most powerful example of heart sacrifice as the final earthly act in which sacrificer and sacrificed stepped into the Black Transformer together to shed their humanity and become gods is the accession ritual of the late Classic Period kings. Scholars have been able to reconstruct the core of this ritual by piecing together before-and-after depictions of it from two different sources. The before scene comes from a funerary ceramic from San José Motul, called by archaeologists the Ik—or "Breath of God"—site, while the after scene appears on a stone slab called Stela 11 from Piedras Negras in Guatemala.

The vase, which is painted with vivid red-brown figures against a tan background and finished with pink hieroglyphs, shows a captive strapped to a wicker scaffold facing a king who has just arrived in a jaguar-hide-covered sedan chair. A priest in white body paint steps forward to meet the king while a kneeling woman shakes a gourd rattle to begin the ceremony. The king steps down from his chair, glowing with red body paint. The scalped captive is tied hand and foot in a seated position in the "cosmic niche" of the scaffold. This niche was a symbol for the 01 Portal center of the Overworld and the topmost branches of the World Tree. The victim stares at the approaching king with an expression of stark terror.

The Piedras Negras stela shows the final stage of the accession rit-

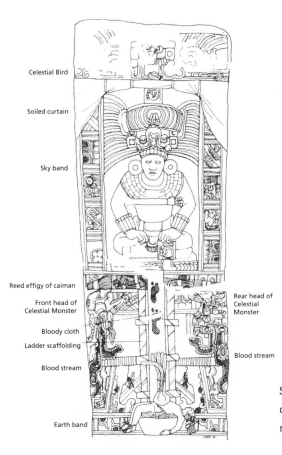

Stela 11 from Piedras Negras, depicting the king's accession ritual.

ual of the so-called Ruler Four. The accompanying hieroglyphs tell us that this event took place on November 13, 729 A.D. Here we see the *king* sitting in the cosmic niche of the scaffold platform.

The sides of the scaffold are decorated with sky-band symbols to depict the body of the Cosmic Monster with planets and stars passing through it. The Principal Bird Deity—in this case, First Father/First Lord in the role of Itzam-na/Itzam-Yeh—shrieks from the roof of the scaffold and spreads its wings in the Overworld. The king wears a magnificent quetzal-feather headdress whose plumes flare out like the rays of the sun and frame a mask portraying First Lord/Chac-Xib-Chac/Venus. The king's head appears to emerge from the god's mouth; his headband is the upper row of the god's teeth. Ruler Four sits cross-legged with his hands on his legs, proclaiming himself the resurrected First Father/First Lord, the new Principal Bird Deity and cosmic wizard, and the ruler of the universe. Blood pours down the sides of the scaffold to symbolize First Lord/Chac-Xib-Chac's sacrifice of First Jaguar—the Cosmic Monster's other head, and his twin brother.

A sacrificial victim lies at the foot of the scaffold across an offering bowl filled with paper strips. The bowl symbolizes the universe. The "terminated one" has just undergone the heart sacrifice. A small wrapped bundle with quetzal feathers representing a sprouting corn plant has been placed in the bloody chest cavity. This quetzal-feather corn plant is a miniature version of the World Tree in its Cosmic Corn Plant aspect. Its placement in the victim's chest cavity means that the unfortunate man has given his life-essence—the very center of his Being—to raise the World Tree and resurrect the universe.

Perhaps the most moving part of this scene is the cloth-covered ladder by which the king has ascended from the sacrifice below to his throne in the cosmic niche. On the cloth we see the bloody footprints the king has left as he walked over the victim's body and climbed the ladder to receive the emblems of his office.

Consistent with the deep mystery we see in the Maya myths of twinship in which the Divine Being sacrifices Itself *to* Itself in order to generate the new creation, the king could grasp his own empowerment only by sacrificing his twin, his alter ego—the captive. We know from the iconography itself and also from comparisons with Aztec practices that the Maya *ahauob* experienced just such a twinship relationship with their captives. Sacrificed enemy kings and nobles became the "brothers" of the victorious lords, and by extension, of all the citizens of the triumphant cities. Having given their lives to increase the flow of *ch'ulel* in the victorious kingdoms, the terminated ones were forever bound as divine protectors to those who had sent them to the Otherworld.

In their accession rituals, the Maya kings symbolically sacrificed themselves *to* themselves in order to re-create their own souls, their kingdoms, and the world. In Jungian terms they sacrificed their shadows. By sacrificing these shadow parts of themselves the Maya kings acceded to their own personal empowerment and became gods ruling from the 01 Portal at the top of the World Tree.

Part three of the partly "Mexicanized" *Popol Vuh* shows three forms of human sacrifice—the heart sacrifice of the Lords of Death and the intended heart sacrifice of Blood Woman after her father discovers that she has disobeyed his orders and gone to see the magical calabash tree with First Father's head in its branches; decapitation sacrifice—the most frequently portrayed in the text, directly and indirectly; and the fire sacrifice. Unlike Classic Period depictions of decapitation as the ultimate form of sacrifice, the *Popol Vuh* makes the Twin Gods' climactic offering a leap into the fire that the Lords of Xibalba have prepared for them. This fire sacrifice is the last and greatest demonstration of the Twin Gods' love for the world they will dream into being.

In voluntarily flinging themselves into the very heart of nonbeing, First Lord/First Jaguar showed every developing Maya soul the final transcendent deed the gods required of it. This final sacrifice from a position of personal empowerment was the last step in implementing the resurrection technology process. With this act, the Twins had done all that they could. Now they had to trust the life-generating side of the Divine Being. Only It could raise new life from the ashes of total destruction. It alone could turn catastrophe into a celebration of even greater Being.

The *Popol Vuh* account of the Twins' self-sacrifice follows the defeat of the demons in the third and last ballgame. First Lord and First Jaguar know that the Lords of Xibalba have planned one final game to destroy them, a game that will end when the demons push them into a huge fiery oven. They summon two Underworld shamans—Xulu and Pacam—who, interestingly, like Blood Woman, are on the side of life. First Lord and First Jaguar tell them "to grind their bones on a stone, just as corn is refined into flour," and throw them into the Underworld river after their deaths.

The messengers of One and Seven Death then bring the Twins to the oven. The text continues:

And here they tried to force them into a game:

"Here, let's jump over our drink four times, clear across, one of us after the other, boys," they were told by One Death.

"You'll never put that one over on us. Don't we know what our death is, you lords? Watch!" they said, then they faced each other. They grabbed each other by the arms and went head first into the oven.

And there they died, together, and now all the Xibalbans were happy, raising their shouts, raising their cheers:

"We've really beaten them!" . . .

After that they summoned Xulu and Pacam, who kept their word: the bones went just where the boys had wanted them . . . the bones were ground and spilled in the river . . . they didn't go far—they just sank to the bottom of the water. . . .

As with the first test in Dark House, it is K'awil power that energizes the Twins' sacrifice and gives it its meaning and life-engendering force. The god of spiritual transformation and manifestation appears in this passage in his two most vital *itz* forms—substance and fire. The substance he manifests and that the Twins become is the corn flour—both physical and spiritual—from which the human body and soul are made. In telling the shaman-seers Xulu and Pacam to grind up their bones and "refine" them, the Twin Gods are asking to be returned to their "corn flour" essence, their primordial state. In doing this they are presenting themselves as "food" and "sustenance" to the God beyond the gods. By reducing themselves to the original sacred substance from which they first arose, and returning their *itz* to the Void, they are, paradoxically, completing the last and most self-empowering this-worldly act in the life cycle of The White Flower Thing.

The Twin Gods are so transported by their voluntary leap into nonbeing that they are instantly incinerated by K'awil's fire. Although prepared by the Lords of Death, from a deeper spiritual perspective, this transforming fire is really their own ecstatic consciousness, the "fire in their blood," that is so intense it melts them into the energy of their origins. Their own spiritual passion, a transcendent state of soul *they* have chosen, ends their finite lives.

Strangely, because of their self-annihilation, death itself is transformed. It becomes more than an enemy, more even than the agent of greater Being—the tester and stimulator of greater wholeness and maturity of soul. By actually choosing death from a position of personal power, the Twin Gods complete the integration of death's final core characteristic—its nonbeing—and thereby mysteriously transform it into a richer, more mature and all-inclusive Being. Like Taoist sages returning to the Way, they take it back with them to the undifferentiated ocean of *ch'ulel* before the appearance of the dualities of good and evil, health and disease, intelligence and stupidity, courage and cowardice, creation and destruction, life and death—back to death's own origin.

The Twins' defeat of death makes it once again, as it was in the beginning, a part of an eternally triumphant life. For the Maya, as for Saint Paul, "Death is swallowed up in victory!" Through the saving acts of the Twin Gods the life-death drama achieves its final resolution and reveals what it has always been beneath the surface of this hallucinated universe—one infinite, eternal, and seamlessly whole Divine Life.

For many of us the horror of human sacrifice as practiced by the ancient Maya may overwhelm any mythological or theological explanations of it. Surely, people who could cut off a living victim's jaw, rip out his intestines, or laboriously hack off his head have nothing to say to us. We are civilized.

Of course, there is no place for the Maya atrocities in our society. But for the Maya, human sacrifice *did* convey powerful truths about owning and integrating the shadow that dwells in the depths of all human souls. Like the ancient shamans, Jung warned that pretending to be all good leads to the crippling of our souls. For Jung this refusal to take responsibility for all of who we are and work with it to achieve a kind of fiercely benevolent wholeness is the greatest moral evil of all, for it leads to the unconscious acting out of our dark impulses. What we do not integrate within ourselves we will inevitably vent on others.

The archetype of human sacrifice—the instinctual need to perform it in *some* way—is a tar baby from which we, as a species, can't seem to free ourselves. The harder we try, the more stuck to it we become, and the more compulsively—and mindlessly—we are forced to act it out.

A large part of our problem may come from Western culture's laudable historical attempt to end the literal practice of human sacrifice, but without, at the same time, showing human beings what to do with their apparently innate need to act it out in some way. The spiritualities of dualism have made this problem worse. The ancient Hebrew prophets stopped the "abomination," as they put it, of human sacrifice. Even the substitute animal sacrifices ended when the Temple of Jerusalem was destroyed in 70 A.D. However, it may not be an accident that after these events the Jewish people themselves became the collective sacrifice of the Christian clerics.

The Christians who believe their savior was the final human sacrifice have been compelled—and compelled it certainly is—to repeat the horrific act over and over again at the expense of the uncountable number of human beings they've forced to play the sacrificial role of their murdered lord. Torture for torture and body for body, the sheer number of Christianity's victims dwarfs the blood offerings of any other religion in the history of the world. Even so, Christians have had a lot of company. While turning in lower body counts, other religions have done their own share of sacrificing the nonbelieving "others" from "outside the city."

Perhaps part of the problem is how to keep the archetype of human sacrifice immediate and present for the faithful, as something that happens to them in real time rather than as a myth from the distant past. Perhaps the dark ecstasy of human sacrifice with its power to confront us with our own mortality and reignite our sense of aliveness and our feelings of oneness with the beautiful terror of God must somehow be made dramatic, palpable, and real, and in such a way that we can neither deny nor escape it. If the blood-ecstasy of human sacrifice really does lie at the heart of all spiritualities—which the foundation myths of dying and resurrecting saviors tell us it does—then we really must find some way to reexperience it in all of its soul-transforming power. We must have *some* way to recapture the intensity of this culminating moment of the divine drama.

When we try to turn away from this demand for the ecstatic embracing of our deaths as "holy and right" sacrifices to the Mystery from which we come and to which we must return, we find other, far less honorable (and spiritually effective) ways to act it out. Are our wars not human sacrifices by another name and on a scale the Maya could never have imagined? Are these and other outbreaks of extravagant violence not dark wallowings in ineptly performed Underworldly rituals?

According to the Maya shamans, choosing self-annihilation from a condition of soul-maturity and personal strength is the last and greatest this-worldly embodiment of K'awil's portal-smashing lightning-serpent strike. Actually *calling for* the god's en-lighten-ment, and leaping into the flames of his Otherworldly oblivion, is the culminating act of faith. If we ourselves could die like this—like *halach uinicob*—what miracles might our deaths evoke from the dreaming Abyss?

The ancient shamans said that only those who can embrace the dark-bright ecstasy of their own deaths can live full earthly lives. Only those who live full earthly lives can choose to die, rush at the Void, and exult in their return to God. And only *they* can live again.

CHAPTER 12

Resurrection

Most of us say we believe in life after death. Many of us go to churches, synagogues, or some other religious center where eternal life is routinely proclaimed. We recite the ritual formulas that affirm our continued existence beyond physical death.

But do we really *believe* it? "Actions speak louder than words," we say. They do. What do our actions tell us about the beliefs that really shape our lives? What does it say about us that more than simple efforts to live healthy lives, diet, health food, and "body beautiful" fads have become obsessions for millions of people, or that more than 50 percent of the health-care costs in the United States alone are spent on the last six months to a year of life in a desperate attempt to stave off our inevitable ends?

If we truly believed in life after death, would we cling so frantically to the body? If we really believed in a last judgment—something all religions teach in some form—would we not do whatever was necessary to prepare for it?

The Maya believed that there really is continued existence beyond the grave. They also knew what the earliest Christians once knew as well—that "many are called, but few are chosen." The only important question for the ancient Maya, as for the most insightful in all religions, was, "What do *I* need to do to be 'chosen'?" As we've seen, for the Maya shamans, the answer to this question was: Embrace death from a condition of intensified Being.

The Maya depicted on their funerary ceramics the miraculous moment—cosmic and individual—in which, against all odds, the *sak-nik-nal* as First Father/Maize burst forth from the Land of Death and rose to glory in the infinite Otherworld. We see this wondrous resurrection in a scene on a Classic Period offering plate. The icon on this plate is different from that on the famous tripod plate, but its purpose is the same: to remind the dead soul of the rebirth it could win for itself if it defeated the Lords of Xibalba.

On this offering plate we see First Father squeezing upward through the crack in the Cosmic Turtle Shell. He's already free from the waist up as he waves a greeting to First Lord. Four quetzal feathers, representing the four quarters of the universe that he is organizing in the time-space dimension, sprout from his headdress. These feathers also symbolize the leaves of the Cosmic Corn Plant/World Tree that he himself is becoming.

The Turtle Shell is slowly and painfully groaning open. The face of the Turtle is contorted, its eyes rolled back in its head, as it gives birth to the transfigured god. From the sides of the Shell emerge the two heads of the Cosmic Monster, showing that the Twin Gods/ecliptic serpent

An offering plate depicting the Twin Gods helping First Father be reborn from the Cosmic Turtle.

flow through this central tear in the fabric of time-space. The monstrous heads of the serpent in turn give rise to the Twins in their humanlike forms. On the right side of the Turtle Shell we see First Jaguar with a large pitcher in his hands, pouring *itz* into the widening crack to lubricate it. On the left we see First Lord reciting a magical incantation to speed his father's passage from eternal death into eternal life.

The power of the event, including the danger and difficulty of the passage through the 01 Portal/birth canal of the Cosmic Turtle Shell, dramatizes the Maya belief that while, in the end, life always triumphs over death, it does so only with enormous suffering. At one level, like the birth onto the earth plane, rebirth into the Otherworld is genuinely dangerous. And, as in human sacrifice, for rebirth to be successful something about us must be "terminated." In this case, the symbol for the part of life and of the soul that must be sacrificed is the Turtle.

The *Popol Vuh* tells the story of this first resurrection in a different way, one that adds to the power and richness of the event. After its description of First Father's failure in his contest with the Underworld demons, and his resulting decapitation, the text says:

> And when his head was put in the fork of the tree, the tree bore fruit. It would not have had any fruit, had not the head of One Hunahpu been put in the fork of the tree. . . .
>
> And then One and Seven Death were amazed at the fruit of the tree. The fruit grows out everywhere, and it isn't clear where the head of One Hunahpu is. . . .

The Lords of Death are afraid of this miraculous Tree of Life, and they forbid anyone to approach it. But one of the demons—Blood Woman, the daughter of One Death, and the Underworld form of First Mother—is overcome with curiosity and wonder. She says to her father,

> "I'm not acquainted with that tree they talk about. 'Its fruit is truly sweet!' they say, I hear," she said.
>
> Next, she went all alone and arrived where the tree stood. It stood at the Place of Ball Game Sacrifice [at the very center of Xibalba]:

"What? Well! What's the fruit of this tree? Shouldn't this tree bear something sweet? . . . Should I pick one?" said the maiden.

And then the bone spoke: . . .

"Why do you want a mere bone, a round thing in the branches of a tree?" said the head of One Hunahpu. . . . "You don't want it," she was told.

"I do want it," said the maiden.

Then First Father tells her to stretch out her hand. As she does so, he spits into her open palm. She draws back in astonishment and looks at her hand. But First Father's spittle has miraculously disappeared, absorbed into her body. The living skull speaks again:

"It is just a sign I have given you, my saliva, my spittle. . . . It's just the same with . . . a great lord: . . . his son is like his saliva, his spittle. . . . The father does not disappear, but goes on being fulfilled. Neither dimmed nor destroyed is the face of a lord, a warrior, craftsman, orator. . . . So it is that I have done likewise through you. Now go up there on the face of the earth; you will not die. . . ." Right away something was generated in her belly . . . and this was the generation of Hunahpu and Xbalanque.

Both the Classic Period offering plate and this *Popol Vuh* passage proclaim the same great Mystery: At the moment of ultimate catastrophe eucatastrophe begins. In the deepest part of the black Abyss of Xibalba's perpetual night, life flickers back on-line. The life force is so powerful and the passion of the Divine Being so great that even total failure on the part of the soul in its confrontation with death is not the end. In its very severing the head becomes the font of life, the wondrous manifestation of the indomitable God beyond God who, insisting on life in the midst of Its ecstatic vision, always finds a way to turn disaster into renewal and rebirth.

The image on the offering plate tells us, once again, that First Father is the Cosmic Corn Plant/Resurrection Body of the universe and of every successful soul.

The Cosmic Turtle Shell is the supernatural maize kernel that bursts open to allow the Resurrection Body to soar up from the realm of death into the world of eternal life. It is the physical body as well, that body which, struck by death's lightning, cracks open in decay and releases the soul. It is the Place of the Ball Game Sacrifice, broken open for us that we "terminated ones" may ascend after we've embraced our own annihilations in the fearful Void.

When Saint Paul was asked by literal-minded Christians about the nature of the Resurrection Body, he replied with a teaching strikingly similar to those of the ancient Maya. He wrote:

> What you sow does not come to life unless it dies. And what you sow is not the body which is to be, but a bare kernel, perhaps of wheat or of some other grain. But God gives it a body as he has chosen, and to each kind of seed its own body. . . . So is it with the resurrection of the dead. What is sown is perishable, what is raised is imperishable. It is sown in . . . weakness, it is raised in power. It is sown a physical body, it is raised a spiritual body. . . . For the trumpet will sound, and the dead will be raised imperishable, and we shall be changed . . . then shall come to pass the saying that is written:

> *"Death is swallowed up in victory."*
> *"O death, where is thy victory?*
> *O death, where is thy sting?"*

The *Popol Vuh* scene between First Father's skull and Blood Woman is charged with images of resurrecting life: the miraculous tree itself recalls all the life-bearing trees of world mythology, including the cross of Christ; the maiden—fresh, courageous, and rebellious—fearlessly, expectantly, standing under that tree asking for life; First Father's skull—his "bone," as the text calls it—making the tree alive and seducing the demon-woman in order to make a world. In the ancient Maya language, the word for "bone" was the same as the word for "seed." So Blood Woman stood before the "seed"—the semen-*itz*—of the Decapitated-Dead-Creating-Thing and begged for her miraculous world-renewing conception.

First Father's skull-seed tests her readiness to enter the Creator Couple partnership with him, telling her, "Why do you want a mere bone, a round thing in the branches of a tree? . . . You don't want it." We can almost see the eagerness and faith shining in her eyes as she says, "Yes. I do! I *do* want to make a world with you!" Then First Father's saliva-semen enters her body and "right away something was generated in her belly," and the resurrection of the universe begins.

The Maya *ah tz'ibob* who wrote this passage were affirming the life-generating connection between death and sex, and the intensified Being that comes from the marriages we ourselves must make between our own Underworlds and Overworlds. Through the figure of Blood Woman, they were also saying that the Xibalba side of God itself yearns for life, betrays its own destructiveness, and sides with creation and fuller Being.

After the miraculous impregnation of the dawning universe, First Father's Decapitated-Dead-Creating-Thing speaks from the fruiting World Tree the ringing affirmation of eternal life. He says, "The father does not disappear [as the Lords of Death had said he would], but goes on being fulfilled. Neither dimmed nor destroyed is the face [the *uich*—the individual personality] of a lord, a warrior, craftsman, orator [a shaman-creator]."

While both the Classic Period iconography and the *Popol Vuh* show First Father as having lost his contest with the Lords of Death, and with it his head, and while on one level his failure was real and eternal death was his sentence, the Maya shamans knew a deeper truth about this god within every soul: As illustrated on the tripod plate and in the *Popol Vuh* text, it is First Father himself who begins the resurrection! Buried in the ground, the corn kernel splits to send up its sprout. Buried under the ballcourt floor in the Classic Period imagery or hung in the *Popol Vuh*'s calabash tree, life begins again from some miraculous process within the seed/head/soul-essence itself.

On those awe-full "stairs of death" at Yaxchilan researchers have recently deciphered yet another important hieroglyph, one that unlocks the greatest mystery of all the Maya mysteries. The hieroglyph reads *ch'akba*. It means "*self*-decapitation." When we add this strange verb to the *hal/ahal*—"descent/conquest/awakening/remembering/evoking/dawning/appearing/creating"—glyph, we see that, like the Twin Gods' leap into the fire in the *Popol Vuh,* the three descent/creations of the Classic Period were all *self*-sacrifices. This means that, like his sons, First Father *willed* his own failure in order to win eternal life and resurrect the universe. Then he "conquered" death by dying, "awakened" in the calabash/World Tree, "remembered" who he was and would be, "appeared" from the cleft Turtle Shell, "evoked" the Twin Gods, and "dawned" as the new world. First Father himself, in the guise of First/Seven Death, defeated his own destructiveness and rose from the Void that he himself was. Now we can grasp First Father's full identity: he was "The-Holy-First-Father/*First Death-Self*-Decapitated-'Dead'-*Self*-Creating-Thing."

For the Classic Period shamans, the first descent of the "father" actually *caused* the second descent of the "sons," which was the continuation in a richer and more complicated way of the first. The second descent with its losing-in-order-to-win theme was only *apparently* different from the first—and seemingly failed—descent. Ultimately, the first and second descents were the same self-decapitating/self-re-creating event—and one that every father and son, and father/son, had to reenact in order to live again as a god.

After recounting the Twin Gods' leap into the Void, the *Popol Vuh* describes their resurrection.

> And on the fifth day they reappeared. They were seen in the water by the people. The two of them looked like channel catfish when their faces were seen by Xibalba. And having germinated in the waters, they appeared the day after that as two vagabonds, with rags before and rags behind, and rags all over too . . . they acted differently now.

These few lines carried a wealth of symbolic meaning for the ancient Maya—most of which is now lost to us. We do know that the Twin Gods' resurrection on the fifth day was probably tied to the cycles of Venus recorded in the surviving codices and reflected in a number of Classic Period inscriptions. While in the ancient Near East the dying-resurrecting gods, including Christ, reappeared on the third day because their rebirths were linked with the phases of the moon, for the Maya, First Lord/Chac-Xib-Chac/Venus was the key player in the drama of death and resurrection—both of the cosmos and of the individual soul.

The fish form of First Lord/Jaguar at the moment of their resurrection is a distant echo of a vanished body of monster-fish myths, only hints of which have survived. This once-important Fish-god appears in various manifestations in Classic Period art. We see it carried on the backracks of the First Father impersonator dancers. The hollow in Pacal's sarcophagus was carved in the shape of the Underworld fish of rebirth. And on the headdresses of Maya kings we see the so-called Xoc-fish eating the water lily that symbolized the transition from death to life.

Some of the magic and mystery the lost fish myths must have stirred in the ancient Maya survive in the modern Chicano legend of the golden carp as told by Rudolfo Anaya in his novel *Bless Me, Ultima*. In the golden carp passage Anaya tells the story of two boys, Tony and Cico, who venture out to an enchanted pond near their pueblo to wait for the appearance of the miraculous fish. Anaya writes:

The pond was dark and clear, and the water trickled and gurgled over the top of the dam. There was plenty of grass along the bank, and on all sides the tall brush and trees rose to shut off the world.

Cico pointed. "The golden carp will come through there." The cool waters of the creek came out of a dark, shadowy grotto of overhanging thicket. . . .

We sat for a long time, waiting for the golden carp. . . .

Then the golden carp came. Cico pointed and I turned to where the stream came out of the dark grotto of overhanging branches. At first I thought I must be dreaming. I had expected to see a carp the size of a river carp, perhaps a little bigger and slightly orange instead of brown. I rubbed my eyes and watched in astonishment.

"Behold the golden carp, Lord of the waters—" I turned and saw Cico standing, his spear held across his chest as if in acknowledgment of the presence of a ruler.

The huge, beautiful form glided through the blue waters. I could not believe its size. It was bigger than me! . . . As he came out of the darkness of the pond the sun caught his shiny scales and the light reflected orange and yellow and red. He swam very close to our feet. His body was round and smooth in the clear water. We watched in silence at the beauty and grandeur of the great fish. . . .

"The golden carp," I whispered in awe. I could not have been more entranced if I had seen the Virgin, or God Himself. The golden carp had seen me. It made a wide sweep, its back making ripples in the dark water. I could have reached out into the water and touched the holy fish! . . .

Then the golden carp swam by Cico and disappeared into the darkness of the pond. I felt my body trembling as I saw the bright golden form disappear. I knew I had witnessed a miraculous thing, the appearance of a pagan god, a thing as miraculous as the curing of my uncle Lucas. . . .

Cico leaned back and stared into the bright sky. "This whole land was once covered by a sea, a long time ago— . . . You know, this land belonged to the fish before it belonged to us. I have no doubt about the prophecy of the golden carp. He will come to rule again! . . ."

He smiled and stood up. "The golden carp is my god, Tony. He will rule the new waters. I will be happy with my god—" . . .

That night in my dreams I walked by the shore of a great lake. A bewitching melody filled the air. . . . I looked into the dark depths of the lake and saw the golden carp, and all around him were the people he had saved.

The fish as a symbol of fertility, sexuality, regenerated life, and instinctual wisdom is ancient and universal. Many ancient peoples saw the fish as an aspect of the life-bearing Sun-god. Sometimes it was associated with a goddess of resurrection. The sign for the ancient Babylonian goddess Ishtar was a house with a fish in it. The fish also stood for the life-generating organs: it looked like the male penis, and it smelled like the female vulva. Gods of resurrection like the Egyptian Osiris and the Phoenician Dagon had fish manifestations, and the secret password of the early Christians was the Greek word for "fish." Depictions of the resurrected Christ as a fish appear in church emblems to this day.

The ancient Maya expressed the aliveness of the Resurrection Body through ecstatic dancing. We know what this Maya dance of resurrection looked like from Classic Period depictions and from the *Popol Vuh* account. This embodied celebration of the final transformation of death into life appears to have included three progressions or stages—the "bone exhumation," the decapitation sacrifice, and the robing and grasping of power emblems while "walking on water." For the bone exhumation stage the dead soul performed a jaunty, hip-swaying, toe-heel strut. Then it burst into ecstatic leaping and swooping as it brandished the executioner's ax in the decapitation sacrifice phase. It returned to the toe-heel strut for its robing and emblem-grasping.

Interestingly, once researchers had decoded the carved and painted images of this ancient dance of rebirth, they suddenly saw the dancelike positions of Classic Period ballplayers in a fascinating new light. Many of the oddly unathletic and seemingly artificial postures—hands pointing in the same direction, ambling toe-heel strolls, and exaggerated leaps—suddenly made sense. Now scholars believe that the ballgame itself was a form of the death and resurrection dance.

The Maya kings performed the great dance many times during their lifetimes in preparation for their final performance beyond the grave. At various stages of the dance they took on the identities of First Father and First Lord as Chac-Xib-Chac. For the bone exhumation they dressed as both together. For the decapitation sacrifice they appeared as Chac-Xib-Chac. And for the accession phases they impersonated the resurrected First Father. Often the stages of the dance were performed at different festivals and timed to resonate with the life-death-rebirth drama as it was reenacted in the "eternal now" of the night sky.

When John Lloyd Stephens and Frederick Catherwood chopped their way through the dense jungle of the Copan valley and broke into the Great Plaza of the ruined city in 1839, they had little idea what they had found. Of all the many mysteries they encountered none was stranger than the elaborately carved "tree-stone" now called Stela H. As Stephens and Catherwood cleared the vines from the limestone slab, a serene face emerged and gazed down at them with regal splendor. Later archaeologists and iconographers struggled to identify this symbol-encrusted figure, but met with little success. Now that we can read the inscription and understand the symbols we know that Stela H is a portrait of Eighteen-Rabbit performing the bone exhumation dance in the guise of First Father/First Lord on the night of December 5, 730 A.D.

The king is dressed in the net skirt of First Father and wears a backrack depicting Itzam-Yeh and an offering bowl for bloodletting sacrifice. He carries the Twin Gods/ecliptic serpent bar clasped to his chest in rapture. Two K'awil heads emerge from the mouths of the Twin Gods' emblem. On the sides of the stela we see the snake-umbilicals of the cos-

The bone exhumation ritual with two kneeling dancers.

mos—the branches of the World Tree that carry the Divine Being's bloody *ch'ulel*-bearing sap of life to all the levels and sections of the universe. White Flower Thing souls emerge from the ends of the umbilical-serpents/World Tree branches.

Across the court is another stela, Stela A, whose inscription describes in greater detail what Eighteen-Rabbit was doing on that momentous night. It says that he conjured a Vision Serpent and entered the Underworld where he endured "nine-deaths"—possibly the six torture houses and three ballgames of Xibalba—and then broke into a royal tomb and dug up the bones of his ancestor Butz'Chan. Stela A refers to this midnight grave robbing with the phrase "bones were cut." Stela H records the magical December 5 date, while Stela A was dedicated sixty days later on February 3. Because we know the positions of the Milky Way and the Orion Cosmic Turtle Shell/Cosmic Hearth on these two dates, can decipher the "bones were cut" inscription, and understand the symbolism of Eighteen-Rabbit's First Father/First Lord costume, we now know that the king was reenacting the Twin Gods' descent, trials, and resurrection in Xibalba, the exhumation of First Father's body from the Place of the Ball Game Sacrifice, and the reattachment of his head.

At the end of this eerie celebration Eighteen-Rabbit became First Father and danced the dance of resurrection and cosmic creation. As Stela H shows, this resurrection was not just First Father's; it was also the regeneration of all the *sak-nik-nalob* that had made their own successful descents into the Land of Death. We can imagine that eerie

December 5th night—the ghoulish exhumation of the ancient corpse, its reassembly by torchlight, and Eighteen-Rabbit's ghostly toe-heel strut in the Great Plaza as the Milky Way/Canoe of Life glowed softly in the vastness overhead and carried the spirit of Butz'Chan/First Father to the place of his rebirth.

The decapitation sacrifice stage of the great dance of life appears in a magnificent painting on a Classic Period funerary vase. Here we see First Lord dancing into the scene from the left toward a Vision Serpent altar on which First Jaguar lies kicking and roaring, waiting for First Lord's ax to fall. First Lord dances on the tips of his toes, raising his right knee high into the air and swinging two sacrificial axes, one in each hand. He gazes up at the ax in his right hand with an expression of wonder. His haughty coiffure waves above his head. His body is richly ornamented and painted with symbols of divinity. He still shows signs of his fish-resurrection: catfish barbels flow from behind his nostrils and scales emerge from the backs of his legs.

First Jaguar is manifesting his so-called Baby Jaguar form. His jaguar tail lashes into the air and he kicks with jaguar ears and paws. His flailing on the altar itself seems like a kind of dance in which he is mirroring First Lord's leaping and swooping. Both seem lost in ecstatic rapture.

On the right side of the altar First Death dances in imitation of First Lord's steps. The demon wears two gouged-out eyeballs on his skeletal head. His emaciated arms and legs and his bloated belly are a pitiful mockery of First Lord's health and energy. First Death wears a back-

A rollout of a vase painting depicting the dance of human sacrifice as performed by the Twin Gods in Xibalba.

First Father being robed by two naked goddesses.

rack made of a human spine and pelvis. He too seems to have entered the ecstatic trance of the decapitation dance.

It's possible that the Maya kings always performed this dance as part of the decapitation sacrifice ritual. Like their victims they too took hallucinogenic drugs to help them enter the Otherworldly death state. Then they donned the costume of First Lord/Chac-Xib-Chac with its resurrection-fish symbols, and imagined themselves dipping and soaring with First Death, their macabre dance partner on the other side of the altar.

The robing and grasping of the sacred symbols of cosmic kingship appears on a carved panel from Palenque. This panel, from Temple Fourteen, shows the dead king Chan-Bahlum's triumphant emergence from Xibalba after his defeat of the Underworld demons. Chan-Bahlum is performing the toe-heel dance. His richly ornamented kilt sways with his jaunty steps. The kilt bears the image of the Underworld Jaguar in its skeleton form, and we see the *k'in* sun sign and a World Tree symbol in his proud headdress. At his feet his mother, Lady Ahpo-Hel, also dead, leans toward him to hand him the K'awil Scepter—the holy image of spiritual transformation. She is wearing the net skirt of her husband First Father, and the Quadripartite Monster emblem adorns her quetzal-feather headdress. By wearing these symbols both Chan-Bahlum and Lady Ahpo-Hel are identifying themselves with the risen sun. Beneath them are three hieroglyphic bands that show that this scene is taking place on the surface of the Otherworld ocean above a supernatural location known only by its glyphic sign—Imix.

The hieroglyphic text describes Chan-Bahlum's Otherworldly accession as like-in-kind to the Dream Time event in which First Mother in her Moon-goddess aspect first gave birth to K'awil and presented him to

First Father. The inscription says that this mythological event took place 932,174 years before Chan-Bahlum's triumph. It identifies Chan-Bahlum with First Father and Lady Ahpo-Hel with First Mother. The moment Chan-Bahlum/First Father grasps his K'awil aspect he completes his resurrection into the Otherworld.

Interestingly, it is his female manifestation—his mother/wife—who helps him over the last hurdle on the way to his apotheosis by bequeathing to him his ecstatic spiritual consciousness, that state of enraptured enlightenment that enabled him to complete his transformation into the infinite Being of the "God beyond God." Of course, K'awil was the fruit of the passionate union of both First Father and First Mother and manifested the life-renewing power of the *merger* of male and female qualities.

The followers of Carl Jung might well interpret this evocative image as an expression of the psychological goal of integrating our male and female aspects to achieve individuation. From Jung's perspective, this wedding of male and female within the soul is vital to the emergence of what he called the "transcendent third." This transcendent third appears

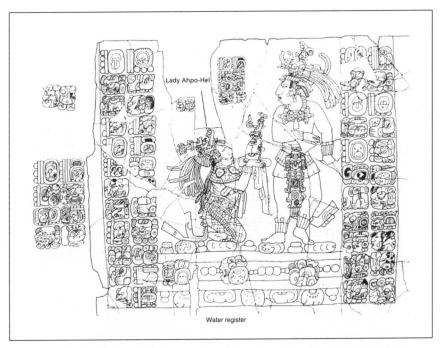

Chan-Bahlum dancing out of the Underworld on the surface of the cosmic ocean as shown on a tablet from Temple XIV at Palenque.

in the myths of many religions in the form of a Divine Child and portrays the rebirth of the soul onto a new level of Being. For Jung, as for the ancient Maya, this Divine Child brings enlightenment and transformation, and It empowers us to grasp the eternal life the Self is always offering the conscious personality.

Chan-Bahlum died on February 2, 702 A.D. and completed his resurrection on November 6, 705. This means that from the point of view of earthly time he spent almost four years in Xibalba. On the other hand, from the Otherworld perspective as portrayed on the sacrificial stairs at Yaxchilan, the descent/decapitation and the awakening/appearing event were one time*less* happening.

The authors of the *Popol Vuh* devoted the last section of Part Three to this miraculous dance of resurrection. Here, the dreamlike quality of the text blossoms fully into the breathtaking finale of First Lord/First Jaguar's triumph over death. The dance begins after they've taken on the identity of traveling magicians. This strange dance includes fantastic feats such as burning houses and instantly restoring them, and sacrificing and resurrecting each other.

The news of these incredible magicians who can turn death into life reaches the Lords of Xibalba, who beg the Twins to come to the palace and perform for them. One Death demands that they sacrifice his dog and bring it back to life, which they do. Then he commands them to burn his house and restore it. They do this as well.

> And then they were asked by the lord:
> "You have yet to kill a person! Make a sacrifice without death!" they were told.
> "Very well," they said.
> And then they took hold of a human sacrifice.
> And they held up a human heart on high.
> And they showed its roundness to the lords.
> And now One and Seven Death admired it, and now that person was brought right back to life. His heart was overjoyed when he came back to life, and the lords were amazed:
> "Sacrifice yet again, even do it to yourselves! Let's see it! At heart, that's the dance we really want from you," the lords said now.

"Very well, lord," they replied, and then they sacrificed themselves. . . . So now, only one of them was dancing here: Xbalanque.

"Get up!" he said, and Hunahpu came back to life.

The Lords of Death were beside themselves. They entered the dark ecstasy of the death state.

And then the hearts of the lords were filled with longing, with yearning for the dance of Hunahpu and Xbalanque, so then came these words from One and Seven Death:

"Do it to us! Sacrifice us!" they said. "Sacrifice both of us!" said One and Seven Death. . . .

"Very well. You ought to come back to life. After all, aren't you Death?" . . .

And this one was the first to be sacrificed: the lord at the very top, the one whose name is One Death, the ruler of Xibalba.

And with One Death dead, the next to be taken was Seven Death. They did not come back to life. . . .

As soon as they had killed the one lord without bringing him back to life, the other lord had been meek and tearful before the dancers. He didn't consent, he didn't accept it. . . .

Such was the defeat of the rulers of Xibalba. The boys accomplished it . . . through self-transformation.

Then the Twin Gods revealed their true identities to the trembling demons and pronounced their judgment upon them.

"All of you listen, you Xibalbans: because of this, your day and your descendants will not be great. . . ."

Such was the beginning of their disappearance and the denial of their worship. . . . Such was the loss of their greatness and brilliance. Their domain did not return to greatness.

And so, the Twin Gods completed the defeat of death through their magical dance of death and resurrection, and, as the text says, "through self-transformation." First Lord and First Jaguar had made the world as safe as possible for the dawning of the human era.

There is a dramatic difference between the idea of resurrection and a belief in the soul's immortality. Resurrection—"raising up again"—means that something has truly died and then been brought back to life. Immortality, on the other hand, assumes the unbroken continuity of the soul's existence after the death of the body.

The ancient Greeks and Romans were horrified by a number of early Christian teachings, but none more so than the Church's belief in the literal resurrection of the physical body. The idea that the eternal life of the soul was dependent on the revival of the decayed corpse was deeply repulsive to Hellenistic spiritual traditions. For thoughtful Jews and Christians, like Saint Paul, the doctrine of physical resurrection was equally abhorrent. It seemed to deny their own belief, inherited from more ancient religions, that a "divine spark"—the *Imago Dei*—dwelled at the core of every soul. Certainly, this divine spark could not die. The idea that its continued existence was somehow dependent on the perishable body was unthinkable. According to the Greeks and Romans and the less literal-minded Jews and Christians, this divine spark returned to God at the very moment of death.

These more thoughtful Greeks, Romans, Jews, and Christians were not alone in their belief in the immortality of the soul. Most religions have affirmed the uninterrupted continuation of the divine life of the human soul. Most modern Christians, while officially subscribing to the doctrine of physical resurrection, seem instead to believe in the soul's immortality.

The ancient Egyptians had a more complicated view. They believed that a part of the many-layered soul was immortal, while another part of it—the part that was bound to the body—had to be resurrected in the tomb through magical incantations and the ritual opening of the eyes, ears, and mouth of the mummy.

The ancient Maya belief, similar in its multidimensional perspective to that of the Egyptians, was even more subtle. On one level, eternal soul-death for those who had failed to develop a durable Resurrection Body was real. In addition, self-sacrificial death meant a leap into the Void in which the individual personality was seemingly obliterated. But since *personal* survival was the goal for the Maya shamans, this destruction of the ego had to be followed by some kind of resurrection.

On another level, even those, like First Father, who were defeated by death possessed an indestructible *ch'ulel*-charged core—a corn kernel/Singing Skull—that would germinate and send up its World Tree/ Vision Serpent/sprout. Their son aspects, as in the scene on the tripod plate, would manifest from their enraptured imaginings and make a second descent into the Underworld to save them. Also, because all human souls were manifestations of the Divine Being's vision, immortality of *some* kind was assured for everyone—even those lost to eternal death.

How did the ancient shamans reconcile these apparently conflicting ideas about eternal death, the necessary resurrection of the personal aspect of the soul, and the soul's core—and foreordained—immortality? As we've seen, the Maya shamans may have believed in something similar to Paul Tillich's doctrine of "essentialization." In this teaching, Tillich tries to reconcile the idea of a loving God with the doctrine of eternal reward in heaven and eternal punishment in hell. Tillich says:

> A solution of this conflict must combine the absolute seriousness of the threat to "lose one's life" with the relativity of finite existence. The . . . symbol of "essentialization" is capable of fulfilling this postulate, for it emphasizes the despair of having wasted one's potentialities yet also assures the elevation of the positive within existence (even in the most unfulfilled life) into eternity.

He goes on to say that:

> This [essentialization] finally answers the question of the meaning of distorted forms of life—forms which, because of physical, biological, psychological, or sociological conditions, are unable to reach a fulfillment of their essential *telos* even to a small degree, as in the case of premature destruction, the death of infants, biological and psychological disease, morally and Spiritually destructive environments. . . . Whoever condemns anyone to eternal death condemns himself, because his essence and that of the other cannot be absolutely separated.

Based on the Jewish belief in a storehouse of virtue and on the Christian idea of the communion of saints, Tillich's doctrine of essentialization says that because the individual soul shares an underlying soul-substance—an essence—with all other individuals, no matter how unfulfilled one's personal life has been, this core essence is saved and lifted into the eternal life of God. The weak and underdeveloped are redeemed by the strong.

The Maya put forward this same idea in their descent myths in which the more spiritually mature Twin Gods save their father. For Tillich and the Maya shamans, then, no matter how unintelligent, unwise, uncreative, immature, fearful, or timid our lives have been, a core part of us lives on. But even with this reassurance, we might ask ourselves just how much of this saved part of us is really *us*—our individual personalities, our unique awarenesses.

There is another solution to the problem of unfulfilled earthly lives, a solution that maintains the seriousness of the soul's failures while at the same time holding out the promise of eventual fullness of Being. That solution is reincarnation.

The ancient Maya hieroglyphic inscriptions and iconography hint that the shamans may have carried this doctrine from their Asian homeland into the New World. In the *Popol Vuh,* First Father affirms his continued existence in his sons, and a Classic Period expression for "descendant" was "replacement." By calling a dead king's heir his "replacement"—his re-place-ment or "placing again"—were the *ah tz'ibob* merely saying that children share the same soul-essence with their parents? Or were they hinting at something more?

We know that the Maya expected to be reborn through the 01 Portal in the northern sky. The Divine Being Itself lived in the Overworld-Otherworld on the other side of this supernatural gash in the fabric of space-time. The topmost branches of the World Tree flowered into *sak-nik-nal* souls in the eternal now beyond this "Heart of Heaven"; and it was through the 01 Portal that these fledgling souls fell onto the earth plane to be born in mortal women. Significantly, Vision Serpents, whose gaping jaws sometimes represent the opening of this portal of rebirth, disgorge both the spirits of the ancestral dead and newborn babies.

The pyramid-tombs of the shaman-kings and nobles were often oriented toward the north, and aligned, as at Palenque, to be activated magically by movements of the stars in that area of the night sky. At Tikal and other cities most of the royal burials are located in the northern quadrant of the acropolises. And the dead were buried with their heads—the source of their divine sight, their intelligence and ecstatic visioning—pointing north toward the 01 Portal. Were the shamans who designed this resurrection machinery positioning the temple-tombs, and the bodies they concealed, simply to make rebirth into the Otherworld easier? Or did they have something else in mind?

There are other clues. As we've seen, according to the *Popol Vuh,* the universe had been sacrificed and re-created three times. The fact that it evolved each time, and that with each new creation the human soul became more complicated, richer, and more godlike, seems to imply a reincarnation-like process—at least on the collective level. Since the individual soul was a fractal version of the universe, and since the universe was ultimately within the soul, the shamans' myth of a recycled cosmos may have hidden a secret teaching about personal reincarnation as well.

The fact is, we don't know if the shaman-kings and others expected to reenter the flesh and dwell in human bodies again or not. But even if they did, it's clear that final liberation and release into a blissful eternal life was their ultimate goal. Reaching paradise was the fulfillment of the this-worldly process of recovering the soul's divine sight and realizing its godlike potential.

The *Popol Vuh* itself says nothing about the Overworld-Otherworld paradise. But from the evidence that has survived from the Classic Period, it seems certain that the most important of the Overworld-Otherworld places to which deified souls journeyed after death was Metawil, the home of First Father, First Mother, and their three sons. Perhaps Metawil, often shown as a giant conch or snail shell enclosing a mysterious alternate reality, was the infinite and eternal ocean of Otherworldly bliss itself, of which the bloody waters of Xibalba were the Underworld expression—the miraculous sea on which Chan-Bahlum and Lady Ahpo-Hel performed the final act of the soul's transfiguration. The image of Chan-Bahlum dancing his toe-heel celebration of eternal life across the surface of this Otherworldly sea, forever reaching out to his mother/First Mother within the Metawil shell—and she rising to empower him with divine ecstasy—lingers in the mind's eye—a vision of destiny fulfilled.

In all cultures, including our own, many of the dying talk about going "Home" or going on a great "voyage." They use these words without any prompting and usually without a trace of exaggerated sentimentality. They apparently believe that their deaths will launch them onto a voyage of spiritual adventure that will finally take them "Home." They don't seem to be thinking of their childhood homes. They seem to be talking about something deeper. They seem to know that earth is not where they came from; and the "Home" they want to return to cannot be found here.

Long before the great voyage seems imminent or the yearning for Home becomes an all-consuming passion, we can feel when something shifts within us and we move into a different—and more intensely alive—time and space. Whenever we feel deep fulfillment and joy, satisfaction with the results of hard work, hope, release, freedom, and peace, we are already experiencing that realm of fuller Being above, below, and behind this world of shadows and illusions. The ancient Greek philosopher Plato, and the medieval troubadours, added being in love to this list of the earthly signs of approaching paradise. Jung said that feelings of wholeness and centeredness, and the satisfaction of integrating our darker impulses with our "ego ideals," and our male with our female aspects, are signs that the soul has already encountered its eternal core. Other psychologists believe that feelings of "groundedness" and "consolidation" are symptoms of the soul's growing "integrity" and authenticity.

In the teachings of the ancient Maya, these feelings are all expressions of godlike ecstatic consciousness. In this ecstatic state, the soul transcends the beautiful terror of the opposites in earthly life and really does go Home. That Home, always and ultimately within the cosmos-embracing soul itself, is its final oneness with the Divine Being in all Its dark and bright splendor.

If the resurrection teachings of the Maya shamans about the nature of God and the created world are fundamentally right, and the real purpose of our earthly lives is to grow ourselves into godlike beings of power and terrible beauty, the third descent we all must make—into the world and into Xibalba—must have a meaning far deeper than mere pleasure or pain. Perhaps if we directed all our energies toward winning life's victory over death for ourselves, others, and the world as a whole, we really could ascend into a dimension of eternal light, taking the cosmos with us. Perhaps we could make our lives—here and now—dances of creation on the surface of an infinite, ever-living Sea. If we could experience our lives in this way, perhaps then we could become the gods we were meant to be.

Epilogue

The Post-Classic Period Maya built one of their last great ritual centers at a place called Tulum—"City of Dawn"—on the east coast of the Yucatan peninsula, about two hours' drive south of modern Cancun. It's one of my favorite places, one I go to frequently to meditate, to reflect, and commune with the gods that have shaped my life.

Tulum is a kind of wonderland built, according to the Maya myths, at the boundary between this world and the next, at the very edge of the earthly manifestation of the Cosmic Turtle Shell/"First True Mountain," where the created world ends and the infinite Otherworld ocean begins. Here the Maya soul found release into a realm of eternal light and danced on the surface of the infinite sea of origin and destiny.

I often sit on the rocks below the strangely constructed temples whose sides flare as they rise into a cloudless blue sky. In the dusty sanctuaries where once the shamans dreamed their dreams and made spirit journeys to other dimensions of reality where the gods and demons dwelled in vividness and passion, lizards and scorpions now make their homes. All about the sun-baked ruins, on the shimmering grass and glaring rocks, iguanas sun, and in the red-flowering bushes and the high palms birds exult in the fresh air.

In the distance, in the silence and peace that wraps itself around

A view of the Castillo at Tulum.

the ruins, I can hear the soft wailing of the clay flutes the vendors sell. I feel the deep calm of the holiness of the earth and the sky and all that is within them, and all that is beyond them.

A powerful Presence haunts this place. It feels somehow beyond our categories of pain and pleasure, beyond our moral codes—though not indifferent to them. It feels like a vast, exuberant Thing that thinks through us, feels through us, and lives through us—Something that sometimes turns around to see Itself reflected in our eyes.

It feels like some kind of force field that calls us up from the earth through the wetness of our parents' passion, and finally calls us back down and through the earth, to some mysterious and wondrous Else-where and Elsewhen.

The world seems alive to me here. It occurs to me how much we've lost by flattening our experiences of it and banishing the gods that made it matter. I wonder, when we flatten the world, where do we find joy, the kind of joy that leads to "eucatastrophe"?

Emersed in the living Presence that infuses this magic place of sun-light and phosphorescent waves, I resolve to live my life passionately, as if every moment held an infinitely precious meaning, as if every day were a Divine Being thundering across the sky. In such moments I feel fearless.

I can grasp the fact that I am going to die no matter what I do, so there is nothing I need to be afraid of about reaching out—now—for the things I want, the things that give me pleasure and creative fulfillment, the things that cause me to feel alive, that bring me a sense of the fullness of Being.

Something else occurs to me here, as I gaze at the white sand beach, the wind-tattered palms, the translucent waves with the sprigs of uprooted waterplants dancing on the white froth. At least for me, if there is no God of grace—of resurrection, of eucatastrophe, of triumphant life—to whom my soul can finally connect, all the spiritual practices and all the "soul-work" in the world mean nothing and lead nowhere. I have rediscovered a God of grace in my sojourns with the Maya. And I *believe* I will live again—and forever.

An ocean breeze stirs the palms. An iguana slides clumsily off its rock, lands with a soft thump, and begins shuffling through the tall grass. I hear Indian flutes wailing in the stillness of the sacredness of Being.

FAMILY TREE O

OVERWORLD AND EARTH PLANE GODS

THE WITZ MONSTER

THE CAUAC MONSTER

THE WATERLILY MONSTER

THE COSMIC TURTLE,
"FIRST TRUE MOUNTAIN,"
THE SINGING SKULL,
THE CORN KERNEL

ITZAM-NA

The Water Wizard, the Cosmic Shaman, one of the *itz'a-tob,* or "Sky Artists"
(Itzam-na may be an aspect of First Father, or First Father may be an aspect of him. In addition, Itzam-na certainly has associations with the Monkey Scribe-Artisans, and may be their "father.")

(All of the above are almost
certainly aspects of First Father.)

UNDERWORLD DEMONS

It's important to remember that the Overworld and Underworld deities are mirror reflections of each other and ultimately express the light and dark sides of a single Divine Being. All the gods and goddesses, and the demons, are kaleidoscopic images of The Holy Thing. As such, their characteristics blend and merge. In the end, no family tree of the Maya gods is fully descriptive of the actual situation in Maya Mythology.

HE MAYA GODS

THE CREATOR COUPLE

FIRST FATHER

"Raised-up-Sky-Lord," Hun-Nal-Yeh:
"First-Tree-Precious," one of the
itz'atob or "Sky Artists," One
Hunahpu

FIRST MOTHER

Ix-Chel (Goddess of the Moon),
"The Painter-in-Red,"
Xbanquiyalo

THE TWIN GODS

THE MONKEY
SCRIBE-ARTISANS

FIRST LORD   FIRST JAGUAR   K'AWIL

Venus   Sun
(together, the Cosmic Monster)

the Paddler Gods

Hunahpu   Xbalanque

GOD L

One/Seven Death

Demon Zero, House Corner,
Blood Gatherer, Pus Master,
Jaundice Master, Bone Scepter,
Skull Scepter, Trash Master, Stab
Master, Wing, Packstrap

UNDERWORLD DEMONS ON
THE SIDE OF LIFE

Blood Woman, Xulu,
Pacam, the Monster-Owls

GLOSSARY OF MAYA
AND OTHER INDIGENOUS
NAMES AND WORDS

Acasaguastlan: A town in Guatemala famous for its ancient Maya ceramics.

ahau: "Lord," an ancient Maya term for shaman-kings and other nobles.

ah tz'ib: "He of the writing," the ancient Maya word for scribe or sage.

ak'bal: "Darkness," a symbol for the Underworld.

Baknal-Chac: A king of the ancient Maya city of Tonina. He built the ballcourt where scholars discovered the image of Six-Sky-Smoke and the central icon of the human soul.

baktun: The ancient Maya cycle of four hundred years.

Balam-U-Xib: "Jaguar-Moon-Lord," a title for the Twin God First Jaguar in his moon aspect.

Balamcanchen: A town in the Yucatan peninsula.

balche: A fermented drink made in part from the bark of the balche tree and used by the ancient Maya to induce trance states.

Bonampak: An ancient Maya city in the Peten (the Classic Period cultural heartland) famous for its murals.

Cacula Huracan: "Lightning One-Leg," the *Popol Vuh* equivalent of the Classic Period god K'awil.

Campeche: A modern Mexican state on the west coast of the Yucatan peninsula.

cauac: "Lightning," for the ancient Maya, a powerful form of creation and enlightenment-engendering divine force, or *ch'ulel.*

Cauac Monster: An ancient Maya representation of this lightning force as embodied in stone. The Cauac Monster was usually shown as a severed skull with a split forehead from which corn plants rise.

cenote: A natural well formed when the limestone surface of the Yucatan peninsula collapses to reveal an underlying river, spring, or lake.

Chaan Muan: A king of the ancient Maya city of Bonampak whose military exploits are depicted in the Bonampak murals.

chacob: The four manifestations of Chac-Xib-Chac—gods of rain, fertility, and human sacrifice. Also the name for the four priestly assistants who held down the arms and legs of sacrificial victims during the heart sacrifice.

Chac-Xib-Chac: The Venus aspect of First Lord, one of the Twin Gods of ancient Maya mythology. Chac-Xib-Chac was the god of rain, fertility, and human sacrifice, and he was the god most responsible (as an aspect of First Father) for the resurrection of the universe and of individual human souls.

ch'akba: "Self-decapitation," one of the most awesome concepts in ancient Maya mythology—the idea that voluntary self-sacrificial death by gods and human beings creates the miracle of rebirth and resurrection.

Chan-Bahlum: The oldest son and first heir of King Pacal of Palenque. He is famous in part for his dance of resurrection as depicted on a carved panel from Temple fourteen.

ch'ay: "Lost energy," "diminished," "expired"—in other words, "died." It was the deciphering of this mysterious hieroglyph that allowed researchers their first glimpse into the nature and fate of the human soul as the ancient Maya envisioned them.

Chiapas: A modern Mexican state in which a number of important ancient Maya cities were located, including Palenque, Bonampak, and Tonina.

Chi-Chaan: The "deer-horned dragon"—a god-demon and an aspect of the Cosmic Vision Serpent.

Chichen Itza: An ancient Maya city in the northern Yucatan peninsula, and the center of a Post-Classic Period empire, famous for its sacred cenote, or "well of sacrifice."

chicle: A rubbery substance taken from the sapodilla tree, used for chewing and for making the rubber balls of the ballgames.

Chilam Balam: "The Jaguar Prophet," a heavily Christianized Colonial Period collection of Maya prophecies. A number of these Jaguar Prophet collections exist.

ch'ul ahau: "Lord of Life," a term both for gods and the ancient Maya shaman-kings. By extension, all "authentic human beings" could become *ch'ul ahauob.*

ch'ulel: "Life force," "life-essence"—the divine energy that created and continually renewed the cosmos and animated the soul.

cizin: "Terrible odor," "fart," also "demon."

Coba: A vast ancient Maya city near the east coast of the Yucatan peninsula, still largely unexplored.

Copan: The easternmost city of the ancient Maya, located in the jungled mountains of western Honduras.

Dzibilchaltun: An ancient Maya city in the northern Yucatan peninsula, famous for its so-called Temple of the Seven Dolls.

hal/ahal: "To wake up," "to dawn," "to appear," "to conquer," "to create." This mysterious hieroglyph, found on the Yaxchilan "stairs of death," and related to the *ah* Knot-Skull glyph and the mythological idea of three descents into the Underworld, shows the profound mystery by which the ancient Maya believed self-sacrificial death resulted in conquest and the dawning and appearing of new life and a regenerated cosmos.

halach uinic: "Authentic human being." This term usually referred to the sacred shaman-king. But it may be related to the Aztec concept of the "real" or "rooted" person, every person who had achieved a "face and heart." If so, Maya *halach uinicob,* like their Aztec counterparts, were human beings who had "rooted themselves in God" through ecstatic experience and achieved the divine identity intended for them by the Supreme Being.

Hasaw-Ka'an-K'awil: A king of ancient Tikal, famous for his depiction as a conquering lord seated on his battle palanquin decorated with a huge image of First Jaguar as his *uay*-protector.

hom: "Abyss," the Abyss of the Underworld, related in the Maya imagination to all holes and clefts in the surface of the earth. The ballcourts were constructed to reproduce this sacred entrance into the "Place of Fright" below.

Huehuetenango: A town in Guatemala famous for its ancient Maya ceramics.

huipil: A Maya blouse, usually ornately decorated.

Hun Ahau: "One Lord" or "First Lord"—the eldest son of First Father and one of the Twin Gods. Hun Ahau was associated with the planet Venus.

Hunahpu: The *Popol Vuh* name for First Lord or Hun Ahau.

Hun-Nal-Yeh: "One Maize Revealed"—the Cosmic Corn Plant, an aspect of the World Tree and a title for First Father after his resurrection.

itz: "Sacred substance"—all sticky, slippery substances like saps and resins, but especially blood. In ancient Maya mythology, *itz* was the carrier of *ch'ulel,* divine soul-essence.

Itzam-na: The "Water Wizard," Lord of the Underworld ocean, leader of the creator gods, and the Cosmic Shaman through whose visions all things came into being. First Father may have been a manifestation of Itzam-na, or vice versa. Itzam-na's Underworld aspect may be the so-called God L/"One," or "First," "Death." During the Colonial Period Itzam-na took on the characteristics of all the gods and goddesses and became identified with Hunab-K'u, the Supreme Being.

itz'at: "Artist" or "sky artist." In ancient Maya mythology several gods, called *itz'atob,* began the creation by painting cosmos-orienting markers on the sky, especially the three stones of the Cosmic Hearth.

Ix-Chebel-Yax: "The Painter-in-Red," an aspect of First Mother in her "sky artist" form. She apparently painted the earth, various plants, and other red things with her sacred menstrual blood.

Ix-Chel: The ancient Maya goddess of the moon and an aspect of First Mother. Ix-Chel was often depicted in two contrasting forms—either as an elegant lady weaving the universe on her magic loom or as a promiscuous temptress.

Izapa: An ancient proto-Maya city on the Pacific coast of Chiapas in modern Mexico.

Jaina: An island off the western coast of the Yucatan peninsula used by the ancient Maya as a burial ground. Many exquisite statuettes from the Classic Period have been recovered from the graves on Jaina.

Kalak'mul: An ancient Maya city in the modern Mexican state of Campeche.

K'an-Hok-Chitam: A king of ancient Palenque.

Kanxoc: A modern Maya town in the Yucatan peninsula.

katun: A sacred twenty-year cycle of time in ancient Maya mythology.

K'awil: The third son of First Father and First Mother. K'awil was the ancient Maya god of materialization, manifestation, energy transformation, and enlightenment. His own "third eye" opened by a lightning strike to the head, he used his lightning-serpent leg to break the foreheads of shamans and bring them enlightenment and personal transformation.

k'in: "Sun" or "day."

k'in ahau: "Sun Lord," a title of the ancient Maya kings, one that identified them with First Jaguar.

K'in Chaac: A famous Maya artist who signed several significant monuments throughout the Usumacinta River valley.

kunil: "Bewitching place" or "dreaming place," a title for the private chapels of the ancient Maya kings and shamans in which they believed they transformed themselves into their animal familiars.

Kunkunul: A modern Maya town in the Yucatan peninsula.

Mac Chaanal: An ancient Maya scribe-chieftain of the city of Copan.

Metawil: The Otherworldly paradise of First Father, First Mother, and their three sons—the Twin Gods and K'awil. Metawil was depicted inside a cosmic conch shell. It may have been identified with the primordial ocean that surrounded all the dimensions of reality.

Muan-bird: The Underworld aspect of the Principal Bird Deity, often shown perched on the head of God L, king of the Underworld.

Naranjo: An ancient Maya city in the southern Yucatan peninsula.

Oaxaca: A state in modern Mexico, in ancient times the area in which the Zapoteca and Mixteca cultures flourished.

ox ahal: "The third decapitation/descent." Found in an inscription on King Bird-Jaguar's "stairs of death" at Yaxchilan, this term seems to refer to the deaths and hoped-for resurrections of sacrificial victims. Apparently these victims were sent on their *ox ahalob* at the conclusion of ritual ballgames.

Pacal: The most famous, and perhaps the greatest, of the kings of Palenque. It was Pacal's tomb that the Mexican archaeologist Alberto Ruz Lhuillier discovered in the Temple of Inscriptions at Palenque.

Pacam: One of the two Underworld shamans who assisted in the resurrection of the Twin Gods as portrayed in the *Popol Vuh.*

Peten: The region in northern Guatemala that lies between the Usumacinta River valley to the northwest, the Yucatan peninsula to the north, and the mountains of western Honduras to the east. The Peten region was the ancient heartland of Maya civilization.

pib na: "Underground house"—a term for the chapels of the ancient Maya shaman-kings in which they believed they made spirit-journeys into the Underworld-Otherworld.

pitz: "Ballgame"—the sacred game that dramatized the cosmic struggle between the forces of life and death in ancient Maya mythology.

pitzlawal: "Ballplayer."

popol na: "Council house"—the building in ancient Maya cities in which the shaman-kings and their councils of nobles met to conduct governmental affairs and prepare for public rituals.

Popol Vuh: "The Book of Council"—the sacred text of the Colonial Period Quiche Maya. The *Popol Vuh* preserves many of the more ancient myths of the Maya in remarkably pristine form while, at the same time, introducing mythological and ritual elements of the Nahua peoples of central Mexico.

Quetzalcoatl: "The Feathered Serpent"—the ancient central Mexican god of storms, fertility, human sacrifice, and creation. Quetzalcoatl was the creator of the present cosmic era and of human beings. He may have had associations with the Cosmic Monster/Vision Serpent of Maya mythology.

Quiche: A Mexicanized Maya people who invaded parts of the Maya homeland in the Post-Classic Period. In the Colonial Period a group of Quiche shamans translated a surviving Maya codex into the written narrative now known as the *Popol Vuh.*

Quirigua: An ancient Maya city in southeastern Guatemala that was the principal rival of Copan in the Classic Period.

sacbe: "White road"—a type of raised road that connected ancient Maya temples and cities and that was used for religious, commercial, and military purposes.

sak-nik-nal: "White Flower Thing"—the ancient Maya term for the human soul.

Seibal: An ancient Maya city in the Peten heartland that shows evidence of having been invaded by Mexicanized Maya peoples in the late Classic Period.

Teotihuacan: The ancient Classic Period city of central Mexico that strongly influenced the development of Maya civilization, including the so-called Tlaloc/Venus form of warfare.

Tikal: An ancient Maya city in the southern Yucatan peninsula originally named Yax Balam for First Jaguar, the second of the Twin Gods. Tikal was the first great Maya city in the Maya heartland.

Tlaloc: The Rain-god of ancient central Mexico whose worship and ritual warfare influenced Maya spirituality and military methods.

Tonina: The southwesternmost ancient Maya city of any importance, famous for its Stucco Wall and the ballcourt marker depicting Six-Sky-Smoke in the Underworld grasping his divine soul in ecstatic trance.

Tulum: A Post-Classic Period Maya city on the east coast of the Yucatan peninsula.

tzompantli: "Skull-rack"—the sculpted stone monument on which the heads of sacrificial victims were impaled.

uay: "Animal familiar" or divine manifestation of a human being or a god. For the ancient Maya the *uayob* dwelled in the shadowy region between individual human identity and the deeper realm of the gods and demons.

u cha???ahal: "The second decapitation/descent"—almost certainly a reference to the death/descent of the Twin Gods into the Underworld to defeat death and resurrect First Father. This phrase is the second element in the Yaxchilan myth of the three descents as recorded on King Bird-Jaguar's "stairs of death."

U-Cit-Tok: The king of Copan at the moment of its collapse.

uich: "Face," an ancient Mesoamerican term that signified both the physical face and what we might call the "ego-personality" or the "persona."

uinal: "Month." In the ancient Maya calendar the *uinalob* consisted of twenty days each and corresponded to the number of human fingers and toes. As such, the *uinalob* were called "human beings."

uinic: "Human being."

u k'ul: "It is the Holy Thing," an ancient Maya phrase that indicates the reader is in the presence of a god.

u na???ahal: "The first decapitation/descent." From King Bird-Jaguar's "stairs of death" at Yaxchilan, this phrase almost certainly refers to First Father's death/descent into the Underworld.

Usumacinta: The great river of the southwestern Yucatan peninsula that flows northward into the Gulf of Mexico, and along whose banks and in whose drainage system many powerful Classic Period Maya cities flourished, among them Bonampak, Yaxchilan, Piedras Negras, and Seibal.

Uxmal: An ancient Maya city in the Puuc Hills of the northern Yucatan peninsula, important in the Post-Classic Period and famous for its elegant architecture.

Waxaklahun-Ubah-Kan: The Vision Serpent in its war manifestation.

Xbalanque: The *Popol Vuh* name for the second of the ancient Maya Twin Gods, and the equivalent of the Classic Period First Jaguar.

Xbanquiyalo: An aspect of First Mother. As recorded in the *Popol Vuh,* the wife of First Father as One Hunahpu.

Xibalba: "The Place of Fright"—the ancient Maya name for the Underworld.

Xibal Be: "The Road of Awe"—the Milky Way road to the Underworld in ancient Maya mythology.

Xmucane: In the *Popol Vuh,* a manifestation of First Mother, the mother of One Hunahpu.

Xulu: With Pacam, one of the Underworld sorcerers in the *Popol Vuh* who is on the side of life, and who helps the Twin Gods achieve their resurrection.

Yax Balam: "First Jaguar," the second of the Twin Gods, and the *uay* of First Lord.

Yaxchilan: An ancient Maya city in northern Guatemala, famous for its magnificent sculpted panels and its important mythological images and theological formulations.

Yaxha: An ancient Maya city in the Peten heartland of Guatemala.

Yax Pac: The last important king of Copan.

Yucatan: The limestone-based peninsula that thrusts northward between Mexico and Central America and separates the Gulf of Mexico from the Caribbean Sea. With Chiapas, Guatemala, western Honduras, and El Salvador, it is the area in which the Maya civilization flourished. Yucatan is also the name of a state in modern Mexico.

Zapotecas: An indigenous people of southern Mexico who created one of the earliest civilized kingdoms in what is now Oaxaca. The Zapotecas may also have been the inventors of the first fully developed hieroglyphic system of writing in the Americas.

NOTES

This Notes section embodies an increasingly used format designed to make chapter notes more accessible to the reader. It avoids chapter note numbers altogether, minimizes citations, and focuses primarily on additional comments and discussions that, had they been included in the main body of the book, would have broken the flow of the text. I have provided an extensive Bibliography for those readers who would like to check references or investigate a particular area in greater depth.

INTRODUCTION

The quote is from John Lloyd Stephens's *Incidents of Travel in Central America, Chiapas, and Yucatan,* the Smithsonian Institution Press edition (1993), page 39.

When I say that many of us need to reenchant the world with a sense of "unutterable force and beauty," I don't mean that we should turn our backs on five hundred years of science, as religious fundamentalists often do. I mean that we would be better off, emotionally and spiritually, if we could move *forward* to what social commentators have called the "postmodern" perspective. Basically, the postmodern experience of ourselves and the world allows us to celebrate the triumphs of the rational mind while at the same time resensitize ourselves to the eerie, inexplicable, and mysterious quality of the universe and our own lives. The postmodern experience rekindles our sense of childlike wonder, a wonder that as cosmology and subatomic physics have shown, is based on a more realistic assessment of the true nature of things than a Newtonian worldview permits. The sense of divine Presence inherent in the experience of wonder immediately and automatically satisfies our hunger for meaning.

1. REDISCOVERING A LOST WORLD

Bringing the Otherworld into our earthly lives is the purpose of all forms of meditation—whether Hindu mantras, Buddhist koans, Taoist breathing exercises, Jewish and Sufi Moslem chanting, Christian revival meetings, or shamanic drug rituals. The goal of these and other practices for achieving altered states of consciousness is to help the soul grasp—or be grasped by—its eternal destiny.

I quote Alberto Ruz Lhuillier's account of his discovery of the tomb of Pacal from the National Geographic Society's book *The Mysterious Maya* (1977), pages 74–75.

What we now know about the institution of Maya kingship—its shamanic role and its coincidence with the founding of Maya civilization—fits the nearly universal pattern of divine or sacred kingships from around the world—from the ancient Egyptian pharaohs to the sage-emperors of China.

How different would our experience of art be if we viewed art objects as concretizations of the spiritual dimension, as ever-present reminders of our mortality, and as guides to the only thing that ultimately matters—living forever beyond the material forms of this world. How much more vivid would this, our true context, make our lives?

The idea that Pacal's sarcophagus is carved in the form of the Maya resurrection fish is my own. (I have subsequently learned that some scholars have come to the same conclusion.) The fact is, unlike ancient Egyptian sarcophagi and coffins, it does not trace the contours of the human body. Instead, it is carved as an elongated oval with a fish tail at the foot. The *Popol Vuh* says that when the Twin Gods rose from the dead in the river of the Underworld, they did so in the guise of channel catfish.

Some anthropologists now believe that the Australian aborigines crossed wide stretches of open ocean—from Southeast Asia to the sub-continent—perhaps as early as sixty thousand years ago. If they are right, it would mean that early *Homo sapiens* had considerable seafaring capabilities.

Amazingly, there is little evidence of materialistic goals in early Maya warfare. Instead, war seems to have been a largely spiritual enterprise—the enactment of the cosmic drama of life's triumph over death. This thoroughgoing religious perspective of the Maya may be hard for modern people to grasp, so accustomed are we to dividing our lives into mutually exclusive "sacred" and "secular" segments, or even eliminating the sacred altogether. The closest parallel to the Maya experience of spiritual warfare in the modern world is the Moslem *jihad* (holy war). Of course, there was some economic motivation for the Maya, in the sense that they believed that by sacrificing war captives they were ensuring the prosperity of their kingdoms. At the same time, they linked the flourishing of their local city-states to the continuing resurrection of the cosmos.

2. A Terrible Beauty

I quote Giorgio De Chirico (page 293) and Franz Marc (page 306) from Aniela Jaffé's "Symbolism in the Visual Arts" (*Man and His Symbols,* 1964).

Throughout this book, when I refer to or quote from the *Popol Vuh,* I'm using Dennis Tedlock's translation and commentary. He has made the *Popol Vuh* his specialty, and is continually updating his translation and interpretations in light of new information from Maya archaeology, linguistics, epigraphy, and anthropology.

In the world's spiritual traditions, "seeing" is always a metaphor for "consciousness" and "awareness." Plato (and later Saint Paul) talked about "seeing in a mirror darkly, but then face-to-face." Jesus used visual images to describe the coming of the Kingdom of God, and then said that the Kingdom is really within—a state of mind. Eastern religions speak of "en-lighten-ment"—the coming of light—and use the image of divine light as the supreme metaphor for God-consciousness.

While all religions teach that a tension exists between the forces of creation and destruction, life and death, and good and evil, it was the ancient Persian prophet Zoroaster (seventh century B.C.) who first proclaimed a belief in their irreconcilable opposition. Zoroastrian thought radically reshaped Jewish, late Hellenistic, and Roman thought, and, through them, the new religions of Christianity and Islam.

The Christian theologian Augustine, intuited that God, above all else, is Being (i.e., Reality) in Its infinitely full form. The religious scholar Huston Smith, paraphrasing Augustine, writes that "Being as being is good; more being is better." The Hindu sages teach that Brahma is more real than the appearances of the material universe. The Christian writer C. S. Lewis maintains that the main reason human beings fail to experience God is that they are not "real" enough to meet Him on His own infinitely vivid level. And the mystics of all religions claim that authentic spiritual experience reveals the really Real, by comparison with which the mundane world seems like a dream.

Many people use love and compassion to deny, or repress, their fierceness and the aggressive assertion of their own agendas. But, as modern psychology has realized, the shameless affirmation of our own needs and desires leads to consolidation of the personal identity. And strengthening the personal identity deepens, rather than negates, our capacity to love and feel compassion.

An account of the restoration of the Bonampak murals appears in *National Geographic* magazine, February 1995, pages 50–69.

3. A Living Cosmos

The great comparative religionist Mircea Eliade, as he did with so many other motifs in human spirituality, made the "eternal return" theme known to modern readers and showed the universality of the practice of making human actions conform to the primordial patterns the gods had instituted in the Dream Time.

We can tell that the magical head at the heart of the Underworld on the tripod plate is envisioning the entire scene because everything in the center of the plate is rising in sequential order from the cleft in the top of its skull—the resurrected First Father, then First Lord, the World Tree, and the life and death struggle between First Jaguar and Itzam-Yeh.

The idea that the figure with the conical head is First Father is my own. Most scholars interpret this being as an Underworld demon. In fact, as the *Popol Vuh* makes clear, one of First Father's aspects was indeed the king of the Underworld, First Death. In addition, my view of the plate as a unified depiction of the process of resurrection—both personal and cosmic—is confirmed by the claim of Mayanists themselves that offering plates like this one were designed to guide the departed soul to victory over the Lords of Death. Furthermore, in the absence of an alternative interpretation of the figure's belt with its three starlike ornaments, and in light of the fact that First Father was reborn through the crack in the

Cosmic Turtle Shell, believed by the Maya to be manifested by the three stars of Orion's belt, I have concluded that this Orion emergence of First Father is exactly what we are seeing depicted on the tripod plate.

I quote Ephesians 1:3–5 from *The Oxford Annotated Bible*, the Revised Standard Version (1962).

Whenever we see blood gushing from an open wound in Maya art we know that a bloodletting rite is being depicted. Scholars know that the function of bloodletting was always to bring on a state of altered consciousness, the ultimate purpose of which was the envisioning of a divine Reality that was continuously creating something from nothing.

It seems clear to me that First Jaguar is represented on the tripod plate as the *uay*, or animal familiar, of First Lord. First Lord was the first Maya king; and we know that the supreme animal manifestation of the *ahauob* was the jaguar. In fact, the hieroglyph for *uay* was a jaguar in the midst of ecstatic trance.

Mircea Eliade, and before him, Sir James Frazer, showed the universal significance of the World Tree in traditional spiritualities as the *axis mundi*, the central life-giving column of the world.

The insight that all vision serpents are aspects of a single Cosmic Vision Serpent, or that all mythological birds are instances of one Cosmic Bird, all virgins local manifestations of one Virgin, and so on, comes from the work of the comparative religionists. Carl Jung used this insight to develop his theory of archetypes.

The original source for the "God is a circle . . ." saying is the Hermetic teachings of the ancient Mediterranean area.

The ancient Maya use of architecture to amplify the "power points" in the surrounding landscape is dramatically illustrated by the artificial "mountain ranges" of Copan's acropolis.

The rending of the fabric of normal time and space by the conch-shell trumpet is illustrated by an incised Classic Period vase. On this vase we see a virtual explosion of Otherworld images carried from the spiritual dimension onto the earth plane by a surging Vision Serpent. Below the Vision Serpent, bending to get out of the way of this supernatural eruption, is a deer-eared figure blowing the conch-shell trumpet whose blast has summoned the vision.

Linda Schele, David Freidel, and other Mayanists have pioneered the application of astro-archaeology to ancient Maya architecture, epigraphy, and iconography with exciting results.

The quote is from Fritjof Capra's *The Tao of Physics* (1975), pages 242–243.

4. Blood and Ecstasy

I define the word "love" here, not in its romantic sense, but as that feeling and force that is willing to sacrifice everything to create life from death, and then nurture that life to its full potential. In this sense, the God of the ancient Maya demonstrated a fierce love for the world and human beings.

The smoke from the bloodletting fires can be thought of equally as spiritual substance materializing *and* as matter transforming into spirit. As usual in Maya thought, seeming opposites were experienced as complementary aspects of the same underlying reality.

The original sacrifice of Isaac is a fascinating idea—and probably correct. In-depth discussion of the theory appears in Patrick Tierney's *The Highest Altar* (1989), pages 369–376. Matthew 6:1 is taken from *The Oxford Annotated Bible*, cited above.

An example of the blood-lined placenta clouds in which gods were born onto the earth plane is a stela from Ixlu. Here a ruler conjures the Paddler gods and the spirits of dead Tlaloc warriors.

Bloodletting was the great preparation for grasping eternal life in several respects. First, it taught, in immediate and undeniable terms, that there really is no creation without pain. Second, through shock and the release of endorphins in the brain, along with the effects of mind-altering drugs, it opened everyday consciousness to dimensions of extraordinary Reality, that same Reality in which the soul—one way or another— would spend eternity. And third, bloodletting gave the soul practical experience of the Otherworld, and through this experience, enabled it to rehearse its defeat of the demons.

That committing atrocities puts the perpetrator in an altered state of consciousness is well documented by the confessions of serial killers, gang members, professional torturers, and those who, to this day, practice rituals of animal sacrifice.

The quote from al-Hallāj is from A. J. Arberry's *Sufism* (1950), page 60. Meister Eckhart's statement appears in Joseph Campbell's *Occidental Mythology* (1964), pages 511–512. The Abulafia quote is taken from Gershom Scholem's *Major Trends in Jewish Mysticism* (1961), page 140.

That the goal of much mystical practice is the extinguishing of the ego is clear from the literature. Evelyn Underhill's *Mysticism* (1911), Swami Nikhilananda's commentaries on the Hindu *Upanishads* (1977), A. J. Arberry's *Sufism*, cited above, and others explicitly enunciate this ideal. And yet, when read closely, what is usually being advocated is not the death of individual identity but its radical expansion.

Linda Schele and David Freidel have shown how Chan-Bahlum of Palenque (the son of Pacal) manipulated the Maya creation story to legitimize his claim to the throne. In the version of the creation story he had carved on the Temple of the Cross he ignored First Father and gave First Mother a greatly expanded role. Researchers believe that First Mother served as the divine archetype for Pacal's mother. Apparently, it was through her, rather than their father, that these men held the kingship.

5. THE CREATIONS OF THE LIGHTNING-SERPENT

An account of Ricardo Agurcia and William Fash's discovery appears in *National Geographic* magazine, September 1991, pages 94–105.

In *Maya Cosmos* (1993), David Freidel, Linda Schele, and Joy Parker provide a fascinating decoding of K'awil imagery (pages 193–202). I have taken their discussion further and linked the ancient (and modern) Maya experiences of life-to-death and death-to-life transformations with the shamans' teachings about enlightenment. In the process of researching this material I realized the striking parallel between K'awil's forehead-piercing torch/hallucinogenic cigar and the "third eye" of Eastern mysticism.

The quote from the Gnostic Gospel of Thomas can be found in a somewhat more pedestrian form in *The Other Bible* (1984), page 305. The D. H. Lawrence quote is from *D. H. Lawrence: Complete Poems* (1993), page 484.

Again, Mircea Eliade is the comparative religionist who has shown the universality of the idea that the cosmos is born from a central, life-engendering point.

The idea that monkeys are imperfect versions of human beings from an earlier creation appears in Part One of the *Popol Vuh*.

6. GOD

The-Holy-First-Father-Decapitated-Dead-Creating-Thing is my term. I use it to condense the complex death-resurrection mythology of the ancient Maya into a single concept and entity. In fact, when we unravel the various threads of this mythology and then tie them back together, something like my formulation presents itself in the original material. Furthermore, the principles I have used in creating this condensed image/dynamic are those routinely used in the field of comparative mythology and religion.

Mircea Eliade has shown that in ancient mythologies "a rose is a rose is a rose." In the case of the severed head icons of the Maya, I maintain (à la Eliade) that a head is a head is a head.

The quotes from Gnostic literature come from *The Nag Hammadi Library*, edited by James M. Robinson (1977), and include passages from the Gospel of Philip (page 132) and the Gospel of the Egyptians (page 197), among others. The translation of the *Bhagavad Gita* I use is that of the Bhaktivedanta Book Trust, *Bhagavad-Gita As It Is* (1968), pages 181–183. Ezekiel's vision can be found in Ezekiel, Chapters 1 and 2.

Joseph Campbell's lifelong work of integrating the insights of comparative religion and depth psychology is foundational to my own.

In his book, *The Idea of the Holy*, Rudolf Otto links the feelings of supernatural horror many of us have from time to time with the supreme spiritual experience of awe and wonder, what he calls the *mysterium tremendum*. The Otto quotations are from *The Idea of the Holy* (1982 edition), pages 18–19. I use *The Oxford Annotated Bible*, cited above, for Revelation 6:12–17.

The startling, and strangely ecological, idea that supposedly inanimate things are carriers of consciousness and can and do revolt against human misuse appears in Part One of the *Popol Vuh*.

First Mother as temptress appears in ceramic figurines from Jaina, an island off the western coast of the Yucatan peninsula in Mexico. The Maya used Jaina as a burial place and put these figurines in the graves of the departed. These figurines depict First Mother pressing her knee against the groins of old men as they cup her breasts with their withered hands.

The reference to Tolkien's use of the word "eucatastrophe" comes from his essay "On Fairy Stories" in *The Tolkien Reader* (1966), pages 68–73. The quote from the *Upanishads* comes from Joseph Campbell's *Creative Mythology* (1970), page 630. The Hermetic Tract quotation comes from E. R. Dodds's *Pagan and Christian in an Age of Anxiety* (1965), page 82. The Buddha's statement comes from his Surangama Sutra. It appears in Dwight Goddard's *A Buddhist Bible* (1966) on pages 135–136. I have taken the Buddha's summary comment from Huston Smith's *Forgotten Truth* (1976), page 60. The quote from Forrest Reid comes from Dodds's *Pagan and Christian*, cited above, pages 82–83.

It may seem strange to readers familiar with the idea that the soul wins immortality by extinguishing the ego, but, for the Maya as for the followers of Jung, eternal life was gained by acquiring a "face and heart"—a powerful individual identity—that, at the same time, experienced a culminating merger with God.

Most of us, thankfully, don't have multiple personalities. We all do, however, have many different moods, and even subpersonalities. How often have we been overcome by an emotion, and later said, "I don't know what came over me!" or "I wasn't myself yesterday"? Jung and Freud both believed they had discovered not only fragments of our individual personalities—like the "shadow" or the "anima" and "animus"— that live below the boundary between who we think we are and the rest of our souls; they also believed they had found, at an even deeper level, the archetypes of transpersonal structures and energies that picture themselves to us as our gods and myths.

The levels of the Maya soul as I've portrayed them are my idea. I believe my reading of Maya iconography is accurate, although it goes beyond even Schele and Freidel's work. My perspective is not only consistent with what we now know about ancient Maya beliefs, but it also places the Maya understanding of the soul in the broad context of world spirituality. In this worldwide context the soul almost always appears as a multileveled being.

The independent decodings of the *uay* hieroglyph were made by Nikolai Grube and Steve Houston in October 1989.

Probably the most primal religious feeling is awe and the sense of ecstatic union with the life force. It seems likely that animals experience these feelings as well, especially during sexual intercourse. It could also be that the so-called rain dance of chimpanzee males during thunderstorms, in which they "display" and shake branches at the threatening sky, is evidence of a kind of religious ritual.

The evidence for the ancient Maya belief in supernatural energy fields includes painted representations of Otherworld places and events, portal iconography, sacred architecture, and the placement of buildings and monuments to establish "power grids." In addition to this evidence, researchers now understand Maya spirituality—past and present—as shamanic in nature. The shamanic interpretation makes sense not only in terms of the physical evidence but also in the context of the Asiatic origins of Native American peoples.

In the "both/and" thinking of what, to my mind, are the most sophisticated theologians, the personal and transpersonal aspects of God are not mutually exclusive. As one of my seminary professors said, "To say that God is a force rather than a person is to make God *sub*human. If God is our Creator, He must be at least what we are."

We find a belief in the preexistence of the soul in such diverse sources as Jewish Kabbalistic thought, Plato, and the writings of the poet William Wordsworth.

In ancient Egyptian mythology, the soul is shown suckling from a paradisal Tree of Life whose branches offer breasts filled with celestial milk.

In reading Richard Wilhelm's translation of *The Secret of the Golden Flower* (1931) I was struck by the similarities between the Taoist and ancient Maya images of the transformed soul. I am also struck by the similarities between Saint Paul's "imperishable body" and the implications of Maya Resurrection Body iconography.

8. THE SHAMAN'S SECRET

I may be overstating the case when I compare the return of Maya souls to the earth plane via vision serpents with the bodhisattvas of Buddhism. But it is known that deified Maya ancestors were regularly summoned to help the living achieve their own victories over the forces of destruction and death.

David Freidel is the Mayanist most responsible for the insight that ancient Maya spirituality, art, and social structures were thoroughly shamanic in nature.

The *Popol Vuh* depicts the Monkey Scribe-Artisans with a strange ambivalence. At times they appear noble and gifted, the cream of Maya society. At other times they are pictured as petty, envious, and foolish. Perhaps this ambivalence toward the educated elite is not so different from that of our own culture.

We can guess what ancient Maya education was like from the material and intellectual remains of their civilization as well as from our detailed knowledge of the Aztec educational system. While including elements of scientific and technical education, the overall scheme was undoubtedly closer to our liberal arts regime. I often think that, more and more, our own educational system creates little more than technologically proficient cultural and spiritual barbarism.

The reverence for art outlasted both literacy and the institution of sacred kingship. To this day, Maya art, while far more limited than its Classic Period expressions, is still impressive.

For the ancient Maya, as for virtually all traditional peoples, the creation of art was part of an overall magical framework in which the cultural expressions of inspired human beings reorganized the "energy fields." Alfred North Whitehead's process philosophy is strikingly similar in its assertions about the influence of finite "occasions" on what he calls the "contingent nature of God." We ourselves try to alter the nature of human psychological and social reality through our attempts at social engineering. And when we reflect on the great events of history, we realize that very often the pen really *is* mightier than the sword.

When I say that, according to the Maya, uncreative souls were cut off from eternal life, I am stressing one level of ancient shamanic belief. It is also true that the sages believed that even those who fell to the ax of the Underworld demons could be saved, at least in part, by the life force that dwelled in the "corn kernel" center of their souls. The Maya reveal their struggle to resolve this seeming contradiction in their myths of First Father and the Twin Gods.

The Paul Tillich quotations come from his *Systematic Theology*: Vol. 3 (1963), pages 406 and 415.

Freidel, Schele, and Parker detail the astro-archaeological view of Palenque's Group of the Cross in *Maya Cosmos,* cited above, pages 144–146.

In the Maya world, cultural creations—whether painted ceramics, buildings, altars, or cooking utensils—had individual personality and consciousness. These things ritually "came into being," as the Maya said, and many were given personal names.

9. Death

When I say that death's most subtle strategy for destroying the soul is to get us to deny its reality, I mean that the denial of death leads us to live less than vigorous and creative lives. It has been my experience that, when the end comes, such lives are often filled with bitterness, fear, and regret. All the great spiritual traditions have taught us that the fullest lives are lived with the continual awareness that our days are numbered.

The Don Juan quotation is taken from Carlos Castaneda's *Journey to Ixtlan* (1974), pages 84–85.

In *Maya Cosmos,* cited above (pages 75–106), Freidel, Schele, and Parker demonstrate the multifaceted view of the Milky Way and the ecliptic held by the ancient Maya. When we realize that the Paddlers, the Canoe of Life, and the double-headed serpent/Cosmic Monster were all aspects of the Twin Gods, the symbolic richness of the Tikal bones and the eccentric flint becomes clear.

Ba'al was the ancient Canaanite god of fertility, civilization, and resurrected life. Tammuz was his Syrian counterpart. Osiris was the ancient Egyptian equivalent to these two, but embodied a more profound spiritual significance. Dionysus, in a more limited way, was also the bearer of resurrection and new life. All of these gods were dying-resurrecting saviors and creators of abundance on earth and eternal life beyond the grave. When viewed in this light, we see that Christianity drew on these more ancient resources in the formulation of its own Christ myth.

One can still see the ancient womb-tomb idea graphically portrayed in museum reproductions of the earliest Egyptian burials. In these burials, the body lies in a fetal position in a womb-shaped hollow in the sand. There is even evidence that similar burials were practiced by the now-extinct Neanderthals.

A discussion of the Yaxchilan three-descents poem appears in Schele and Freidel's "The Courts of Creation" from Vernon Scarborough and David Wilcox's *The Mesoamerican Ballgame* (1991), an anthology of articles about various themes in ballgame research.

According to Freud's theory of the "primal father" of the "primal horde," deep in the prehistoric past, when humankind existed as a single tribe, a great chieftain seized power and ruled with absolute authority. As an expression of his authority he claimed all the eligible women as his own, and forbade his sons to have sexual relations with them. Starved for sex and female companionship, the sons revolted, killed the father, and divided the women among themselves.

But there was a catch. Since there is a strong, instinctual prohibition against sons murdering their fathers, the sons were overwhelmed by feelings of guilt for their terrible deed. The father reappeared in their imaginations and haunted their guilty consciences. The sons kept the women they had won, but to assuage their guilt they resurrected the father into the spiritual world and made him a god.

From the perspective of modern psychology, not believing that we ourselves will die is a form of *hubris*—godlike pretension. The ancient Greek dramatists moralized about this form of arrogance in their tragedies. In all religions, the attempt by mortals to achieve divine invulnerability is followed by the gods' punishments. The *Popol Vuh* even applies this teaching to lesser divinities—the Monkey Scribe-Artisans and Seven Macaw and his sons.

10. THE TRIALS OF XIBALBA

The ancient Maya belief that human cruelty is a specialized form of natural cruelty finds confirmation in the study of chimpanzees and other primates. Chimpanzees show nearly all the forms of interpersonal cruelty human beings are capable of: child abuse, intimidation, rape, beatings, torture, and warfare.

That minor nobles may have turned to witchcraft as a means of economic gain and to intimidate others becomes probable in light of a similar development in Aztec society.

The Maya and other Mesoamerican peoples may have been aided in the practice of indifference toward suffering and cruelty by their characteristic emotional makeup, a makeup that may have been at least partly biological. In his extraordinary analysis of the conquest of Mexico, *Cortés* (1993), Richard Marks says that the Spanish were struck by how different Indian psychology was from their own. On pages 215–218 Marks writes:

> During . . . rare moments of repose the Spaniards were able to perceive that there was a great calm middle span in the emotional nature of the Indians, an unaffected calmness that had little counterpart in the Spanish make-up. . . . Yet the Spaniards had to wonder: How could the same human beings who created . . . beguiling, lassitudinous bliss be the ones who in the frenzy of their ceremonies tore the hearts from living victims and frolicked in human skins? Untold millennia of evolution had produced these two strains of human beings on different sides of the world unknown to each other. . . . The Spaniards were also aware of a dim, dull end in the emotional span of the Indians, an absence of resentment alien to the Spaniards and amounting almost to apathy. . . . Although puzzled, the Spaniards, as Christians, sensed that the structure of Indian society with its almost incomprehensible extremes was held to-

gether . . . by . . . a hypnosis of horror. Yet in the Indian's
very long, emotional middle span of patience and grace there
was hope for the future.

As understood by anthropologists and depth psychologists, the universal
idea of the "road of trials" is always a part of some form of initiatory
process by which the soul dies to its former life, passes through a physical and/or emotional crisis, and is finally released into a state of larger
and more complex Being.

The Maya belief that the soul has lived before in a heavenly paradise and then been called down to the earth plane to be tested finds a
powerful parallel in the poetry of the Aztecs. Also, the Aztec birthing ritual included an address by the midwife to the newborn baby that urged
it to remember its paradisal origins and, through the courageous conduct
of its earthly life, to seek to return to that blissful realm.

Because the *Popol Vuh* presents the House of Fire almost as an
afterthought and uses a different form for its name, the Maya specialist
Dennis Tedlock believes the original version of the manuscript depicted
only five torture houses, which, according to Tedlock, may have represented the five cycles of Chac-Xib-Chac/Venus celebrated throughout
the Maya area in ancient times. Even if this is true, the fact that the later
version of the text describes six houses and three ballgames may show
that at least by late Post-Classic Period times the shamans had synchro-
nized the number of tests with the *bolon-iplah*—"nine deaths" or "nine
strengths"—the nine hours of the night and their nine manifestations of
the Lord(s) of Death.

We don't know what the Classic Period scheme was, but it seems
probable that at least some of the Maya tortures from this epoch were
modeled on the trials later portrayed in the *Popol Vuh*. It could be that the
extended process of captive torture was patterned on the cycles of Venus
and/or on the "nine deaths" of the Underworld demons.

The Church fathers Irenaeus and Origen proposed the ransom theory of salvation that was later depicted as God fishing for Satan with
Christ as the bait. Joseph Campbell provides an illustration of a twelfth-
century version of this myth in his *Creative Mythology* (1968), page 18.

Some psychologists believe that the ego can partially restructure
the unconscious and change its attitudes and outlook. These psychologists recommend that their clients go back into their nightmares and en-
gineer a positive outcome.

The idea that if one can name the demon one can have power over it is an ancient and universal belief. Jesus named possessing demons in order to cast them out, and some exorcists use this technique to free their clients from diabolical forces even today. Similarly, in psychology, the "spell" of a neurotic complex is often broken when the client understands its origin and true intent—its "name" or nature.

The quote from Thomas Berry comes from a PBS miniseries broadcast a number of years ago. The particular episode was called *Beliefs: Soul.*

Jung believed that what we do not face about ourselves we will be forced to encounter or act out in the external world. He claimed that this is a much more destructive way of handling what he called "shadow" elements than working with them creatively within the psyche. The British psychiatrist Anthony Storr provides an insightful analysis of violence as the last resort of legitimate self-affirmation in his book *Human Destructiveness* (1991), pages 3–33.

11. THE BALLGAME AND HUMAN SACRIFICE

Some evidence exists that there may occasionally have been more than one or two ballplayers per team.

In his commentary on the *Popol Vuh,* Dennis Tedlock discusses the symbolism of "dawning and rebirth." The rabbit as a substitute ball is pictured in Classic Period art and hints at a now only partly understood rabbit-in-the-moon myth. In Classic Period art, the Moon-goddess—Ix-Chel—is often shown sitting on a crescent moon cradling a rabbit in her arms. The rabbit is a symbol of her sexual unfaithfulness and her tricksterishness. The queens who opened the ballgames at Yaxchilan may have been thought of as incarnations of Ix-Chel. If so, the rabbit-as-ball may have been their Moon-goddess *uayob* playing the decoy role of the rabbit in the *Popol Vuh.* The fact that the rabbit enters the *Popol Vuh* game to lead the Lords of Death away from First Lord as (in this case) the sun in order to give him a chance to regenerate himself (with the help of his *uay,* First Jaguar) may reflect a far more ancient myth in which the monthly menstrual (*moon*-struel) blood of women diverted the Underworld demons from the blood of men. Women's monthly "bloodletting"—as an expression of the *ch'ulel* of the moon—may have reduced the obligations of men—the representatives of the sun—to let their blood.

One reading of ballgame iconography emphasizes the astronomical over the agricultural aspect of the game. While the corn "dies" during the spring planting and "resurrects" in the fall, the "true sun"—First Jaguar—"resurrects" in the *spring* when, at the vernal equinox, it is moving northward. The Jaguar Sun "dies" in the fall as it moves to the south. Even from the agricultural point of view, the corn actually begins its resurrection in the spring as its sprouts push up from the "Underworld," and it submits to "decapitation sacrifice" in the fall when it is harvested. Because of the sprouting of the corn and the northward movement of the sun, the dry season—the season of death—is also the season of life. And as the sun moves southward and the corn is harvested the rainy season—the season of life—is also the season of death. Like the mingled identities of the Twin Gods themselves, this interweaving of the images of life and death in ballgame mythology dramatized the miraculous, eternally recurring life/death event that was the core essence of the ballgame as it was of all aspects of Maya life.

In his exhaustive study of Aztec myths, *The Phoenix of the Western World: Quetzalcóatl and the Sky Religion* (1982), Burr Cartwright Brundage discusses in detail the relationship between the planet Venus and the sacrificial death and resurrection of the sun. It is probable that Maya mythology, now lost in its original scope and complexity, paralleled much of this Aztec scheme.

The quote from Saint Paul is taken from Romans 6:3–5, *The Oxford Annotated Bible,* cited above.

The idea that voluntarily embracing one's own sacrificial death leads to rebirth of the individual and/or the cosmos is virtually universal in the spiritual traditions of the world. The most obvious example is the mythology of Christianity, but this theme can be found in Judaism, Hinduism, and Buddhism as well. In the Hindu *Rāmāyana,* we learn that Ravana, the archdemon, has willed his own death at the hands of Rama in order to create a new world order. In a somewhat different vein, the Buddhist bodhisattvas give up their own entry into nirvana in order to save the lost beings they have left behind in the created world. Moslem suicide bombers believe that their deaths will not only gain them immediate entry into paradise but will also renew the world by cleansing it of unbelievers. And the rhetoric that urges men, and now women, to war has always enlisted this primal archetype.

Clendinnen's understanding of human sacrifice in the Aztec context is impressive. Patrick Tierney's more wide-ranging analysis in *The Highest Altar,* cited above, is equally arresting.

A dramatic non-Maya depiction of the sacrificial victim's intestines hung on a lattice to symbolize the life-bearing branches of the World

Tree comes from El Tajin in Veracruz, Mexico. On a carved column erected by King Thirteen-Rabbit (ninth century A.D.), we see a decapitated victim lying on a bench. His exposed intestines are spread above him on a rack decorated with tasseled corn plants.

There was still another Post-Classic Period form of human sacrifice, one that has captured the imaginations of generations of explorers and travelers. This was the water sacrifice at the famous sacred cenote of Chichen Itza. This natural well is a huge hole in the limestone rock that underlies most of the Yucatan peninsula. An underground river flows beneath the surface at Chichen Itza. After centuries of erosion by the river from below and rainfall from above the limestone surface collapsed, leaving the 190-foot-wide mouth of the cenote with its vine and root-shrouded walls and its sheer drop to the surface of the water.

The Itza Maya believed that the cenote was one of the most powerful portals to the Underworld. Its waters were the living embodiment of the "black waters" of Xibalba, and its rocky walls were the skeletal jaws of the White-Bone Snake. Beneath the visible water welled the supernatural "bloody water" that filled the Underworld. Long after the fall of Chichen Itza, the sacred cenote was a place of pilgrimage for all the surviving Maya.

In ancient times the shaman-priests led sacrificial victims from the great central pyramid in the main plaza, past the skull-rack hung with the severed heads of war captives, down the tree-lined sacbe—"white road"—to a platform built over the edge of the cenote. Then, to the eerie sounds of chanting, flutes, conch-shell trumpets, gourd rattles, and drums, they swung the victims out over the rim and threw them as far toward the center of the White-Bone Snake's gullet as they could. The "terminated ones" hung in midair for one terrifying instant and then plunged into the muddy waters sixty feet below. In the Post-Classic era these victims were dedicated to the chacob—the four gods of rain and fertility—and were expected to carry messages from the world of the living to the demons who lurked in the bottomless Abyss.

By studying the scenes from the San José Motul vase and the Piedras Negras stela, and comparing them to other scenes of royal accession, I believe I have been able to understand their symbolic meaning. The captive, bound in the cosmic niche, represented Itzam-Yeh—the false sun and the Overworld and earth plane manifestation of the power of death. At the same time, he may have portrayed First Jaguar, First Lord's uay and the true sun, which in order to be reborn each day and every year at the spring equinox had to subject himself to the sacrificial ax of his brother.

I believe that for a Maya king to accede to power he had to simultaneously reenact these two myths of the Twin Gods' victory over the forces of destruction and death. As we see in the scene on the tripod plate, First Father/Lord/Jaguar had to knock Itzam-Yeh—the false ruler of the cosmos—from his perch in the World Tree, kill him, and thereby limit the power of Xibalba in the new creation. At the same time, First Lord had to sacrifice his brother—the sun—and resurrect him within his own person. The human king accomplished both of these things by dethroning the captive, throwing him from the cosmic niche to the ground, sacrificing him, and raising the World Tree/Cosmic Corn Plant from his open chest—the same gashed and bleeding chest Itzam-Yeh displays in the scene on the tripod plate. Then the king ascended the cloth-covered ladder and received the insignia of his newly won divinity—the Twin Gods/ecliptic serpent bar and the K'awil scepter.

The idea that the sacrificial fire into which the Twin Gods leap symbolizes their own K'awil consciousness is mine, as is the belief that by having their bones ground down and thrown into the water they were reducing themselves to their essence and resubmerging themselves in the divine energy fields. My interpretations are consistent with what we now know about K'awil imagery and the structure of the Maya Cosmos.

I confess that I am at a loss to say how modern people might recapture the intensity and immediacy of human sacrifice. Perhaps what we could work for would be a fuller consciousness of the ways in which we act out the sacrificial archetype in our own lives and on the world stage. Greater consciousness, according to Jung, always brings us greater control of our impulses.

12. RESURRECTION

The citations here are Matthew 22:14, and I Corinthians 15:35–38, 43–44, 52, 54–55, *The Oxford Annotated Bible,* cited above.

The belief that destructiveness and death betray themselves and side with creation and life is widespread. Hinduism, Buddhism, and Taoism, not to mention the more ancient religions of duality that lie behind them, all maintain that the darkness transforms itself into the light. (Of course, they also maintain that the light transforms itself into the darkness, but ultimately in the service of creating a richer, more whole light.) Even the religions of dualism—Judaism, Christianity, and Islam—show Satan as furthering God's purposes, albeit against his will.

The golden carp story comes from Rudolfo Anaya's *Bless Me, Ultima* (1972), pages 112–119.

Freidel, Schele, and Parker offer a masterful reconstruction of ancient Maya dance in *Maya Cosmos,* cited above, pages 257–286.

My eight years of experience as a pastor in the United Church of Christ convinced me that even those who regularly attend church overwhelmingly believe in the soul's immortality rather than in its resurrection. Few maintain, even at the level of lip service, that the decayed remains in the grave will somehow be revived at the end of the world, or that the soul has to wait until that distant day to enter heaven.

The Tillich quotes come from his *Systematic Theology,* Vol. 3, cited above, pages 407 and 409.

Modern psychology, while almost never explicitly embracing a spiritual framework or goal for its efforts, nonetheless is aiming at essentially the same target as the most enlightened seekers in the religious traditions. That target for both is a deeper, more powerful, more complete human identity.

SELECT BIBLIOGRAPHY

Allegro, John M. *The Sacred Mushroom and the Cross.* New York: Bantam Books, 1971.

Anaya, Rudolfo. *Bless Me, Ultima.* New York: Warner Books, 1972.

Arberry, A. J. *Sufism: An Account of the Mystics of Islam.* New York: Harper & Row/Harper Torchbooks, 1970.

Armstrong, Karen. *A History of God: The 4,000-Year Quest of Judaism, Christianity, and Islam.* New York: Ballantine Books, 1993.

Baba, Pagal. *Temple of the Phallic King: The Mind of India: Yogis, Swamis, Sufis, and Avatars.* New York: Simon & Schuster, 1973.

Barnstone, Willis, ed. *The Other Bible.* San Francisco: Harper & Row, 1984.

Basham, Arthur L. *The Wonder That Was India: A Survey of the Culture of the Indian Sub-Continent Before the Coming of the Muslims.* London: Sidgwick & Jackson, 1954; New York: Grove Press, 1959.

Baudez, Claude, and Sydney Picasso. *Lost Cities of the Maya.* New York: Harry N. Abrams, 1992.

Beahrs, John O. *Unity and Multiplicity: Multilevel Consciousness of Self in Hypnosis, Psychiatric Disorder, and Mental Health.* New York: Brunner/Mazel, 1981.

Bernal, Ignacio. *The Olmec World.* Translated from the Spanish by Doris

Heyden and Fernando Horcasitas. Berkeley: University of California Press, 1969. Paperback printing 1976. First published as *El Mundo Olmeca* by Porrua Hermanos, Mexico City, 1968.

Berrin, Kathleen, and Esther Pasztory, eds. *Teotihuacan: Art from the City of the Gods.* New York: Thames and Hudson, 1993.

Bettelheim, Bruno. *Freud and Man's Soul.* New York: Alfred A. Knopf, 1983.

Bierhorst, John. *The Mythology of Mexico and Central America.* New York: William Morrow, 1990.

Blacker, Irwin R., and *Horizon* Magazine Editors. *Cortés and the Aztec Conquest.* New York: American Heritage, 1965.

Braden, William. *The Private Sea: LSD and the Search for God.* New York: Bantam Books, 1967.

Bricker, Victoria Reifler. *The Indian Christ, the Indian King: The Historical Substrate of Maya Myth and Ritual.* Austin: University of Texas Press, 1981.

Browning, Don S. *Generative Man: Psychoanalytic Perspectives.* Philadelphia: Westminster Press, 1973; New York: Dell, 1975.

Brundage, Burr Cartwright. *The Phoenix of the Western World: Quetzalcóatl and the Sky Religion.* Norman: University of Oklahoma Press, 1982.

Buck, William. *Rāmāyana.* Berkeley: University of California Press, 1976.

Budge, E. A. Wallis. *The Egyptian Book of the Dead (The Papyrus of Ani): Egyptian Text, Transliteration, and Translation.* New York: Dover, 1976.

Bunson, Margaret R., and Stephen M. Bunson. *Encyclopedia of Ancient Mesoamerica.* New York: Facts on File, 1996.

Campbell, Joseph. *The Hero with a Thousand Faces,* rev. ed. Princeton: Princeton University Press, 1968.

———. *Historical Atlas of World Mythology.* Vol. 2, *The Way of the Seeded Earth.* Part 1: *The Sacrifice.* New York: Harper & Row/Perennial Library, 1988.

———. *The Masks of God: Creative Mythology.* New York: Penguin, 1970.

———. *The Masks of God: Occidental Mythology.* New York: Viking Press, 1964; New York: Penguin, 1976.

———. *The Mythic Image.* Princeton: Princeton University Press, 1974.

———. *The Power of Myth.* Garden City, NY: Doubleday, 1988.

Capra, Fritjof. *The Tao of Physics.* Boulder: Shambhala, 1975.

Carmichael, Elizabeth, and Chloë Sayer. *The Skeleton at the Feast: The Day of the Dead in Mexico.* Austin: University of Texas Press, 1991.

Carrasco, David. *Quetzalcoatl and the Irony of Empire: Myths and Prophecies in the Aztec Tradition.* Chicago: University of Chicago Press, 1982.

Carrasco, David, and Eduardo Matos Moctezuma. *Moctezuma's Mexico: Visions of the Aztec World.* Niwot: The University Press of Colorado, 1992.

Castaneda, Carlos. *A Separate Reality: Further Conversations with Don Juan.* New York: Simon & Schuster/Pocket Books, 1971.

———. *Journey to Ixtlan: The Lessons of Don Juan.* New York: Simon & Schuster/Pocket Books, 1974.

———. *The Teachings of Don Juan: A Yaqui Way of Knowledge.* New York: Ballantine Books, 1968.

Ceram, C. W. *Gods, Graves, and Scholars.* New York: Alfred A. Knopf, 1967.

Chaplin, Gordon. *The Fever Coast Log.* New York: Simon & Schuster, 1992.

Cleator, P. E. *Lost Languages.* New York: New American Library, 1962.

Clendinnen, Inga. *Aztecs.* New York: Cambridge University Press, 1991.

Coe, Michael D. *Breaking the Maya Code.* New York: Thames and Hudson, 1992.

———. *Mexico: From the Olmecs to the Aztecs,* 2nd ed. New York: Thames and Hudson, 1982.

———. *The Maya,* 5th ed. New York: Thames and Hudson, 1993.

Coe, Michael D., et al. *The Olmec World: Ritual and Rulership.* Princeton: The Art Museum, Princeton University, 1995.

Cumont, Franz. *The Mysteries of Mithra.* Translated from the 2nd revised French edition by Thomas J. McCormack. LaSalle, IL: Open Court, 1903; New York: Dover Publications, 1956.

Day, Jane S. *Aztec: The World of Moctezuma.* Niwot: Roberts Rinehart Publishers, 1992.

de Landa, Friar Diego. *Yucatan Before and After the Conquest.* Translated with notes by William Gates. New York: Dover Publications, 1978.

De Vries, Ad. *Dictionary of Symbols and Imagery.* Amsterdam: North-Holland Publishing Co., 1984.

Dodds, E. R. *Pagan and Christian in an Age of Anxiety: Some Aspects of Religious Experience from Marcus Aurelius to Constantine.* New York: W. W. Norton, 1965.

Doore, Gary, ed. *Shaman's Path: Healing, Personal Growth, and Empowerment.* Boston: Shambhala, 1988.

Dupont-Sommer, André. *The Essene Writings from Qumran.* New York: World/Meridian Books, 1961.

Edinger, Edward F. *Ego and Archetype: Individuation and the Religious Function of the Psyche.* New York: G. P. Putnam's Sons (for the C. G. Jung Foundation for Analytical Psychology), 1972; New York: Penguin Books, 1974.

——. *The Creation of Consciousness: Jung's Myth for Modern Man.* Toronto: Inner City Books, 1984.

Eliade, Mircea. *Cosmos and History: The Myth of the Eternal Return.* Princeton: Bollingen Foundation, 1954; New York: Harper & Row, 1959.

——. *Myth and Reality.* New York: Harper & Row/Harper Torchbooks, 1963.

——. *Patterns in Comparative Religion.* New York: World Publishing, 1963. Originally published in French as *Traité d'histoire des religions.* Paris: Editions Payot.

——. *Rites and Symbols of Initiation: The Mysteries of Birth and Rebirth.* New York: Harper & Row, 1958.

——. *The Sacred and the Profane: The Nature of Religion: The Significance of Religious Myth, Symbolism, and Ritual Within Life and Culture.* New York: Harcourt, Brace and World, 1959. Originally published in German by Rowohlt Taschenbuch Verlag, 1957.

Engnell, Ivan. *Studies in Divine Kingship in the Ancient Near East,* 2nd ed. Oxford: Basil Blackwell, 1967.

Evans-Wentz, Walter Y., ed. *The Tibetan Book of the Dead,* 3rd ed. New York: Oxford University Press, 1960.

——. *The Tibetan Book of the Great Liberation; or the Method of Realizing Nirvana Through Knowing the Mind.* London: Oxford University Press, 1954.

Fagan, Brian M. *Kingdoms of Gold, Kingdoms of Jade: The Americas Before Columbus.* London: Thames and Hudson, 1991.

——. *The Journey from Eden: The Peopling of Our World.* London: Thames and Hudson, 1990.

Fasquelle, Ricardo Agurcia, and William L. Fash, Jr. "Maya Artistry Unearthed." *National Geographic,* September 1991.

Ferris, Timothy. *The Red Limit: The Search for the Edge of the Universe.* New York: William Morrow, 1977; New York: Bantam Books, 1979.

Forsyth, Neil. *The Old Enemy: Satan and the Combat Myth.* Princeton: Princeton University Press, 1987.

Frankfort, Henri. *Ancient Egyptian Religion.* New York: Columbia University Press, 1948; New York: Harper & Row, 1961.

————. *Kingship and the Gods: A Study of Ancient Near Eastern Religion as the Integration of Society and Nature.* Chicago: University of Chicago Press, 1948.

————. *The Birth of Civilization in the Near East.* Garden City, NY: Doubleday, 1956; Bloomington, IN: Indiana University Press, 1959.

Frazer, James G. *The Golden Bough: A Study in Magic and Religion.* 12 vols. 3rd ed. London, 1915. Reprint, paperback edition published by Macmillan, 1963.

Freidel, David, Linda Schele, and Joy Parker. *Maya Cosmos: Three Thousand Years on the Shaman's Path.* New York: William Morrow, 1993.

Freud, Sigmund. *Moses and Monotheism.* Translated by Katherine Jones. New York: Alfred A. Knopf, 1939.

————. *Totem and Taboo: Some Points of Agreement Between the Mental Lives of Savages and Neurotics.* Translated by James Strachey. New York: W. W. Norton, 1950; London: Routledge & Kegan Paul, 1950.

Gaer, Joseph. *How the Great Religions Began.* New York: Dodd, Mead, 1929. New revised edition, New York: Dodd, Mead, 1938; New York: New American Library/Signet Books, 1954.

Gallenkamp, Charles. *Maya: The Riddle and Rediscovery of a Lost Civilization,* 3rd ed. New York: Penguin, 1985.

Garrison, Jim. *The Darkness of God: Theology After Hiroshima.* Grand Rapids, MI: William B. Eerdmans, 1982.

Gillespie, Susan D. *The Aztec Kings: The Construction of Rulership in Mexican History.* Tucson: The University of Arizona Press, 1970.

Goddard, Dwight, ed. *A Buddhist Bible.* Boston: Beacon Press, 1970.

Godwin, Joscelyn. *Mystery Religions in the Ancient World.* San Francisco: Harper & Row, 1981; London: Thames and Hudson, 1981.

Gonda, Jan. "Ancient Indian Kingship from the Religious Point of View." *Numen 3* (1955): 36–71, 122–155; *Numen 4* (1956): 4, 24–58, 127–164.

Grant, Robert M. *Gnosticism and Early Christianity.* New York: Columbia University Press, 1959; New York: Harper & Row/Harper Torchbooks, 1966.

Hadfield, Percival. *Traits of Divine Kingship in Africa.* Westport, CT: Greenwood Press, 1979.

Halifax, Joan. *Shamanic Voices: A Survey of Visionary Narratives.* New York: E. P. Dutton, 1979.

Hartshore, Charles, and Creighton Peden. *Whitehead's View of Reality.* New York: The Pilgrim Press, 1981.

Heinberg, Richard. *Memories and Visions of Paradise: Exploring the Universal Myth of a Lost Golden Age.* Los Angeles: Jeremy P. Tarcher, 1989.

Henderson, Joseph L. *Thresholds of Initiation.* Middletown, CT: Wesleyan University Press, 1967.

Heschel, Abraham Joshua. *Man Is Not Alone: A Philosophy of Religion.* New York: Farrar, Straus and Giroux, 1951.

Hooke, Samuel H. *Middle Eastern Mythology.* New York: Viking Penguin, 1963.

Jacobi, Jolande. *Complex, Archetype, Symbol in the Psychology of C. G. Jung.* Princeton: Princeton University Press, 1959. Originally published in German as *Komplex/Archetypus/Symbol in der Psychologie C. G. Jung.* Zurich and Stuttgart: Rascher Verlag, 1957.

———. *The Psychology of C. G. Jung.* London: Routledge & Kegan Paul, 1942; New Haven: Yale University Press, 1973.

Jaffé, Aniela. *The Myth of Meaning: Jung and the Expansion of Consciousness.* New York: Penguin Books, 1975.

James, William. *The Varieties of Religious Experience: A Study in Human Nature.* Gifford Lectures. London: Longmans Green, 1902. Reprint, paperback edition, with foreword by Jacques Barzun, New York: New American Library, 1958.

Jobes, Gertrude. *Dictionary of Mythology, Folklore, and Symbols.* Metuchen, NJ: Scarecrow Press, 1962.

Johnson, Robert A. *Ecstasy: Understanding the Psychology of Joy.* San Francisco: Harper & Row, 1989.

Jung, Carl G. *Aion: Researches into the Phenomenology of the Self.* Vol. 9 of *The Collected Works of C. G. Jung.* Princeton: Princeton University Press, 1959.

———. *Civilization in Transition.* Vol. 10 of *The Collected Works of C. G. Jung.* Princeton: Princeton University Press, 1970.

———. *Man and His Symbols.* New York: Dell, 1964; London: Aldus Books, 1964.

———. *Modern Man in Search of a Soul.* New York: Harcourt, Brace, 1933.

———. *Mysterium Coniunctionis: An Inquiry into the Separation and Synthesis of Psychic Opposites in Alchemy,* 2nd ed. Princeton: Princeton University Press, 1970.

———. *The Portable Jung.* Edited by Joseph Campbell. New York: Penguin Books, 1971. Reprint of Jung's work in *Aion,* pp. 148ff.

———. *Psyche and Symbol: A Selection from the Writings of C. G. Jung.* Edited by Violet deLaszlo. Garden City, NY: Doubleday, 1958.

———. *Psychology and Alchemy,* 2nd ed. New York: Bollingen Foundation, 1953; Princeton: Princeton University Press, 1980.

————. *Psychology and Religion: West and East*. 2nd ed. Vol. 11 of *The Collected Works of C. G. Jung*. Princeton: Princeton University Press, 1958.

Kramer, Samuel Noah. *Sumerian Mythology: A Study of Spiritual and Literary Achievement in the Third Millennium B.C.* New York: Harper, 1961.

Krickeberg, Walter, et al. *Pre-Columbian American Religions*. Translated from the German by Stanley Davis. New York: Holt, Rinehart and Winston, 1968; London: Weidenfeld & Nicolson, 1968.

Lafaye, Jacques. *Quetzalcóatl and Guadalupe: The Formation of Mexican National Consciousness, 1531–1813*. Chicago: The University of Chicago Press, 1976. Translated by Benjamin Keen. Originally published as *Quetzalcóatl et Guadelupe*. Paris: Editions Gallimard, 1974.

Larsen, Stephen. *The Shaman's Doorway: Opening the Mythic Imagination to Contemporary Consciousness*. San Francisco: Harper & Row/Harper Colophon Books, 1976.

Lauzun, Gérard. *Sigmund Freud: The Man and His Theories*. Translated by Patrick Evans. Greenwich, CT: Fawcett, 1962; Paris: Pierre Seghers, 1962.

Lawrence, D. H. *Complete Poems*. Edited by Vivian De Sola Pinto and Warren Roberts. New York: Penguin, 1993.

Lemaitre, Solange. *Hinduism*. New York: Hawthorn Books, 1959. Translated from the French by John-Francis Brown.

León-Portilla, Miguel. *Aztec Thought and Culture: A Study of the Ancient Nahuatl Mind*. Norman: University of Oklahoma Press, 1963. Translated from the Spanish by Jack Emory Davis.

————. *Fifteen Poets of the Aztec World*. Norman: University of Oklahoma Press, 1992.

————. *Time and Reality in the Thought of the Maya,* 2nd ed. Norman: University of Oklahoma Press, 1988. Translated from the Spanish by Charles L. Boilès, Fernando Horcasitas, and Miguel León-Portilla. Originally published as *Tiempo y realidad en el pensamiento Maya: Ensayo de acercamiento* by Universidad Nacional Autónoma de México, Ciudad Universitaria México D. F.

Leonard, Jonathan Norton, and the Editors of Time-Life Books. *Ancient America*. New York: Time Incorporated, 1967.

Lewis, C. S. *Till We Have Faces*. New York: Harcourt, Brace and World, 1956.

MacLachlan, Colin M., and Jaime E. Rodríguez O. *The Forging of the Cosmic Race: A Reinterpretation of Colonial Mexico*. Berkeley: University of California Press, 1980.

Mahdi, Louise Carus, Steven Foster, and Meredith Little, eds. *Betwixt and*

Between: Patterns of Masculine and Feminine Initiation. LaSalle, IL: Open Court, 1987.

Malandra, William W. *An Introduction to Ancient Iranian Religion: Readings from the "Avesta" and "Achaemenid" Inscriptions.* Minneapolis: University of Minnesota Press, 1983.

Marcuse, Herbert. *Eros and Civilization: A Philosophical Inquiry into Freud.* Boston: Beacon Press, 1955.

Marks, Richard Lee. *Cortés: The Great Adventurer and the Fate of Aztec Mexico.* New York: Alfred A. Knopf, 1993.

May, Herbert G., and Bruce M. Metzger, eds. *The Oxford Annotated Bible: The Holy Bible.* New York: Oxford University Press, 1962.

Meyerowitz, Eva L. R. *The Divine Kingship in Ghana and Ancient Egypt.* London: Faber & Faber, 1940.

Miller, Mary. "Maya Masterpiece Revealed at Bonampak." *National Geographic,* February 1995.

Miller, Mary, and Karl Taube. *The Gods and Symbols of Ancient Mexico and the Maya.* London: Thames and Hudson, 1993.

Moctezuma, Eduardo Matos. *Life and Death in the Templo Mayor.* Niwot: The University Press of Colorado, 1995. Translated from the Spanish by Bernard R. Ortiz de Montellano and Thelma Ortiz de Montellano.

Monick, Eugene. *Phallos: Sacred Image of the Masculine.* Toronto: Inner City Books, 1987.

Moody, Raymond A. *Life After Life: The Investigation of a Phenomenon—Survival of Bodily Death.* With Introduction by Elisabeth Kübler-Ross. New York: Bantam Books, 1975.

Moore, Robert, and Douglas Gillette. *King, Warrior, Magician, Lover: Rediscovering the Archetypes of Mature Masculinity.* San Francisco: HarperCollins, 1990.

———. *The King Within: Accessing the King in the Male Psyche.* New York: William Morrow, 1992.

———. *The Magician Within: Accessing the Shaman in the Male Psyche.* New York: William Morrow, 1993.

Morley, Sylvanus G., and George W. Brainerd. *The Ancient Maya,* 4th ed. Revised by Robert J. Sharer. Stanford, CA: Stanford University Press, 1963.

Morris, Richard. *Time's Arrows: Scientific Attitudes Toward Time.* New York: Simon & Schuster, 1984.

Mylonas, George E. *Eleusis and the Eleusinian Mysteries.* Princeton: Princeton University Press, 1961.

Neumann, Erich. *Art and the Creative Unconscious.* Princeton: Princeton University Press, 1959.

Nicholas of Cusa. *The Vision of God.* Translated by O. R. Gurney. Edited by Evelyn Underhill. New York: Ungar, 1960.

Nicholson, Shirley, ed. *Shamanism.* Wheaton, IL: Theosophical Publishing House, 1987.

Niehardt, John G. *Black Elk Speaks.* New York: Simon & Schuster/Pocket Books, 1972.

Nikhilananda, Swami. *The Upanishads.* New York: Ramakrishna-Vivekananda Center, 1949.

Norris, Richard A., Jr., and William G. Rusch, eds. *The Christological Controversy.* Translated by Richard A. Norris. Philadelphia: Fortress Press, 1980.

Otto, Rudolf. *The Idea of the Holy.* New York: Oxford University Press, 1923.

Pagden, Anthony, trans. and ed. *Hernan Cortés: Letters from Mexico.* New Haven: Yale University Press, 1986.

Pagels, Elaine. *The Gnostic Gospels.* New York: Random House, 1979.

Parkes, Henry Bamford. *A History of Mexico.* London: Eyre and Spottiswoode, 1962.

Peck, M. Scott. *People of the Lie: The Hope for Healing Human Evil.* New York: Simon & Schuster, 1983.

————. *The Road Less Traveled: A New Psychology of Love, Traditional Values, and Spiritual Growth.* New York: Simon & Schuster, 1978.

Penrose, Thomas. *Mayan Cryptoquantum Numerations.* Franklin Park, N.J.: Liberty Bell Associates, 1924.

Perowne, Stewart. *Roman Mythology.* London: Hamlan, 1969.

Perry, John Weir. *Lord of the Four Quarters: The Mythology of Kingship.* Mahwah, NJ: Paulist Press, 1991.

Peterson, Frederick. *Ancient Mexico: An Introduction to the Pre-Hispanic Cultures.* Toms River, NJ: Capricorn Books, 1962. Originally published 1959.

Pickthall, Marmaduke. *The Meaning of the Glorious Koran.* New York: New American Library, 1953.

Plato. *Apology, Crito, Phaedo, Symposium, Republic.* Translated by Benjamin Jowett. Edited with introduction by Lousie R. Loomis. Roslyn, NY: Walter J. Black, 1942.

Prabhupada, A. C., Bhaktivedanta Swami. *Bhagavad-Gita As It Is.* Bhaktivedanta Book Trust, 1968; New York: Macmillan/Collier Books, 1972.

Pritchard, James B., ed. *The Ancient Near East: An Anthology of Texts and Pictures.* Princeton: Princeton University Press, 1958.

Proskouriakoff, Tatiana. *An Album of Maya Architecture.* Norman: University of Oklahoma Press, 1963.

Reents-Budet, Dorie, et al. *Painting the Maya Universe: Royal Ceramics of the Classic Period.* Durham: Duke University Press, 1994.

Reichel-Dolmatoff, Gerardo. *Amazonian Cosmos: The Sexual and Religious Symbolism of the Tukano Indians.* Translated from Spanish. Chicago: University of Chicago Press, 1971.

Richards, J. W. "Sacral Kings of Iran." *Mankind Quarterly 20,* nos. 1–2 (1979): 143–160.

Riding, Alan. *Distant Neighbors: A Portrait of the Mexicans.* New York: Random House, 1989.

Robinson, James M., ed. *The Nag Hammadi Library.* San Francisco: Harper & Row, 1977.

Rojas, Pedro. *The Art and Architecture of Mexico: A Comprehensive Survey.* Translated by J. M. Cohen. Feltham, Middlesex: Hamlyn House, 1968.

Sabloff, Jeremy A. *The Cities of Ancient Mexico: Reconstructing a Lost World.* New York: Thames and Hudson, 1989.

Sanford, John A. *Dreams: God's Forgotten Language.* New York: J. B. Lippincott, 1968.

————. *Evil: The Shadow Side of Reality.* New York: Crossroad, 1981.

Scarborough, Vernon L., and David R. Wilcox, eds. *The Mesoamerican Ballgame.* Tucson: The University of Arizona Press, 1991.

Schele, Linda, and David A. Freidel. *A Forest of Kings: The Untold Story of the Ancient Maya.* New York: William Morrow, 1990.

Schele, Linda, and Mary Ellen Miller. *The Blood of Kings: Dynasty and Ritual in Maya Art.* London: Thames and Hudson, 1992.

Scholem, Gershom. *Major Trends in Jewish Mysticism.* New York: Schocken Books, 1961.

The Secret of the Golden Flower: A Chinese Book of Life. Translated by Richard Wilhelm. New York: Harcourt Brace Jovanovich, 1931.

Seltman, Charles T. *The Twelve Olympians.* New York: Thomas Y. Crowell, 1960.

Silverberg, Robert. *Lost Cities and Vanished Civilizations.* New York: Bantam Books, 1963.

Smith, Huston. *Beyond the Post-Modern Mind.* Wheaton, IL: The Theosophical Publishing House, 1982.

————. *Forgotten Truth: The Primordial Tradition.* New York: Harper & Row/Harper Colophon Books, 1976.

————. *The Religions of Man.* New York: Harper & Row, 1965.

Smith, Morton. *Jesus the Magician.* San Francisco: Harper & Row, 1978.

Snelling, John. *The Elements of Buddhism.* Rockport, ME: Element Books, 1991.

Spores, Ronald. *The Mixtecs in Ancient and Colonial Times.* Norman: University of Oklahoma Press, 1984.

Stephens, John Lloyd. *Incidents of Travel in Central America, Chiapas, and Yucatan.* Washington: Smithsonian Institution Press, 1993.

————. *Incidents of Travel in Yucatán.* Volumes 1 and 2. Panorama Editorial, S.A., 1988. Originally published by Harper and Brothers, New York, 1843.

Stevens, Anthony. *Archetypes: A Natural History of the Self.* New York: Quill, 1983. Originally published as *Archetype: A Natural History of the Self.* London: Routledge & Kegan Paul, 1982.

Storr, Anthony. *Human Aggression.* New York: Atheneum, 1968; New York: Bantam Books, 1970.

————. *Human Destructiveness.* New York: Basic Books, 1972; New York: Grove Weidenfeld, 1991.

————. *The Integrity of the Personality.* New York: Atheneum, 1960; New York: Random House, 1992.

Stuart, George, and Gene S. Stuart. *The Mighty Aztecs.* Washington: National Geographic Society, 1981.

————. *The Mysterious Maya.* Washington: National Geographic Society, 1977.

Tedlock, Dennis. *Popol Vuh: The Definitive Edition of the Mayan Book of the Dawn of Life and the Glories of Gods and Kings.* New York: Simon & Schuster, 1985.

Thomas, Hugh. *Conquest: Montezuma, Cortés, and the Fall of Old Mexico.* New York: Simon & Schuster, 1993.

Thompson, John Eric S. *Maya History and Religion.* Norman: University of Oklahoma Press, 1970.

————. *The Rise and Fall of Maya Civilization.* Norman: University of Oklahoma Press, 1954.

Tierney, Patrick. *The Highest Altar: Unveiling the Mystery of Human Sacrifice.* New York: Penguin Books, 1989.

Tillich, Paul. *The Courage to Be.* New Haven: Yale University Press, 1952.

————. *The Eternal Now.* New York: Charles Scribner's Sons, 1963.

————. *Systematic Theology*. Vol. 3. Chicago: University of Chicago Press, 1963.

Time-Life Books Editors. *The Age of the God-Kings, 3000–1500 B.C.* New York: Time-Life Books, 1990.

————. *Aztecs: Reign of Blood and Splendor*. Alexandria, VA: Time-Life Books, 1992.

Tolkien, J. R. R. *The Tolkien Reader*. New York: Ballantine Books, 1966.

Townsend, Richard F. *The Aztecs*. London: Thames and Hudson, 1992.

Tucci, Giuseppe. "The Secret Characters of the Kings of Ancient Tibet." *East and West 6*, no. 3 (October 1955): 197–205.

Turner, Victor. *The Ritual Process: Structure and Anti-Structure*. Ithaca: Cornell University Press, 1969.

Underhill, Evelyn. *Mysticism*. New York: E. P. Dutton, 1911.

Valeri, Valerio. *Kingship and Sacrifice: Ritual and Society in Ancient Hawaii*. Translated from Hawaiian by Paula Wissing. Chicago: University of Chicago Press, 1985.

Vermes, Geza. *The Dead Sea Scrolls in English*. Baltimore: Penguin Books, 1962.

Von Franz, Marie-Louise. *Number and Time*. Evanston, IL: Northwestern University Press, 1974.

————. *Projection and Recollection in Jungian Psychology*. LaSalle, IL: Open Court, 1980. Originally published in German as *Spiegelungen der Seele: Projektion und innere Sammlung*. Stuttgart: Kreuz Verlag, 1978.

von Hagen, Victor Wolfgang. *Maya Explorer: John Lloyd Stephens and the Lost Cities of Central America and Yucatán*. San Francisco: Chronicle Books, 1990.

Wales, Horace G. *The Mountain of God: A Study in Early Religion and Kingship*. London: Bernard Quaritch, 1953.

Watts, Alan. *The Supreme Identity: An Essay on Oriental Metaphysic and the Christian Religion*. New York: Random House/Vintage Books, 1972.

Watts, Alan, and Eliot Elisofon. *Erotic Spirituality: The Vision of Konarak*. New York: Macmillan/Collier Books, 1971.

Wei, Henry. *The Guiding Light of Lao Tze*. Wheaton, IL: Theosophical Publishing House, 1982.

Whitecotton, Joseph W. *The Zapotecs: Princes, Priests, and Peasants*. Norman: University of Oklahoma Press, 1977.

Whitehead, Alfred North. *Adventures of Ideas*. New York: Macmillan, 1933; New York: Free Press, 1967.

————. *Process and Reality.* Edited by David Ray Griffin and Donald W. Sherburne. New York: Collier Macmillan Publishers, 1978.

Willey, Gordon Randolph. *Essays in Maya Archaeology.* Albuquerque: University of New Mexico Press, 1987.

Wilson, John A. *The Culture of Ancient Egypt.* Chicago: University of Chicago Press, 1951. Originally published as *The Burden of Egypt.*

Winter, Marcus, Coordinator. *Monte Alban: Estudios Recientes.* Contribución No. 2 del Proyecto Especial Monte Albán 1992–1994, Oaxaca, 1994.

Wolf, Fred Alan. *The Eagle's Quest: A Physicist's Search for Truth in the Heart of the Shamanic World.* New York: Simon & Schuster/Summit Books, 1991.

▰▱▰▱▰▱▰
• • • • • • • • • • • • • • •

ABOUT THE AUTHOR

DOUGLAS GILLETTE has an M.A. from the University of Chicago Divinity School in religion and literature and an M.Div. from Chicago Theological Seminary in religion and psychology. He is an author, a lecturer, an internationally known workshop leader, and a counselor in private practice.

Douglas Gillette is also the author of *Primal Love: Reclaiming Our Instincts for Lasting Passion,* which traces the relationship problems between the genders to our evolutionary heritage and shows how to work with the "primate patterns" that guide our lives. *Primal Love* includes a Foreword by John Bradshaw and a Preface by Harville Hendrix.

In addition, Mr. Gillette is the coauthor of five books on masculine psychology and spirituality. His first book, the best-selling *King/Warrior/Magician/Lover,* is regarded by many as the most important "decoding" of the male psyche ever undertaken.

A former pastor in the United Church of Christ, Mr. Gillette is a lifelong student of comparative religion and mythology. His special area of interest and expertise is the cultures and spiritual traditions of "Mesoamerica"—Mexico and Central America. He has made numerous trips, including extended stays, to Mexico, Honduras, and Costa Rica to research these ancient spiritualities. He has spent much of his time studying the most spiritually powerful sites, especially those of the ancient

Maya, including Chichen Itza, Copan, Tulum, Coba, Ake, Uxmal, and Dzibilchaltun. A fluent speaker of Spanish, he has a rich personal experience of the people of Mesoamerica.

Mr. Gillette brings to his writing, counseling, and workshop facilitation a lifetime of study in the fields of comparative mythology and religion, depth psychology, and anthropology. He is the cofounder of the Institute for World Spirituality, a nonprofit organization that fosters communication among many different spiritual traditions around the world.

Mr. Gillette lives in Chicago where he divides his time between writing, counseling, and enjoying his new family.

INDEX

ILLUSTRATION CREDITS

The author is grateful for permission to use the illustrations that appear on the following pages:

Pages 3, 35, 39, 65, 86, 87, 96, 103, 112, 171, 177, 204, 206. From *Maya Cosmos: Three Thousand Years on the Shaman's Path* by David Freidel, Linda Schele, and Joy Parker. Copyright © 1993 by Linda Schele, David Freidel, and Joy Parker. New York: William Morrow, 1993. Illustrations courtesy of Linda Schele.

Page 5. Alberto Ruz Lhuillier.

Page 8. From *A Guide to Ancient Maya Ruins* by Bruce C. Hunter, by permission of the University of Oklahoma Press. First edition copyright © 1974 by The University of Oklahoma Press, Norman, Publishing Division of the University. Second printing of the first edition, 1975; third printing, 1976; fourth printing, 1977. Second edition copyright © 1986 by the University of Oklahoma Press. All rights reserved.

Page 11. From *The Olmec World* by Bernal Ignacio, translated from the Spanish by Doris Heyden and Fernando Horcasitas. Berkeley: University of California Press, 1969. Paperback printing 1976. First published as *El Mundo Olmeca* by Porrua Hermanos, Mexico City, 1968. Illustration courtesy of John Bigelow Taylor.

Pages 13, 105, 216. From *The Ancient Maya*, fifth edition, by Robert J. Sharer, with the permission of the publishers, Stanford University Press. Copyright © 1946, 1947, 1956, 1983, 1994 by the Board of Trustees of the Leland Stanford Junior University.

Pages 16, 43, 76, 145, 174. From the author's collection.